Joanne

(509) 329-

# Birds of Passage

## A memoir

*Denae Veselits*

*gwen Dubigk*

The Veselits Family:
Denae, Elaine, Karen,
Diane, Gail, Gwen, and Keith

## *Good Words Press*
### *Guilford, CT*

Cover photo: Denae Veselits and her father, Frank

ISBN  978-0-9988028-0-0

Printed in the United States of America

Interior design by booknook.biz

For Dad and Mom

# CONTENTS

*There was a crooked man, and he walked a crooked mile*
*He found a crooked sixpence upon a crooked stile*
*He bought a crooked cat, which caught a crooked mouse*
*And they all lived together in a little crooked house*

.....

Pretty soon the crooked man got himself a wife
Who became crooked too, it was part of that life
And she got herself a child –all the way to number nine
And they were crooked too, as they stood there in a line

The cat danced with a bat beneath a sickled moon
While the crooked man demented a tuneless little spoon
The song seemed to go on forever, from mouth to crooked mouse
As we all lived together in that cracked and crooked house

# PART ONE

# BEGINNINGS

Front: Gail, Gwen, Denae, Keith, Karen  Back: Charles, Mom, Elaine, Diane

I knew I should not be in the room. It was forbidden. But I wanted to see her. "Summer-set Mom." I wanted to see the portrait daddy was painting of mom. But why the odd title? In front of us kids, he always called her "your mother."

Crouched behind a dresser in the cramped bedroom, my scrawny nine-year-old shoulders pressed against the wall, I was holding my breath, my heart pounding like a jackhammer – because daddy was in the room with me. Seconds earlier, when I heard the approach of his metal-toed boots outside the door, I had dived behind the clothes chest to hide, recalling his repeated warnings: "Don't you *ever* enter that room when I'm working on a painting!"

Not noticing me, he sat down heavily at his drawing table – an old school desk shoved against the sagging bed for support – and stared fixedly at the image on his canvas. Reaching for an open bottle of beer standing between his charcoal sticks and sardine-can spittoon, he drained it down his throat, then slowly, painstakingly, began applying charcoal to the facial contours. Periodically, he would rub the carbon with the tip of his little finger to soften edges and create shadows.

Crash! A slamming door somewhere in the house rattled the window and desk, toppling the beer bottle onto the floor.

"Son of a bitch!" Daddy's body jerked upright like he had just hooked a barracuda, leaving behind a thick charcoal gash across the artwork. Picking up his spittoon, he flung it at the portrait, the pool of black spittle flash-flooding its surface and the nearby white bedspread. Airborne droplets spattered my hair and forehead, too, forming dark rivulets as they ran down my eyelids and nose. At the same time, the sardine can bounced twice across the bed like a stone being skipped and landed with a tinny clang at my feet.

Daddy charged out of the room like a bear after deer. Now was my chance! Jumping up as the door slammed shut, I somersaulted over the bed to get one quick look at Summer-set Mom – at least what could be seen of her beneath the tobacco juice. Why was he painting her, anyway? Most of the time, he acted like he didn't even like her, constantly criticizing her with, "You stupid Norwegian, with your half-assed, one-track mind." And he would hit her almost as often as he hit us nine kids.

So I stared hard at the ruined image. Why, it didn't look like mother in the least. There was even a pipe sticking out of the mouth. It wasn't a woman at all!

Glancing down at the desktop, I realized my hand was resting on a book opened to the back dustjacket. The print on top read *The Razor's Edge,* and the man's photo beneath looked a lot like the face daddy had been working on. Somerset Maugham … oh.

It's one of my earliest memories connecting my father with the world of art.


Elaine

I remember falling, falling down the mountainside, my red chapped hands both hot and cold as the crusty packed snow rushed hard against my bare palms, scraping my legs, tearing at my cheeks.

It had been sunny there on the top, before I stumbled. And now I was plunging into the darkness, falling farther and farther away from the light.

"Help me, mommy, help me!" I wanted to cry out. Where was she? Could she even hear me?

I had stopped falling – all alone now in a crumpled heap at the bottom of a crevasse. High above me I could see the sky – a narrow ribbon of blue, so far away.

"Mama, mama, come get me! I'm afraid. Help me!" I screamed and screamed. Somewhere above me on the steep mountainside, an avalanche had begun.

We lived at the base of the Trinity Alps in Northern California.

I was three years old. Mommy was in the house taking care of my six-month-old twin sisters, Diane and Denae – too busy and too tired to watch me, while daddy worked in the mountains. So I had gone outside, forgetting my mittens, playing on top of the 7-foot high snowdrifts surrounding our cabin, when I slipped and fell.

Gwen

Write a story about growing up? Why in hell would I want to do that? That requires opening the door – that immense, heavy, menacing separation between today and everything that happened as a child. I have spent years laboring to keep that door bolted shut, but I couldn't. Some force beyond me, beyond reason and understanding, kept pushing it open.

*I don't want to look. I don't want to see, I don't want to remember what is behind that door. I want to keep pretending that today doesn't have anything to do with yesterday.*

Why would I want to remember the image of dad pulling out of the driveway with Curt in the car, leaving me and Charles, with not a shred of understanding as to why we would be left behind? Interesting that I feel no sadness for myself, only for Charles. It's as if I had no expectation whatsoever that dad would have included me.

What's the point in remembering? I always feel sad. I know there are good memories, but the bad, the sadness, seem always to overlay the good.

How many years of therapy will it take to put all this to rest? To reconcile a childhood I've tried to forget but couldn't? What could possibly be healing in remembering mom outside on Saturday – when the whole world is home – banging pots and pans together? What on earth is she doing? I have a crazy mother, and now everyone in the neighborhood knows it, too.

The only birthday I can remember is the last year daddy was home – in first or second grade. Coming home from school, walking toward the front door, I was a little hopeful, a little excited. This is *my* special day. It's the only day that is all about me, not anyone else. It's still "light" on this side of the door. If I open the door, will the light flood into the house, or will the darkness suck me in? If I don't open the door, I won't have to risk losing the precious little that I do have. But what if I open it and there are balloons and streamers and a cake and presents and everyone is smiling and happy to see me, and they all yell, "Surprise!".

I push open the door and daddy is standing there. "It's your day to take the garbage out." That's all.

Oh no, the darkness is starting to suck me in. I feel it pulling me straight toward daddy. I don't want to go there. I empty the garbage. I'm numb. Go walk on the path to the signboards, I tell myself; then you can cry.

It's too much to feel. It's bigger than I am. By the time I get to the path, I can't feel; I can think, though. Don't feel. Don't hope. Don't hurt. Just be. Why couldn't I have just hated *him* instead of me?

Rarely do I revisit my earliest memory – lying in my bed in a very small bedroom. I look in one of the corners and see a large black spider. The spider terrifies me. Equally terrifying is the response daddy might have to my fear of it. I am paralyzed with fear of a large spider and a frightening father. I am encased in fear, inside my little body, inside my little bedroom, within a world with no way out.

Diane

*Mother that was not a person. Father that was not human. There are no questions. There is only waiting. The child cannot face the memory. Blind-eyed I see the past… The mother cannot stop it. She will not see.*

I open my eyes and look around. The school bus is empty. I must have fallen asleep and missed my stop. Where is Denae? My heart starts beating really fast. I am too terrified to cry, fearing that I will never see my family again. I feel more alone than I have ever felt in my seven years. Will the bus ever stop? Will I be lost forever on this long, winding country road? I am afraid to speak to the driver, feeling ashamed for missing my stop. I can't tell him how to get back to my house; the landscape is too unfamiliar. I am afraid to ask him to take me home – afraid he will say no – that this is my punishment for missing my bus stop.

Years later, when I look back on this memory, it helps me understand how this incident shaped my adult perception of the world. When I'm driving, I have a great fear of getting lost, especially on backroads. I'm never quite sure where I'm going even if I have been there before. Throughout my school years, I often got lost in the corridors, experiencing panic, not knowing where to find my classrooms. I often feel disconnected from life – like the experience on the bus where I felt adrift, cut off from my family and alone.

To this day, I can never take naps – possibly due to that long-ago fateful nap which felt like it would cost me my family and my life. The memory of how I eventually got home has vanished. This remains part of the mystery.

Karen

Whenever mom was pregnant and just days from delivering, daddy would drive us cross-country in one of his old clunkers to Grandma Hartmann, my maternal grandmother, who lived on a farm in St. Cloud, Minnesota.

To be exact, I emerged on Sept. 20, 1949, from my mother's worn and tired body in Bemidji, Minnesota. (But I always said Cass Lake to make it sound more upscale; address gentrification was to be a compulsive habit until my 20s). I came home from the hospital wrapped in Grandma Hartmann's flannel nightgown because an early snow had fallen the night before. She weighed 215 pounds, while I weighed in at a measly six.

Shortly after I was born, mom had no milk to nurse me. Years later, she told me she had gone to the icebox and found only an onion inside. It made her cry, so she brought me back over to Grandma Hartmann's where food was always plentiful.

Along with milk cows and pigs, grandma also kept chickens. After our family left Minnesota for the West Coast, she would cry when she scattered the cornmeal and scratch for them because she knew they were eating better than her own grandchildren. Over the years, she sent mom what must have been a small fortune in emergency money, but she never let Grandpa Hartmann know.

The swing is a difficult image for me, summoning up a sense of deep sadness and isolation. By the age of two, my babysitter was a primitive swing dad had built. It hung from two hooks in the ceiling over the extra bed in the living room, in case I should fall out. The lengths of rope were so short my bare legs dangled high above the bed – not close enough to be able to touch any of my three sisters. If they stood on tiptoe on the mattress, they could just reach my feet to give me a little push to start me in motion. But the sagging mattress and height of my perch discouraged their efforts, leaving me most of the time on my own. I sat motionless for hours in the warmer air near the ceiling, gazing down at them playing, listening to their voices. It was like being alone without actually being alone.

<u>Denae</u>
My earliest memory, at age 4 or 5, remains to this day, more than 50 years later, the most vivid, the most beautiful of my entire life. At the time our family of six – mom, dad, Elaine, Diane, Karen and myself – lived in rural Minnesota in a ramshackle old farmhouse, deep in the backwoods. It must have been fairly late in the evening because I remember how very dark and quiet it was –not even a cricket was chirping – when daddy ordered me outside for some infraction I had committed. Wet cheek pressed tightly for comfort against the peeling wood of a fence at the back of the house, I felt alone, scared, and desperately sad. *Would I be out here all night?* We often heard wolves and coyotes howling after dark, and daddy had put no time limit on my expulsion.

It could have been minutes, or it could have been hours. All I know is eventually I merged with the darkness and the quiet, waiting, just waiting like the night, for morning to come with its bird calls and warm sunshine. I had no expectation of rescue or reprieve, no ability to transform the moment into anything beyond what it was.

Then, I don't know why, I happened to look up. And that changed everything – my punishment, my fear, and ultimately the rest of my life.

Looking out beyond the sooty darkness that had become me, I saw wide glowing bands of pure color streaming all the way across the sky from horizon to horizon. It was as though someone had inverted vast rows of tulips and irises at the peak of their bloom, parallel rows bursting with fuchsias, pomegranate reds, teals, ocean blues, tangerine pinks, lime greens and lemony yellows. No stars could be seen, nor any of the blackness of an evening sky. Instead, were these impossibly colored, luminous swathes, shimmering, reveling across the Cimmerian expanse of that Minnesota night.

So unexpected, so spectacular was the scene, I could not look for too long. In an instant, I knew what it all meant and raced inside to tell my family. Breathless, wild-eyed, I announced with all the emotion a 4-year-old could express, "It's the end of the world! Come and look! It's the end of the world!!"

Of course, everyone jumped up to follow me, even daddy. For several minutes we all stood there, gazing up at this astonishing sight. Beyond that, I cannot say – because my memory stops there.

In the years that followed, I would ask family members from time to time what they recalled of that night. Unbelievably, *no one* remembered – no one but me. Which has confounded and baffled me my entire life. *How could anyone forget a night that remarkable?*

It has taken a long time to unravel this mystery, but I think I finally know the answer. Neither dad, mom, nor my sisters remember it because I'm the only one who saw all those blazing colors. That heavenly spectacle was created just for me. And, no, it was not the aurora borealis on an exceptionally good night. Not only have I viewed these elusive light displays in Minnesota and Canada, I've also spent exhaustive library hours researching them to determine if the celestial phenomenon I witnessed bore any resemblance to the northern lights. There was simply no comparison between the two.

That one exceptional night imparted a special grace to my life which has never lapsed. In times of deepest sorrow – the plane crash deaths of my youngest brothers, the five suicide attempts in our family – I have never felt alone nor abandoned. It is clear to me that not only was I given the gift of extraordinary beauty that evening, I was also given the gift of unconditional love.

Keith

It was the summer of 1957 and our family was now living in Peshastin, Washington, in the middle of an apple orchard. Dad worked as a picker and a pruner – no doubt feeling his larger talents and abilities were degraded by this menial employment. He held many jobs like this one, jobs that attracted migrant laborers or men hiding from the law – men with suspicious histories. His meager income barely provided food and shelter for us.

Our house, one of the many pickers' shacks, was covered in oily, black tarpaper. I don't remember the inside, only that the two small rooms were inadequate for a family of seven, and that in the absence of running water, the toilet was outside in a shed close to the house.

One day dad walked in the door with a great gift for me – a full Indian headdress! As a 5-year-old I was speechless and just stood there looking at it. Rarely did we receive gifts of any kind, so I felt quite important. Unfortunately, its downside was soon revealed. Setting the crown of red feathers on my head, dad said, "Son, when I'm gone, you'll be the man of the house." His words didn't mean a thing until the federal marshal drove up, handcuffed him and hauled him away. You see, dad had gone AWOL from the army many years earlier; Uncle Sam had finally caught up with him. I found out later it was mom who had called the military authorities, because dad had started to hear voices and was displaying bizarre behaviors.

"1 little, 2 little, 3 little Indians, 4 little, 5 little, 6 little Indians ..." How clearly I remember standing outside our tarpaper shack with the fruit trees as a backdrop, proudly wearing my red war bonnet as dad was driven away to face justice. Yep, there I was, heap big chief Keith

– Chief-in-Charge.

For years afterward, the scene haunted me, because being so young at the time I was hardly prepared to be the man of the house. I felt my inadequacy deeply, not knowing how to measure up to dad's expectations. Later on in my teens, dad was hauled off again, but for different reasons. This time I *was* old enough to assume some responsibility, but didn't. Mom had returned to college for her A.A. degree, and acquired a good job with the state, thus enabling us to get off welfare. She needed me to help out at home, but by then I was too involved in drugs and alcohol to offer her any support.

Gail

My earliest memory is being very sick at age five. With a raging temperature of 106 degrees, mom and daddy had me bundled up so tight I could barely breathe. Finally, they drove me to the hospital. The doctor took one look at me and asked, "Why in God's name do you have so many blankets on her? Can't you see she's burning up with fever?" Stripping me down to my underpants, he turned me over to a nurse who gave me a sponge bath with cool water.

After being admitted and assigned to a bed, I heard the doctors discussing my "convulsions." No one explained what they were, but I wished I could have them every day. I had never been treated so well in my life. If simple convulsions were all it took to land you in a place like this, then you could definitely count me in.

A lovely nurse with long pink fingernails took care of me. Every day she bathed me, combed my hair, read me stories – and the food was out of this world. I thought I had died and gone to heaven.

I remember Elaine, only 13 at the time, visiting me every day. Each afternoon at the lunch hour she would ask to be excused and then walked the mile from school to the hospital to check in on me. Her face always had such a look of concern. I wondered if she thought I was going to die. I hoped I wouldn't, because I just wanted to stay here forever: a bed all to myself, unlimited amounts of ice cream and Jell-O, and nurses constantly checking on me to see if there was anything I needed. I never had it so good!

The doctors finally determined I had a kidney infection and that the convulsions had been caused by my extremely high fever. Regrettably, I improved after a few days, so I was sent home. And even though I waited weeks for the symptoms to reoccur, they never did.

A few years later I suffered from chronically infected tonsils. Rejoicing in my good fortune, I prayed each night they would need to be surgically removed so I could experience once again the sheer joy of being at the hospital.

Elaine

Weekends are always an adventure because daddy takes us camping to Chimacum Creek, a wild, hilly forested area in Western Washington state.

Keith and Karen, at 2 and 5, are tethered to a tree by a long length of rope, while mom is squatting down at the creek washing out dirty diapers. I try not to look at her raw, bleeding knuckles as she scrubs up and down against the metal-ribbed washboard, while the rippling current rinses away her blood and the diaper debris. All that clean sparkling water spilling down from the hills into the sandy-bottomed pools hopping with water-skimmers – too bad it has to be polluted everywhere we go by all those grubby diapers.

Daddy is fishing higher up in the thick timber and underbrush, trying to catch his limit to grill for our lunch, along with pan-fried potatoes. Deliberately smacking his lips while we eat, he always says, "Who'd want a fat old lake trout when you can catch these fresh brook trout – nothin' tastier in the world!"

Sometimes Denae, Diane, and I tag along with him, pushing away the low-hanging branches laced with spider webs as we hike higher up along the creek. Daddy thinks we're old enough to toss out the line from his bamboo pole, hoping to get a nibble. But mostly we sit together up on the bank, watching him wade in the icy spring water in his old leather shoes, around slippery boulders and beneath skinny waterfalls. On the way back to camp we walk behind him carrying his silvery wet trout, which have been strung through the gills on a cut tree branch. Water squishes out from his shoe tops, making squeaky sounds as though a mouse were hiding somewhere inside his socks.

A lot of mornings we get up early, the sky still streaked with pink, and go clam digging on the Puget Sound beaches before the tide can return, looking for the long necked geoducks, sooty-backed mussels or razor clams. The little spitting geysers pock-marking the sand give away their locations, and we all yell, "Gooey-duck!" so mom and daddy can run over with their buckets to dig them before they get away.

At night we sleep under the stars on beds made of cut evergreen boughs, covered with old woolen army blankets. Mom reminds us to check for pine cones before lying down. We worry about the ticks too; but since you can't see them at night, the skin check will have to wait until morning. With the bullfrogs croaking like bass drums beneath the waterfalls, we fall asleep watching for shooting stars.

# SUN RUNNING

Diane and Denae

*I have waited so long to be free, so much longer than I have been myself...*

–Diane, *journal entry*

<u>Denae</u>

At age 22, my twin Diane wrote "To Where We Did and Were" – a troubling, yet compelling reminiscence of our childhood.

> Hunched inside a vault fault
> of strained dry cry,
> where matter splattered
> in spot dotting
> strains of restraints
> and faint paint-waiting
>
> i was trying dying
> scorn born,
> birth worthless
> why crier
> that I had become –
> sometime
> in mind finding
> or self shelving
>
> and the fast past
> never passed
> i was too dead to pant,
> besides, tombs are so tight
> and why fight night?
> light was a right turn
> but I was left.
>
> borrow from tomorrow?
> but you can't
> when you owe for yesterday

and mortgaged today
for the still bill
that's paid in delays.

and I sold old dreams
for stocks that bankruptured me
into lie ability
and a closed account of myself
but you knew me before
we would have laughed then
at "trying dying"
"birth worthless"

we played leap frog
over the green streams
of the mirrored meadows
where our reflections knew us
and smiles were easy
we did. . .didn't we?

sun running
winding windless
to nowhere

we learned by touching
much was our knowledge of moving things.
our hands were our minds
and cupped thoughts in astonishment

tameless
and nameless
we were then. . .weren't we?

but time climbed between us
and fixed a city
that mixed us
up and down in misdirection
and we lost our ways

i urbanized
but you synthesized
and found green streams
in my city pity

untame me now,
unname me now
and I shall sun run
with you again
to where we did
and to where we were...

This journey is a remembered vision of a time reeling with horror, joy, pain and inquisitiveness – a *Grand Guignol* tableau spinning out more questions than answers for a young mind desperately seeking order. How aptly this term references the anchoring theme of our past. Original to Paris of 1897, it is a genre of theater specializing in brutality, mayhem and insanity – translated as the Big Puppet. As a tableau, it becomes a stage set with costumed actors who neither move nor speak.

Childhood is not always the idyllic paradise we wish it to be. The villains and monsters of fairy tales can be confused with real-life parents who can also be villains and monsters. Reality is a changeable commodity, especially with parenting such as ours – a hurricane mix of schizophrenia, alcoholism, sadistic violence and sexual abuse.

The house lights have been dimmed for calamity and doom – a stage-noir whose curtain rises and falls like a guillotine of the French Revolution upon the terrified players fleeing in chaos from the lead actor/director... our father. Sets, scenes, costumes change so fast that a child becomes disoriented, benumbed. We look always to center stage. Our very lives depend on the persona occupying that space: Captain Hook? Sinbad? Quasimodo? Dracula? Daddy...?

time climbed between us
and fixed a city
that mixed us
up and down in misdirection
and we lost our ways

tameless
and nameless
we were then. . . weren't we?


Reality plays tag with fiction, then steals the clothing of truth and wants to become a fairy tale – but fancies it knows more than the storyteller – so it changes the words, and then no one knows the story anymore. Since words can't be trusted, and witches and ogres are everywhere, "sun running" becomes impossible. Maybe the sun is really the moon—the difference between Light and Darkness a masterful illusion. Has the "fast past" really passed? Or is it still at the train station, only pretending to move? One can't be certain of anything, so life becomes a whirling carousel without a STOP button, a shattered kaleidoscope. No longer a joyful thing, it has become a burden, a frantic effort to reclaim those happier times before the witch came to visit, when:

we played leap frog
over the green streams
of the mirrored meadows
where our reflections knew us
and smiles were easy

Yes, indeed, the power of the fairy tale. Consider a perennial favorite, *Little Red Riding Hood*. That prim, vermilion-caped blonde. I still think of her with the same indignant wrath I felt as a child. How *could* she be so stupid as to look upon the wolf in granny's bed, wearing her flannel gown and cap, and not realize he was definitely *not* grandma? Any fool could see that furry wolf snout and long red tongue poking out from the ruffles was certainly not anyone's grandmother! Even if blondie had entered the room blindfolded, surely she could have smelled the difference between dirty, wet animal fur and the lavender soap, chocolate-chip cookie aroma – which everyone knows is how a grandmother's house smells.

Little Red Cape's powers of observation were appalling. She deserved to be eaten by the wolf, and I was sorry that in the end she was rescued by the woodsman.

Unlike her, we learned to be acutely tuned to the dangers in our environment – most specifically to "daddy." Many days as I approached the house with an armload of schoolbooks and assignment notes, I would see a dense black cloud hovering above the door, prelude to calamity.

Psychic phenomenon? Imagination? What did it matter? I only knew, once inside, to tread lightly, to escape to an upstairs bedroom, where the rest of my siblings would be. Daddy was clearly in a frightful mood – the mood for the misbegotten. He and the spittoon can and his beer bottle – that odious brown, rancid-breath-smelling bottle that I avoid even now in grocery stores and supermarkets, veering sharply off-course when I spy it in the wine and beverage aisle. As though mere proximity could carry me back to the realm of those dreadful memories.

Elaine

I grew up one of six sisters, but most of the time I felt lost, isolated and maltreated, disconnected from my family and my feelings – trapped inside a space filled with terrible secrets. From this private hell, wardened by fear and shame, I escaped by reading books, most often fairy tales. As the oldest and the only half-sister, I related to the story of Cinderella, seeing myself toiling among the ashes. On school mornings my responsibility was to rise first and collect wood for the stove, tending the fire until the breakfast cereal was cooked. For many long years, the dull routine of meals, laundry and housecleaning fell to me. I dreamed of being rescued by a kind and handsome prince –delivered from drudgery and mind-numbing isolation into a state of cherished royalty. I looked for glimmers of hope, wondering if it would ever be possible to escape my intolerable existence.

Denae

It is an August morning, and really hot. Our family is camping in a wooded area along the Spokane River. I smell potatoes frying, so I stumble from the tent where almost everyone else is still sleeping. I guess I'll help peel more potatoes for breakfast. Looking over at the picnic table a few yards away, I see mom sitting there. She looks funny because there is a white diaper wrapped around her head. She's opening a can of lard to add more grease to the frying pan. As she turns away from the wood fire, I see a big red spot on the cloth over her forehead. I feel sick to my stomach, remembering daddy yelling at her last night when we were supposed to be asleep. I don't want to know what made that big red spot on her forehead. I don't want any breakfast.

Karen

"Stormy weather" is the usual, the only forecast at our house. This particular day, a full-on gale is advancing in the living room as daddy, dish plate in hand, addresses mom: "I'll teach you to defy me. Why can't you do as I say? How many times do I have to tell you, you thick-skulled Norwegian, to do what I say?!" All seven of us kids watch in horror as he draws his arm back and then hurls the platter at mom. She ducks, and it hits Keith, a skinny eight-year-old in the head. Stunned by the blow, he doesn't make a sound, just bleeds a lot, and is taken to the hospital. The doctor on duty asks a few questions – none of them the right ones – and gives Keith 40 stitches.

Scars are like memories; some go away and some remain, like Keith's – a little reminder every time he looks in the mirror.

Another evening a year later, dad is upstairs yelling at Keith, both out of our sight at the top of the enclosed stairwell. Lunging in anger, he pushes at Keith's back, and we listen in alarm to the sound of a body rolling over and over, down the 15 bare wood steps. Fearfully, we await the sight of our brother. Amazingly, it is dad whose body appears. Our brother dodged instinctively at the critical second. Overwhelmed with hysteria and the irony of this outcome, we all run outside as fast as we can to the railroad ditch beyond the sign boards. There, safe from dad's rage, we laugh until we puke. And then we laugh some more.

Denae

Vigilant, ever vigilant. Those were the watchwords of our youth. To drop one's guard, even for a moment, was to invite peril and calamity. Like soldiers on the battlefield, we trained ourselves to discern

20

intent and movement, to identify the enemy whether it be high noon, dawn or midnight.

And when you do sleep, don't sleep too soundly, don't be lulled into relaxation when prayers are over and the sandman has turned out the lights. Because if you do, you might not hear the door begin to creak as the knob is stealthily turned... and you are pulled from your bed. Lecture time or punishment time or – something much worse. Daddy is *back* on center stage. So, forget about being alert for the history exam in school tomorrow. Keep your eyes open; pretend to listen and nod at the appropriate times. Practice falling asleep while you are standing there in your nightgown, wide awake.

Can you understand now why Little Red Riding Hood infuriated me so?

# SNAPSHOTS
# OF the UNCONVENTIONAL

Front: Charles, Diane, Gwen, Dad, Curt
Back: Karen, Denae, Keith, Elaine, Gail

*From childhood's hour I have not been as others were –*

Edgar Allan Poe

How do you know if you are unconventional? Is it a good thing or a bad thing? Isolation negates the question because without neighbors there is no society, and without society there can be no comparisons. If no one is watching, then who really cares?

We kids certainly didn't – that is until we moved out of the woods and into a neighborhood. Then the question became inescapable, and we did care. A lot. So when the answer arrived—and it didn't take long – not wishing to kill the messenger, we befriended him instead. Especially since it was obvious he would not be leaving anytime soon. However, lurking in the linguistic shadows was that churlish mongrel, dysfunctional, whose company we did disdain. He lacked the quixotic flair of *unorthodox, bohemian, eccentric, bizarre, crazy* – all chums of unconventional.

Gail

Who would have imagined that my choosing to wear red rather than blue shorts one summer day would result in such a humiliating outcome? It was a sultry July afternoon, and daddy was hurrying Keith, 10, me, 9, Gwen, 6, Charles, 5, and Curt, 2, into our old station wagon after purchasing a stack of lumber for a fencing project.

"Hey, mister," a millworker called out. "You're not going anywhere without red-flagging those boards. They're sticking out at least four feet behind you!"

Exasperated, daddy looked under car seats and into the glove compartment for a scrap of material to tie to the lumber. When he began eyeballing the boys' clothes, I began to sweat, knowing full well the lengths he would go to get what he wanted. Why, why had I chosen the red shorts when I could just have easily put on the blue?

I held my breath as daddy scanned the drab colors of the boys' clothing, then moved on to scrutinize Gwen. Wouldn't you know, even at six, she had the foresight to choose green shorts and a white shirt. So there she sat, confident and relaxed in the front seat, in no danger of being parted from her clothes, while I was counting the seconds until his eyes reached me. My fear was not so much the surrendering of my shorts as it was that their removal would render me *naked* from the waist down.

Since I owned only three underpants, it was mathematically impossible to put on a clean pair each day of the week. Even by turning them inside-out to extend their wearability, come Saturday I was simply out of clean underwear. In the past when I ran out, I would sneak a pair of Keith's. However, that little caper ended the day in Phys Ed when my classmates discovered me wearing his Fruit-of-the-Looms and laughed me out of the locker room. Better to go undy-less, I reasoned, than to suffer that humiliation again.

Finally, daddy's gaze fell upon my blood-red shorts. Like the wolf salivating over Red Riding Hood, his eyes glittered with triumph. "Take off those shorts right now! You *knew* I was looking for something red!" he demanded.

Trying to postpone the inevitable, I squirmed and hung my head, hoping by some miracle he would change his mind. "But daddy," I wailed, "I can't take them off; I'm not wearing any underpants."

"Do you think I give a good goddamn if you're sitting there in your birthday suit? I need those shorts. If you don't pull them off right now, I'll take them off you myself!"

Realizing it was futile to argue, I slowly pushed them down my legs and handed them over. As he tied them to the board ends, I hissed to Charles and Curt sitting alongside me, "If you take one look at me, I'll scratch your eyes out with my bare hands when we get home!"

I must have made my point because for the rest of the trip they both looked straight ahead, absolutely inert, as though rigor mortis had claimed their bodies. Not a word was uttered as I sat with my legs tightly crossed – now wondering how I might be reunited with my shorts at journey's end.

Luckily, Keith came to the rescue when we reached home, by grabbing them off the lumber and tossing them to me through the open window. From that day on, wardrobe selection took on a whole new meaning. Never again would I wear anything that might fulfill any function other than clothing my body. Red was banished from my closets: to this day I am reluctant to wear the color.

Denae

In political terms, our household was definitely not a democracy, but rather a dictatorship, with dad as commander-in-chief. There was no second in command. Mom was as powerless as the rest of us, except on Saturday, laundry day, when dad would leave the house until suppertime. She could be as terrifying as dad, albeit over something as trivial as our dirty clothes. It was a day we dreaded all week and cowered in subservience for the six to eight hours it took to launder 11 people's clothing.

Gwen

Make eight, nine, ten piles of dirty clothes. Make each pile the same distance from the next one. Line them up in rows. Don't look around the basement – at the walls or ceilings that are dirty, filled with ancient spider webs and other unimaginable things. And don't even glance into the lower basement, with the dirt floor and the darkness and that secret passageway that all the mice use to get up into our house. Don't look down there – you might see something.

Be careful with the wringer. Remember the last time you got your hair caught in it and no one was there to help you. Pray that mom doesn't come downstairs to check and see if you've changed the water. Don't let her see how dirty the wash water is. Put the clothes in the rinse water. That water is dirty, too.

Hurry up. Hurry up and get the clothes on the line. Line them up perfectly. Put the same amount of fabric in each clothespin. Hang all the shirts in a row, all the pants in a row, all the socks together and all the towels together. For the moment, I feel there is order to life; at least something is in my control.

Finish the last load. Don't leave anything lying on the floor in that scary basement room. Don't glance into the pitch-black lower level as you climb up the stairs to the dining room. Close the door quick. Latch it with the hook and eye clasp that masquerades as a lock. Now I'm "safe." Funny how we have no key for the front door, no protection from the outside world. But there's a deadbolt on the door that leads down into the basement, into the darkness, into the bowels of our life.

Gail

One afternoon, I was nonchalantly walking through the kitchen past mom, wearing some of Keith's clothes and his baseball cap. Out of nowhere, mom grabbed me and started pounding my head against the floor. Lucky for me, with all the shaking, my cap fell off and she realized I was Gail and not Keith. It was Keith she wanted, now more upset because she had wasted her energies banging the wrong head. With that, I was allowed to put the cap back on and go about my business. I did warn Keith a few minutes later that it might be prudent for him to avoid mom for the rest of the day.

Denae

Winter laundry was the worst. None of us wanted to leave the warm house to be exposed to the icy blast of Arctic air in order to hang the dozens of diapers, bed sheets and clothing on the outside lines. It might take all day, but eventually those articles would be dry enough to be returned inside to complete the process. So with the wan afternoon light fast fading from a frosty January sky, we would pit our energies against the wooden clothespins, trying to detach them, now solidly frozen to the cotton fabrics.

We had no need for a clothes basket because the shirts, diapers and pants were all stiff as boards. If we tried to bend them to make them more manageable, they would snap apart as quickly and cleanly as though sheared by a scissors. These flat planks would be stacked like firewood and then carefully maneuvered through the kitchen door to the warmer air of the dining room, where the one heat vent was located.

Blue jeans were carried in horizontally as one might convey the sawed-off limbs of cadavers. Those trouser legs were not flat like the sheets, but rounded due to the gusting winds, which slowly froze them into place on the lines.

They would be deposited in standing positions on the floors. Unable to resist the theatric possibilities, we would rearrange them in conversational groups throughout the living and dining rooms. As the pants defrosted, they would become more pliant, whereupon we would bend the knees and seat them on chairs and sofas, occasionally pairing them with a thawing party dress.

Due to our isolation during the long winter months, we derived great amusement from these clothesline mannequins. However, in the midst of the frivolity, we had to be mindful that other items as well, like pillow cases and sheets, needed thawing so that they too could eventually dry. Since the 3-by-3-foot grating in the dining room was the only heat vent, situated over the oil furnace in the basement, mom had nailed a large metal hook in the ceiling above it. Elaine, the tallest, would hang the sheets one at a time from the hook, where the surging air would extend the billowing fabric like some cheap Arab tent filling with desert wind.

Meanwhile, the rest of us, shivering in our wool sweaters and jackets could hardly wait for the laundry to dry so we could reassemble over that coveted warm space. Then like a remake of Marilyn Monroe pushing down her white dress over a New York sidewalk grate, we would bunch together, holding down our own skirts, flapping puckishly around our waists.

Elaine, more mindful of architectural supports and stresses, could not entirely dismiss her chronic fear that eventually the combined weight of our six or seven bodies would collapse that fragile 3-foot square. Like the buccaneer movies we watched of prisoners dropping through false castle floors to the dungeons below, we too would one day plummet through the dining room floor into the fiery red jaws of our overheated furnace.

It's not surprising that, until the ages of 12 or 13, we older girls lacked a vocabulary by which to describe our home environment, since we lived most of those years without neighbors. (In later years Karen would declare, not without humor, that our family saga was one part American Dream and several parts American Gothic).

Because dad was AWOL, we pulled up stakes once, and often twice, every year to keep a few miles between us and the CIA or FBI, whichever group dad believed was pursuing him. We seemed always to be on the run, and our possessions amounted to what we could cram into the car trunk or tie to its roof. The shacks, cabins, leaking farmhouses and other assorted shelters which we lived in –from California to Minnesota, Idaho and Washington —were always in isolated areas, which meant no neighbors to visit or observe by way of comparison. Under such circumstances, it was inevitable that for the first decade together we just assumed our household was normal.

Our settling in Greenacres, a suburb of Spokane, Washington in 1959 was a watershed moment for our intrepid family, now numbering eight. As we pulled out wool blankets, cardboard boxes of pans and dishes, and a few torn paper bags overfull with clothing from our old Buick, mom looked at dad and announced with finality, "I am *never* going to move again, Frank. This is it!!"

The places we live –do they find us, or do we find them? Late 1950s Spokane was not without its Steinbeckian features, though still bearing traces of a frontier town patina. The state's second largest city, with a river running through its center, was bordered by three Indian reservations and a sprawling mental hospital.

Southwest of downtown was Vinegar Flats, a patchwork of small Asian truck farms and shantytown buildings skirting the vinegar works plant, which employed most of the locals. Irrigation came from Hangman Creek, a ribbon of a stream, so named because of the lynching of several Indian chiefs, decades earlier.

Situated to the north along the banks of the Spokane River was Peaceful Valley, remnant of a rowdy 1930s squatters' camp, and now a languid pre-era Woodstock where the more ambitious worked at the nearby coffin factory.

Sprague Avenue, an east-west arterial was home to a number of gypsy families. The colorfully garbed, black haired women sat inside large glassed storefronts, beneath cardboard signs lettered with: PALM READING and FORTUNE TELLING. On the opposite side of town was Skid Row, a mean streets slum of homeless transients, dimly lit bars and crumbling brick tenements grafted with swaying black iron ladders for emergency exits.

Monroe Street Bridge at city center, adorned with cow-skull gargoyles, not only spanned the river for convenient crossing, but unfortunately, was also used as a point of departure for suicide jumpers. Of course, as newly arrived residents, we had yet to learn such details. Mindful of our ignorance, an omniscient destiny had found for us in Spokane and Greenacres a perfect match for the outré, decidedly unconventional nature of our existence.

Diane

The house itself sat at the base of a triangle, its construction like a ransom note – cut and pasted, pieced together by a random assortment of mismatched wood, chunks of brick, discarded railroad ties, tarpaper and burlap. Broken windows were grafted with cardboard and plastic strips, while old rags were used to seal the caulking cracks.

The railroad tracks behind the house paralleled Appleway, the main road, forming one side of the triangle. Sprague Avenue, the street in front, formed the other side. Where Sprague, Appleway and the tracks intersected was the apex of the triangle – a perfect arrow pointing to Greenacres Junior High, my nemesis.

Mom and Diane

On the left, beyond our half-acre vegetable garden were the gigantic, two-story signboards. We couldn't see what they were advertising because we faced them from the back. Dad was paid $50 a year for allowing them at the edge of our land.

When we first moved into our house, the billboards seemed a strange architecture in the backyard, like looking at scaffolding that was holding up the sky – a protective shield concealing us from the curious eyes in passing cars. The longer we lived in Greenacres, the larger the signboards seemed. Maybe it was my wishful thinking causing them to grow taller and taller, hoping my classmates would not notice the rundown house beyond the dry, yellow field through the cross-hatching of two-by-fours and gigantic posts. Hoping they would be distracted by the pretty advertisements. If people could not see our property, our poverty, then maybe it would not exist – a way of thinking that set me on the path to practicing the art of being invisible.

Equally fascinating were the railroad tracks running just behind the billboards – a magical place for me. Occasionally, on the way home from school, I would follow the tracks instead of Sprague Avenue. Looking ahead to the east were pine-covered hills and bleached-out fields colored with purple thistles and blue bachelor buttons that led eventually to the Bitterroot Mountains in Idaho. Looking west toward town, the tracks disappeared into a landscape of metal sheds, trailer parks, taverns, gun shops and more trailer parks, with wagon wheels and deer antlers everywhere – in yards, hanging on signs, in storefronts, by mailboxes. The buildings were so square, so utilitarian, so prefab, so aluminum, so in a row – no grass, just dirt, rocks and asphalt.

I liked to put my hands on the tracks while they were still warm from the passing train, then practice my ballet steps, using them like a gymnast on a balancing beam. I was mesmerized by the rail lines and the ties connecting them – always evenly spaced, always orderly. The symmetry was calming, affording me a kind of emotional security. Sometimes I laid my ear against the tracks, like in the cowboy movies, listening for a coming train. I loved the sound it made as it sped by – a moment of pure power – and loud enough to drown out my father's drunken screaming.

The clamor of the train awakened a power within me. That sound became a siren call promising freedom at the end of the tracks. I loved standing between the still vibrating rails as the train disappeared, watching the cloudy strata of its wake. The tracks seemed to lead to a magical world where there was always plenty of food, where all shoes were beautiful, and where no one was hurt or crying.

In later years the tracks did become my path to freedom, when at 27, my boyfriend had punched me in the face. I had to work that night as a barmaid in a popular nightspot. One of my first customers was a guy I knew from high school. I handed him his beer, trying to dodge his gaze from my swollen black eye – like so many black eyes mom had suffered at my father's fist. If there is an emotion beyond humiliation, that is what I was feeling. When I returned home, my boyfriend was gone, so I collected what belongings I could carry in my arms and left. No car. I headed for the railroad tracks, knowing it would be a long, dark five-mile trip to mom's house in Greenacres. I began running over the ties like I was the train. I became the train – running and running. The miles sped by like the wind was pushing me. I was a stream of power, an ecstasy of liberation. Never again would I be victim to a man's fist as my mother had been. Instead, I would be the train – this torrent of steel. In what seemed like only seconds, I was there – at the signboards and the ditch. I collapsed after I jumped off the tracks, then ran to the house. Mom was there crying, but she was happy, too, because I had made my escape.

The garden was the centerpiece of our property – the prize between the signboards and ransom note construction of our house. It glittered green, an oasis in the barren landscape of thistles and dandelions. Yet it was an oasis of unnatural shape –a shape determined by the hostile terrain, or perhaps, as I often imagined, by a UFO that had once landed there, imprinting its irregular contours onto the ground.

But it wasn't a UFO, it was mom. She was the true architect of the garden, with its latticework of irrigation canals. While she worked, dad would sit nearby in the broken shade of a ragged line of pine trees, a beer bottle in his hand, complaining about the heat and swatting at the flies. He would watch as the oncoming water would spill effortlessly into an intricate pattern of smaller furrows running alongside the carefully weeded kohlrabi, beets, zucchini, cucumbers, onions, rutabagas and tomatoes. When the stream flowed evenly, it was beautiful to see the wet blueness filling the garden row by row, etching its landscape in shimmering, liquid frames of water.

Conversely, there would be times when the driving current would overrun rock-clogged rows, threatening to flood the entire area, and mom would scream out, "Diane! Someone! Shut off the water!" If I couldn't find dad's big wrench, in desperation I would hold up my hands against the rushing torrent as the wall of water cascaded over me.

One time when dad came home from the tavern in a drunken rage, mom grabbed us kids, yelling "Run to the ditch!" I remember being surprised at how fast she was, keeping pace with all seven of us as we fled across the field. We jumped down the bank and lay on our stomachs in the mud. I wasn't that scared because she seemed so assured, so capable of protecting us. When outside, she had a will and determination that could not be broken – unlike the way dad victimized her inside the house.

I will never forget the afternoon several of us were in the kitchen, when I opened the broom closet looking for a mop – and found mom crouched inside, hiding there after dad had punched her in the face and kicked her in the ribs. Running out to the garden, I knelt in the dirt by the cukes and tomatoes and kept seeing my mother's eyes in the broom closet. Like a wounded animal afraid to move, so beaten she didn't know she was our mother. She just stared – looking like she wanted us to disappear – as if we were a burden and she felt the guilt of wanting us gone. I prayed to God that He would spare me from my mother's fate, hoping to avoid marriage and having children. For years, I lived with the constant fear that I would not be able to love my own children.

Denae

We were all elated to be moving into a real house with a real bathroom, complete with porcelain tub. But best of all, we had neighbors. From an upstairs bedroom window, we could glimpse Greenacres Junior High, the school that would help immeasurably in defining us as individuals and as scholars. It was here that Diane and I as eighth-graders brought our 4-year-old brother for show and tell on the invitation of our math instructor – after informing him that Curt was a child prodigy. Of course he wasn't, but that didn't stop us. Each night after supper we coached him in memorizing simple geometric theorems to be sure he would be well prepared for his academic debut.

At the point that we had him comfortably settled in a chair before the class, we prompted him with, "Now, Curt, will you please explain to Mr. Kallas and the students what the Pythagorean Theorem is?"

Quick as a wink, little apple-cheeked Curt replied, "The square of the hypotenuse is equal to the sum of the square of the other two sides." Following that, he spoke briefly of Euclid, "paralyzed" lines, "rheumatoid angels," pyramids and trapeze "prisons." Geometry had never been so exciting. The entire class applauded, along with our teacher. Eminently gratified, Diane and I returned Curt –now an acclaimed genius –back home to his sandbox.

Karen has her own inimitable way of describing the community bordering our home at 17907 E. Sprague Avenue. She refers to it as "the phenomenon known as Greenacres."

Karen

Greenacres during the 1950s and 1960s was unlike any suburb in America. Simultaneously ahead of the times and seriously behind them, it knew little of the nuclear family structure, June Cleaver moms, or kitchens filled with new-fangled appliances. Rather, it was a veritable Poker Flats of misfits, felons, alcoholics, abandoned cars, treadle sewing machines – and did I mention the chronically unemployed?

Notable among Greenacreites was Oral Fraker, our 88-year old neighbor whose bed we inherited after his death. We called it the TB Bed because Oral had died of tuberculosis. With nine children and only four beds in our house, at "lights out," we all scrambled to claim our places in the safer beds, knowing the slowest and last would be left to crawl uneasily beneath the covers of the fatally infected TB bed.

For reasons long since forgotten, somehow Oral ended up being buried next to our Grandma Hartmann in the cemetery plot that had been designated for her second husband, Lawrence, who was interred instead in Minnesota next to his first wife.

As eccentric as Oral, was mom's best friend Mrs. Applegate, aka Johnny, who had retired to a two-room trailer after an illustrious past in Las Vegas. No one asked why she had decided upon our neighborhood, but there she was on foot (barefoot, that is) ambling back and forth between the assorted taverns, beauty parlors and food stops on Greenacres Road and Sprague Avenue. Totally nonjudgmental, as she had tried everything at least once, Johnny counseled mom on finances, motherhood and men. Mom referred to her visits with Johnny as her "R and R's" (furloughs away from us) and looked forward to being pampered there once a week.

"Rose, honey, come on in," she would croon. "You look beat. Take off your shoes and I'll make you a hot cup of blackberry tea. Now you just forget about your troubles, dearie; don't let those pecker necks get to you. Make yourself comfy on the couch, and we'll have a nice little chat."

A little of the Southern belle and a lot of Southern hospitality was innate to good-natured Johnny's personality. Once a ravishing beauty (she told us), her current indigent circumstances had reduced her to one cosmetic aid, a tube of blood red lipstick. She arched her eyebrows with it, rouged her ample cheeks, outlined her hazel eyes and colored her lumpy lips with it. Sitting below her over-permanented, dyed crimson hair, Johnny's face gave the appearance of a red-hot torch.

Denae

Next to Johnny Applegate, Helen Gentle was for years mom's closest friend and confidante. And like Johnny, Helen had a passion for fire engine-red lipstick, which always seemed over-generously applied to her thin lips, such that the overflow found its way onto her upper teeth and chin. Her only other beauty aid was a jet-black eyebrow pencil, which was also applied over-zealously to her brow – the effect of which was akin to two blackbirds in perpetual flight from her face. Helen was extremely protective of mom and was generous in availing her home as a welcoming sanctuary, an escape from dad's abuse and the stress of raising too many children.

The other occupant of Helen's home, besides her two tabbies, was her son, Jerry. "Gentle Fingers," as we called him, or "Crazy Fingers," as he called himself. Liberace was his mentor and calendar pin-up. It was with the sole intent of gaining this icon's attention that Jerry pursued his piano ambitions. His spare time was spent gilding himself in like fashion – amassing dozens of bejeweled jumpsuits and flaring capes in flashy reds, golds and hot pinks. His coiffure was heavily shellacked by hairspray, while his hands glittered with an assortment of oversized cocktail rings.

It was with tremendous interest that we older girls, Diane, Karen and myself, fixated on Jerry. Albeit, he was a pariah of sorts in the neighborhood – infamous, even as a teenager. To be precise, he was openly gay and reveled in flaunting his sexuality. Such frankly outrageous behavior appealed to us enormously, because compared to him we did not seem like such odd ducks, coming as we did from our own Twilight Zone household. So, we embraced Jerry as a soul mate and followed his musical career and antics with keen enthusiasm.

How could we not? Especially when we learned that he was the first person in Greenacres to undergo cosmetic facial surgery (he was only 19). What was even more remarkable was that he performed the surgery himself! Incisions, sutures and post-ops. This unprecedented revelation came about not through hearsay or rumor but rather from the reddened lips of his own mother – a conversation I overheard while Helen and mom were sitting together in our kitchen, drinking Sanka coffee.

"And Rose, you cannot believe…" Helen's voice dropped to a whisper, alerting me to lean closer to the doorway from the adjoining room to hear what would follow. Apparently, that very morning she had returned a tad early from a hair appointment and found Jerry in the bathroom, gazing purposefully into the mirror as he sutured a small incision on his cheek, using Helen's sewing needle, pink thread dangling.

Acne? Old scar tissue? An abscess? Shrieking, she ran to the bedroom for her nitroglycerine pills. Weeks of mandatory grounding, phone deprivation, a padlock to her sewing room, midnight lectures – nothing, it seemed, could deter Jerry from his now unstoppable obsession of altering and (hopefully) improving his face. Our obsession paralleled his in the months to come as each interaction with Jerry began with our rapt inspection of his nose, forehead, cheeks and jaw line. There were always detectable changes, and we discussed their success or lack thereof with the seriousness of surgeons at a medical conference.

36

Jerry was the Greenacres rock star. Like any other music groupies, we would attend his ragtime piano concerts at the Greenacres Grill or Savage House Pizza Parlor. In fact, so impressed were we by his musical abilities (or perhaps because he was the only musician we knew), that upon the death of our beloved grandma Hartmann, we asked if he would be the pianist for her funeral.

Jerry was thrilled by the invitation, already envisioning the event as he remarked, "I should probably wear my pink jumpsuit; it's always been one of her best colors."

He was on a roll. We had no idea, that in anticipation of his performance, Jerry had already conferred with grandma, months earlier, on music as well as floral arrangements. "You do know the number she wants played as her casket is wheeled down the aisle to the altar, don't you?" continued Jerry, not noticing we hadn't yet recovered from the image of him performing in flamingo-pink satin. It was to be, after all, the first funeral in our family. Unruffled, he finished with, "Yes, 'Raindrops Keep Falling on My Head.' It will liven up the mood a little."

He couldn't be serious. Of course, he knew it was impossible for us to confirm this with grandma since she was already in the process of being embalmed. However, to Jerry's credit, "Raindrops" was indeed played. After considerable family discussion, we all had agreed that it really was one of her favorites.

But we did put our foot down when he asked to do her makeup. You might think his request unusual. Actually, it was not, because I forgot to mention that Jerry's third passion (besides his piano playing and the reconstruction of his face) was his dream of opening a funeral parlor. He was going to call it "The Gentle Rest."

His small home library was crammed with books on embalming procedures, morticians, cremations and coffin designs. He really was expertly informed and conversant in these matters; as a matter of fact, he was employed part-time after school at the Thornhill Valley Funeral Home as a makeup assistant. On occasion, when short-staffed, the manager permitted him to usher in grieving families for viewings and also to chauffeur the lead hearse for interments.

So we did not doubt Jerry's abilities to capably rouge grandma's cheeks and coif her snowy white hair. Rather, it was that we knew him too well. He did so have a tendency to overdramatize in his showmanship. Had we allowed him access to grandma at this crucial time, we would have had no guarantees that in a moment of inspired staging, he might re-dress her in something more glamorous from his own well-stocked closets—a sequined, mink-lined bedjacket, perhaps, with matching brooch. Or, discover moments before the service, rising from the rim of her casket, the tailfeathers of some unhappy pheasant –ascending in resurrection—adornment to a felt hat topping her matronly hairdo. No, best to leave grandma's final gilding to the sensibilities of the funeral home's more conventional-minded staff.

There is a postscript to this story, and it has nothing to do with Jerry Gentle. In fact, he carried out his musical responsibilities with great aplomb. The problem was with mom. In the morning as we were all dressing for the funeral, she surprised us with, "I don't want to see *any* of you dressed in black today. It's spring. Grandma Hartmann lived a good life, and now she's with her beloved Lawrence in heaven. So wear pastels and whites for her funeral service. This is a time for rejoicing!"

The very idea! Unconventional as we usually were, this pronouncement seemed inexcusable, a deliberate heresy – maybe even a mortal sin by Catholic standards. "Rejoicing? Wearing *white*?" I for one, was not at all happy that grandma was gone; as a matter of fact, I was perfectly miserable. But, more to the point, every funeral we had ever seen, whether on television (think John Kennedy with the splendidly-veiled Jackie) or in newspapers, the grieving family always, *always* wore black. Mourning became Electra, and it certainly, we thought, suited us. Just this once, we had really looked forward to observing conventions. We had even practiced in front of our mirror, imitating the stately walk and controlled expression of the indomitable Jackie.

The day had dropped to a lower level of somber. We had to conform to mom's wishes, no matter how desperately wrong we knew her to be. And just imagine how horrified our proper, conservative grandmother would be to see us – her spit-polished, loving grandchildren, sitting teary-eyed in the front row, attired in pale pinks and whites, from our shoes, knee-highs and dresses to our all-white cotton gloves.

Can you blame me then, when I say that forever after, each time an occasion has arisen to recall or speak of this event, I always, always refer to it as "Grandma's Wedding." I can't help myself.

# A PASTICHE OF THE ABNORMAL

Diane, Dad, Karen, Denae, Elaine

*Time spins through the friction of the mind's apprehension, and pulls the universe into winds of change that blow thoughts into hurricanes.*

–Diane, journal entry

Conspiracy Theory. The bane, no, the nightmare of the paranoid-schizophrenic, and dad surely was one – although it would take years for us to learn the term and subsequently his place within its membership.

We lived in a Cold War climate. In essence, dad was as fearful of us as we were of him. He had a lot to hide, a lot of ragged, toxic memories that had mutated over time into vile, unpredictable behaviors. And if we were ever to figure him out and then band against him in protest … well, with nine kids and a wife, we would be a virtual army to his one.

Now that we lived in Greenacres, a real neighborhood, after years of leap-frogging from one outpost to the next, dad was not about to blithely deliver us into a carte blanche existence without a fight. The well-being of his malfunctioning persona was utterly dependent on keeping mom and the rest of us malleable, ignorant and submissive. Not unlike children born into cults, our reality had been profoundly tainted by his paranoias and indoctrinations. Many times in the middle of his inescapable lectures, he would stop to remind us of the movie cameras and tape recorders hidden throughout the house:

"*I'm* the one who runs this ship … and don't you ever forget it. This place is booby-trapped with cameras and recorders; I've got them hidden all over the goddamn place. So if you think any one of you is going to get the upper hand, think again! Whether I'm here, or in the next country, I know every move you make, so just put *that* in your pipe and smoke it!"

We dared not criticize dad, or even question mom about his violence and abnormal behaviors by way of piecing together our domestic dysfunction. How could we, when our house – every single room – was trip-wired, audio-taped and video-recorded? Home, like our father, had become the enemy with this ongoing threat of 24 hour surveillance.

### Elaine

I recall as a 16 year old, sitting on the bench next to dad at the dining table, nauseous with fear as I tried to eat the spaghetti in front of me. Mom was in the kitchen washing pots and pans while dad was in mid-lecture, spewing criticism and profanities, his face a thundercloud of wrath. Glancing in my direction like a passing storm, he snarled out, "I don't like the way you're looking at me. Wipe that look off your face!"

Quickly, I tried to unclench my jaw and readjust my demeanor into something between *blank* and *benign*.

Fiasco.

"Godamn son of a bitch. I'll teach you to give me your snotty-nosed looks." Lifting his plate piled high with spaghetti, he dumped it over my head. Meatballs, foot long pasta and tomato sauce spilled across my face, hair and shoulders, finally pooling into blood puddles at my feet.

The humiliation was so absolute I could neither speak nor move; nor could Keith, Gail, Karen, Diane, Charles – the rest sitting around the table, staring at me.

Crucifixion, Veselits style.

### Denae

Dad also reminded us from time to time that he could read our minds, which really compounded our sense of powerlessness and violation. Although, to his credit, despite his domineering tendencies, in his finer moments he was a huge and vocal advocate of free thinking: "You've all got good minds, not a dummy in the bunch. Be independent thinkers; nothing worse than being goddamn sheep following the rest of the herd." So it was definitely an uphill battle for him to keep us docile and obedient, while at the same time exhorting us to be free-thinkers.

However, back to dad's mind-reading abilities. Once indoctrinated into his paranoid, delusional world, we were virtually prisoners to his will. His access to us – from our bodies to our minds – was absolute. Nowhere was safe. No house, no matter how many rooms it contained, would be large enough to hide from him. His presence was ubiquitous. Even when away, the specter of his presence sullied every surface. With hidden tape recorders and cameras documenting our every conversation and move – didn't everyone live like this? – we felt we could never escape.

This feeling of being trapped permeated even our sleep. From the time I was five through adolescence, I suffered from a recurring nightmare, so terrifying that it numbed my very movements. In sleep I could not cry out, could only clutch in horror at Diane's arm in bed next to me, clutch with such force that she would wake and then stumble into dad and mom's bedroom: "Denae's having that dream again. Would you come and get her? She keeps waking me up."

The dream had a name; I called it "The Devil Is Holding Me." Always the same: black, swarthy blackness … and some indiscernible form, like a demon in the dark, wrapping its straitjacket arms around me … smothering me. No escape.

*Unconventional.* To put it mildly. Could dad really read our minds? Of course he could, and proved it more than once. One evening after a series of beatings by dad, and after long hours of degrading criticism, which we had all been forced to witness, mom decided to leave.

The 1960s were an inhospitable time for women in crisis, especially poor women with lots of children and no independent sources of money. No women's shelters existed in Spokane in those days, no domestic crisis hotlines, no parish priests who would sanction (much less assist) a battered wife trying to leave her husband.

Divorce? One could be excommunicated from the church for that sacrilege. No options. That's a hard place to be when both your eyes are swollen shut and your ribs and arms have black and blue marks. And your heart...? No amount of surgery could ever make that right again.

So mom decided to leave. Was it to Helen Gentle's? To Johnny

Applegate's? I doubt that she had formulated much of a plan. She didn't even pack a suitcase; there was nowhere to hide it. Early the next morning – even Cisco our pet rooster was still asleep – she crept out of bed, dressed, and reached for the doorknob. Dad was there, waiting. With a gun. Pointed at her.

"Don't you ever try to leave me again, Rose, you stupid Norwegian. Haven't I told you time after time that I can read your mind? It's as easy as reading a book!" Jabbing the gun against her temple, he continued, "I knew from the moment the thought entered your brain what you had planned."

"Go ahead, Frank, shoot me," was mom's wooden reply.

The commotion had wakened us all and we stood there in the kitchen, barefoot, mute, our faces ashen as the white nightgowns we were wearing. If mom could not oppose him, how could we? The reign of terror was never going to end.

As complicated and difficult as dad made our lives, periodically other forces too, of equal intensity would emerge to disrupt the precarious equilibrium of our household. Consider the notion of repossession. When abbreviated to repo – its slang counterpart – an entirely different connotation comes to mind, more in the nature of that dreaded bogeyman common to the financially strapped – the repo man. We were not immune to his attentions.

He called unexpectedly one chilly spring morning when all of us sat around the breakfast table noisily scraping away the last streaks of oatmeal from the sides of our bowls. Looking grim, mom gently replaced the black phone into its cradle, took a deep breath and then addressed us tonelessly with, "A man is coming by to pick up our furniture and appliances because we're so far behind on the bills. I want all of you to stay upstairs until he leaves."

Before she could finish speaking, dad had bolted outside to rev up the engine of our old panel station wagon, trying to decide the best place to hide it.

An eerie 15 minutes passed as we older girls warily peeked out the second-floor bedroom window. The suspense was palpable. Diane sought relief in distraction. She picked up a pink plastic hand mirror and the metal tongs of her eyelash curler. Grateful for the diversion, we all watched as she carefully coiled her long black eyelashes between the flat rods. Too much pressure and her lashes would stand at rigid right angles to her blue eyes. Worse yet, miscalculated force could shear them off entirely... no doubt the reason why this dubious beauty aid has dwindled into disfavor.

But more pressing misfortune returned our gaze to the driveway below as an ominously large truck pulled up next to the kitchen door. Dread and uncertainty sat on our chests like great roosting vultures. No one spoke, not even to whisper. The little kids: Keith, Gail, Gwen and Charles huddled on the floor, leaning against the bed frame, while Elaine, Diane, Karen and myself on top of the bed ducked our heads below the sill, clenching our eyes shut, not wanting to see our belongings hauled out the front door by a stranger.

How would the lower rooms look without furniture? Would he take our old, out-of-tune, upright piano that we all loved to play "Chopsticks" on? The kitchen stove? Our dining room table?

I imagined us sitting cross-legged, Indian-style, in a circle on the floor, as we dipped our spoons into a central bowl of soup. Not so long ago we had sat on peach crates around a large, wooden wire spool dad had salvaged from the dump. He had sawed off the bottom half to keep it in proportion for eating, and had covered the gaping hole in the middle with an oversized platter to keep glasses of water or food bowls from accidentally toppling into that great dark pit.

Now sitting crouched beneath our window, helpless to prevent the activities of the collections man, we wondered how many of our neighbors were home, discreetly peering through parted curtains, witness to our disgrace, as couches and chairs were piled high onto the waiting truck.

We seemed always to be the object of pity or ridicule: "Oh, those poor Veselits – nine kids and their father doesn't even work." Each Thanksgiving and Christmas, our closest neighbors, the Porters,

Skeens and Ingalls, observed the procession of charity baskets and boxes being delivered to our front door. Granted, these food drops usually took place after dark to minimize the embarrassment of the recipients. To alleviate my own humiliation on these holidays, I would sometimes hop on my bike and pedal around the neighborhood, peering inside porches and atop stair steps hoping to find a charity box neatly placed at someone else's door. After all, there were plenty of other poor folk living in our area.

As we awaited our fate, mom's voice hailed us from the kitchen below: "You can come down now. He's gone."

Descending the stairs with all the enthusiasm of turkeys at Thanksgiving, we raised our eyes fearfully at the bottom step to view the desolation. Unbelievably, not a stick of furniture was missing! God was good. We had been spared.

However, despite the jubilation of the moment, a dark horse of a thought reframed the situation for me: was it comic or outright tragic that our household furnishings were of such little value that even a low-life repossession man could find nothing, not one solitary item to take away with him for resale?

Karen

Denae's description of the unpredictable nature of our home life and our charity-box holidays makes me long for some happy, nostalgic remembrance. I wish I had "A Christmas Memory" like the one Truman Capote captures in his touching memoir of Buddy and Miss Sook Faulk, his elderly rural Alabama cousin. Wistfully, he details "fruitcake weather ... gathering windfall pecans and buying moonshine whiskey" for the annual baking of fruitcakes to be distributed among friends and "favorite strangers."

My own holiday memories are fragmented and scattered, like everything else in our early lives. However, given my Sept 20 birth date – I was conceived at Christmas – I'm finally able to muster some enthusiasm after several seasons of not celebrating at all.

Holidays in our home were not a given – perhaps on the wall

calendar, but not in practice. Many a Christmas ended prematurely, when dad pitched the fully decorated tree out the back door, or through the front window. The crashing of glass always spectacular.

Those were the heavy drinking years, the years of biting poverty when we were all on edge – from hunger and need and abuse. Some of dad's holiday frustration was sheer guilt for not providing for his family; some was self-pity for what he never had as a child; and the balance was his Bohemian nature, his chronic restlessness.

In theory, dad liked Christmas. It brought out the kid in him, and there was a lot of kid on his good days. He always knew where the best trees were, from his countless fishing trips and our many huckleberry-picking expeditions in the Idaho and Montana forests.

Finding and cutting the perfect Yule tree was my favorite holiday tradition. After driving for miles along icy country roads, we would finally pile out of the car, sometimes in waist-deep snow, with no boots and bare hands – but we didn't care. Of course we were always trespassing on someone else's property, thus perpetually on the lookout for a homeowner with a gun, all of us staying clear of open spaces, hugging the tree line or brushy patches for cover, while dad, blissfully preoccupied, would be chopping away at the tree trunk. Nothing ever fazed him (except responsibility); he simply took what he wanted with no regrets.

Our exchanged gifts were usually homemade. Mom's best year was the Christmas we kids earned $7.50 by selling cookies and centerpiece candles, made from melting down our school crayons. Fortunately, the nearby Horseman's Meat Market had a small jewelry display featuring a pair of brown cut-glass star earrings, right in our price range.

Dad usually received a gaudily decorated spittoon, which amounted to ribbon and plastic pearls, or beads from broken rosaries, glued onto an empty tin can – the larger the better. Family size Pork & Bean cans were the best since dad was not always good with his aim, and we took exception when his tobacco juice hit the floor for us to clean up.

One memorable Christmas, dad was in such a bad mood that he

wouldn't let mom wrap and label our church-donated gifts. Instead, he placed them in a pile at one end of the living room, then drew a thick charcoal line at the other end for us kids to stand behind. Raising his arm like the flagman at a race track, he blew a whistle and yelled, "Go get 'em!" We all lunged forward to grab what we could, unfortunately trampling the little kids in the process. Young as I was, I recall thinking the proceedings seemed more than a little barbaric, even for our family.

Denae

*Unconventional*. I remember the time dad found some dried egg on a dinner plate after it had been washed. Furious, he approached the six of us sitting at the table waiting for supper to begin – three of us on each side and mom at the foot. "Pick up your plates," he ordered, "and follow me outside."

*What in the world?* The neighbor's dog was yapping inquisitively as our subdued little parade, dishes in hand, followed him like the Pied Piper to a rotting mound of soil next to the woodshed. Stopping there, he motioned downward, "Scoop that up and smear it on your plates; then go on back to the table."

I think we had all guessed by now what our punishment was to be for that dab of overlooked yolk. On the way back to the house, mindful of our waiting dinner, we held the dishes behind our backs, shaking them like tambourines, hoping to dislodge more of the filthy dirt.

Once inside, mom spooned tuna casserole onto our blackened plates while I focused on dad's charcoal portrait of Somerset Maugham hanging on the opposite wall above the red Chinese cabinet. The absurdity of it all had me on the verge of the giggles. Mom was playing her part flawlessly, as though it was a perfectly normal dinner routine. "Next dish, please. Watch your milk, Gwen." Wouldn't our school chums be amazed to see such crazy conduct! Not to mention the artful plate maneuver daddy had taught us in the (rare) event of dessert. First licking our plates clean – like dogs – we would then flip them upside-down onto the table. And voila! mom would neatly place the pie or cake in the center of that tight clean circle.

I dared not laugh, hysterical as I might feel. Glancing over at Elaine, Diane and Karen, I realized that their hunched shoulders and pressed lips betrayed a corresponding urgency to spasm into the giggles. Instead, we soberly lifted noodles and tuna to our mouths, after a few more hopeful taps to free the sticky soil.

As an added precaution, fearing my extreme need to laugh might be evident on my face, I readjusted my demeanor to be more expressive of woe. After all, daddy was expecting distress, so we didn't want to disappoint him.


The insanity never stopped. Who could forget the time we had all assembled for supper, realizing as we looked around us that the walls of the room had been redecorated in a novel manner. The painting The Last Supper, which customarily hung above dad's head at his end of the table, was conspicuously absent. In its place was a torn-out page from Playboy magazine, the centerfold. Draped across the little wall lamp next to it was a soiled B-cup cotton bra. Randomly tacked to the adjoining walls were numerous explicitly photographed women from Playboy, all of them naked in varying seductive poses – on Caribbean beaches, in sports cars, powdering themselves in front of boudoir mirrors.

Our shabby, drab dining room had become a French Quarter bordello, a Middle Eastern casbah of languorous, wanton concubines and odalisques. We dared not move, even to draw a breath, for fear of brushing up against the pendulous breasts and fleshy buttocks. Careful, lest our cotton school blouses be smeared by lusty crimson lips – lips which could have defrocked a dozen priests. Porcine thighs, creamy rounded shoulders and heavy-lidded temptatious eyes promised forbidden pleasures. The fleshpots of Sodom surrounded us; pagan temples of harlots and courtesans had transformed our eating space into a seraglio oozing with libidinous desires and unspeakable carnal appetites.

Tense and mute like Quaker maids, we girls stood in awe of this decadence. What *were* those women doing up on our walls, anyway?

They surely bore no resemblance to our mother, a different species entirely. Head bowed, she sat limply at the table, her short brown hair bobby-pinned unstylishly behind her ears. A faded housedress hung from her lanky shoulders and bony arms – hung almost apologetically from limbs that were starved for calories and protein, not to mention love and protection. No, these lusty femme fatales were no sisters of hers.

So blatant were the faces and bodies of these women draped shamelessly about us, they fairly screamed, "Sex … and plenty of it!" into our defenseless ears. We were a household of nine children who practiced scrupulous modesty. The old days of the humiliating, middle-of-the-living-room washtub baths had long ceased once we moved into the Greenacres house, furnished with its small bathroom and stationary tub. When changing clothes, we always turned our backs to each other, clinging to our modesty like bark to a tree. Sex and its attendant elements was a strictly taboo subject.

As often as we had observed mom's swelling belly and the subsequent arrivals of pink-faced infants, we had no concept of the body parts or physical interactions involved to produce these results. It was not until age 17 that I learned from a neighbor girl what intercourse was.

However, despite the naivete and ignorance of our sexual training, our minds were vast repositories of linguistic vulgarities. Daddy's verbal tirades, which occurred almost daily from our earliest years, were liberally peppered with sexually charged invectives: "cunts, whores, sluts, striptease artists." With beer bottle in hand, he was only warming up as he volleyed us with increasingly obscene descriptions of our sex and the sexual act.

Yet, accustomed as we were to his extremes, this photo-plastered violation of our dining room was excessive, even for him. Cheeks rouged by the redness of our shame, eyes burning with unshed tears, it was not necessary to look around at each other to know we all were equally mortified.

"Cleanliness is next to godliness," began daddy, pointing up toward the offending bra, which dangled just above his head. *Whose was it?*

*Why had he been rummaging through our dirty clothes and bedroom drawers in the first place?* I wondered. *If you couldn't put your soiled underwear in the laundry basket, where were you supposed to put it?*

My thoughts were silenced as his voice crescendoed louder and louder in self-righteous anger. He denounced our collective "dirtiness" (We were always punished as a group; one person's crime was everyone's crime.) as spiritual defilement, then spiraled illogically into abstruse realms of sacrilege and heresy – esoteric dogmas of which I was certain only priests, rabbis and other holy men could comprehend.

"Aren't you all ever so saintly, lining up for church every Sunday, praying with three hands? Sanctimonious holy rollers. Hypocrites, every single one of you!" he roared, blue eyes glacial with contempt. "This, this is the path you Jezebels are treading, the destiny of god-forsaken sluts like you!" His hand splayed toward the display of naked women.

With that careless passing of his hand, like a mad magician with his wand, he had transformed the lot of us into scarlet women, Lolitas all. Ten-, 14-, 16-year-old Hester Prynnes, scarlet of face, not of letter, as we stood there silent with shame, silent like our mother – guilty of crimes that had no meaning to us. We were the Whores of Babylon, and dad demanded we look long and hard at our sisters-in-sin there upon the walls as he continued to drain the Bible of verses and parables describing our doom.

It was a challenge to find a place to safely rest one's eyes with all the nakedness besieging us. I could not look at the towering inferno which was dad, his arms still flailing wildly, like *Night of the Iguana's* Reverend T. Lawrence Shannon calling down thunderclouds of damnation upon the lot of us. Finally my eyes settled on that forlorn little B-cup bra which had begun this whole drama. With only three changes of underwear apiece, we liked to keep them on as long as possible, especially with the ongoing threat of the "underpants check," a dreaded daddy ritual, devised to ensure our cleanliness. Any time, day or night, he could approach us with, "Underwear check!" and we were expected to drop our drawers on the spot for inspection.

The very thought made me instinctively press my fingertips

against the lower edge of my panties. *Surely he would not call out that command to complete this night of disgrace.* No, he was far too busy calling down the gods of pestilence and retribution – a straw pontiff delivering his Sermon on the Mount.

It would never end. Shutting my ears as best I could, I looked up to the space above dad's head where The Last Supper used to hang, now occupied by the fleshy, red-lipped centerfold. Mentally, I took paintbrush and palette, squeezing out an assortment of blues, yellow, greens, white and browns. Then painstakingly, inch by inch, I restored sanctity and order to that space by re-creating one brushstroke at a time: Christ, his twelve disciples, the loaves of bread and finally the linen-draped table.

It seemed to us kids that the dining room and its attendant table, no matter which house we lived in, afforded a stage of sorts for dad. It was his theatre-in-the-round, guaranteeing a captive and attentive audience. Conversation was generally discouraged at mealtime, not a friendly place for family discourse. Rather, it was a convenient venue for dad to vent, criticize, educate or entertain, as per his mood.

One memorable evening, after a full day of picnicking and swimming down at the river, dad decided to enrich our knowledge of metaphysics with a demonstration. Apparently, he knew something of the spiritualist Edgar Cayce. Both of them seemed to be keen advocates of "mind over matter." Directing all ten of us, including mom, to stand in a circle around the dining room table, he shut off the lights and then continued, "Close your eyes. Now, with your fingers extended, just barely touch the edge of the tabletop."

Considerably apprehensive, we did as we were told, not eager to hear some long deceased relative's voice or to see some dimly lit apparition hovering above our heads. We were no strangers to séances; Alfred Hitchcock movies and horror comic books had provided us with ample insights into such fare.

Sensing our reluctance, dad countered with, "Hey, what's the matter with all of you? We're not trying to communicate with the dead;

we're just trying to raise the dining room table!" *Phew.* "Empty your minds of all thoughts," he continued. "The power of the focused brain increases exponentially with the size of the group. Trust me, there is no question we can raise this table off the floor. It just requires our complete concentration. And no talking! Mind over matter is a powerful tool which most people underestimate." (It always amazed us how quickly dad could switch from his folksy slangs and idioms to informed rhetoric as effortlessly as boiling water becoming steam).

So with tightly closed eyes and taut bodies, we willed our minds to unite with the metaphysical universe so that together we could lift our dining room table off the floor. None of us had much faith that such a miracle would indeed occur. Dad had already warned us that if the experiment failed, it would be due to our collective lack of concentration, not because the feat itself was impossible.

Mon dieu! To our amazement, after about 15 minutes that old pine table started swaying unevenly, then slowly rose one, two, almost three inches above the floor! albeit dipping a little on the younger kids' side. Hugely satisfied and empowered, we realized the experience had not only afforded us a glimpse into the mysterious realm of metaphysics, but it had also provided us with a sense of our capacities to explore and interact with it.

That said, I will allow that the greater part of our family entertainment took place on less esoteric planes. In fact, much of it was downright mundane, once dad brought home a used 19-inch, black-and-white television set. No matter that we were the last family in Greenacres to own one; we kids were ecstatic!! For years we had longed for the talking box. We listened with something akin to lust when our school chums rapturously described "The Ed Sullivan Show," "Laurel and Hardy" movies, "American Bandstand," or the forbidden late-night shows.

We yearned for the day we too could knowingly and nonchalantly drop the words "idiot box" and "boob tube" from our tongues to prove we were part of mainstream culture – and not some backwoods ignoramuses who didn't know a soap opera from a Wagnerian opera.

With the introduction of television into our home, Rod Serling's

"Twilight Zone" and "Alfred Hitchcock Presents" became descriptive terms that we used interchangeably as fractured versions of our home life. Karen has an almost photographic recollection of those early programs:

"Do you remember," she asks me, "that first Alfred Hitchcock episode we watched, called "Mrs. Fiske," where the husband strangles his wife with her pearl necklace and then tries to hide the crime? To us the story did not seem that unusual."

I nod in agreement as I think back to another Hitchcock episode where a malcontent wife kills her husband with a frozen leg of lamb. Later in the evening, a policeman is in the home questioning the widow and looking for evidence – most specifically the murder weapon. The story ends with the two amiably sitting down to dinner, feasting on succulent roast leg of lamb and mashed potatoes as the detective compliments his hostess on her fine culinary skills.

On just such an ironic note, I find myself cringing at the memory of a long ago morning in Greenacres, which began innocently enough as we children lined our daffodil-edged driveway awaiting the arrival of the Liens, our Everett cousins. En route to Glacier National Park, our house was stopover for a brief visit – a place to kennel their pet ducks Wanda and Willie, since none of their neighbors had been available to duck-sit.

Considerately, as the noon hour approached, they prepared to leave, not wanting to embarrass mom and dad – compelling them to admit that there was not enough lunch for five extra guests. All our relatives were only too aware of our chronic food shortages.

"Bye Bobby; bye Uncle Clarence," our mouths bulging with the jawbreakers Aunt Mary had brought us, we waved our goodbyes while awkwardly grasping the two flapping, quacking ducks. With some difficulty we maneuvered them into our backyard rabbit hutches.

So what explanation can I offer when several days later the cousins returned, bursting with tales of a great vacation and anxious to reclaim their much-missed pets? Dad met them at the door, arms folded across his chest. The rest of us were hiding upstairs, too ashamed and upset to face our relatives, knowing what dad had done. With no remorse, he informed them that Wanda and Willie were at present in our freezer, wrapped in butcher paper, reclining next to the frozen peas and hamburger. Alas, in our household, *any* game was fair game.

## Karen

We were both fascinated and delighted by the ongoing parallels between the weekly television episodes and our daily affairs. Yet to come in our appetites for the extreme was an awareness of filmmaker Frederico Fellini's surreal, often grotesque interpretations of the human condition.

Diane and I will never forget a memorable night in 1972 when we watched Dylan Thomas' *Under Milk Wood* in a West End London theatre. Like the American Absurdists who followed, Thomas had captured a community on the edge – characters like us who did not fit the norm. The residents of the wee Welsh village of Llareggub were not unfamiliar. Their extravagant fantasies and bizarre behaviors seemed much like our own, right down to the subconscious desire to poison our father. We particularly loved the finale when the entire community collects on the beach in their pajamas to dance beneath the light of the full moon. How the English audience interpreted the play remains a mystery to me; but as for Diane and myself, we found a little slice of Greenacres that night in London town.

Elaine and I had a similar response to the film *Mommie Dearest*. We were the only two viewers in the packed theatre who laughed hysterically throughout the movie, amazed to be witnessing another family which functioned so much like our own.

## Denae

We must have been looking for the aberrant in film and in literature because subconsciously it justified or at least partially explained our own peculiar environment. Doesn't every species seek out the familiar? I was deeply imprinted by Victor Hugo's story of *Laughing Boy* from our home library long before I came to know *The Hunchback of Notre Dame* or *The Phantom of the Opera*.

Paradox can cut deeply into the psyche, even in that of an adolescent teen. For indeed, "Laughing Boy's" life was no laughing matter. Enemies of his family had deliberately disfigured his young face by taking a knife and extending his smile by several inches. They also cut away his lips, thus permanently exposing his gums and teeth, leaving him to look like a hideously grinning skull. When his lesions had healed, he was exhibited as a sideshow freak on theater stages and in travelling circuses. None could control their laughter upon seeing him.

I had begun reading the story by believing its title, expecting to be laughing myself within a few pages. Not only was there little humor in the tale, but it became ever more bleak as the story unfolded. Laughing Boy was really "Crying Boy." But in seeking entertainment, the book's 17th century audience saw only his big fat smile and thought he was the happiest kid they'd ever seen. As Hugo aptly wrote of the irony: "His face laughed; his thoughts did not."

I was pretty sure I knew how he felt behind that sham grin, because we did a lot of pretending ourselves at home and at school – hiding behind expressions of well-being when inside what we were really feeling was despair, fear and isolation. Oh yes, at home we understood all about pretending, about acting – about stage smiles, "crocodile" tears, disappearing acts, dramatic effect and prompts.

"Yes, daddy, if you and mom get a divorce, *of course* you are the one I'd pick to live with. I love you so much." We always knew our lines. Perfectly. Acting was a big thing in our house. Real feelings were not exactly appreciated: "If you have to cry, then go up to your room where no one has to hear you" was the usual unsympathetic parental response to tears.

So when I finally met up with the Hunchback and the Phantom, I felt like I already knew them, old friends, really. Extreme criticism, rejection, abuse and ridicule can turn *anyone* into a Quasimodo or a Phantom, a pariah-at-large. The exterior details are inconsequential: details like scissor hands, humpbacks, scars, oversized heads or stump legs. Stage makeup, if you will, that either accentuates or else entirely conceals the real problems that lay beneath.

56

One can easily imagine the worst about one's self, whether true or not. Illusion and reality become interchangeable – uncertain, relative terms. Damaged children can look into mirrors and see monsters (or nothing at all), the same as anorexics can look into mirrors and see fatties. Anything is possible under these conditions – anything.

Elaine

Criticism and abuse were all I knew. The few times I did dare look in the mirror, my face would change shape – sometimes growing longer or flattening like a plate, sometimes bulging out monstrously – like watching a psychotic episode. I had no idea what I really looked like.

During my college years I once peered in the mirror to find the front of my neck horribly swollen. Thinking I had a goiter, I called for a doctor's appointment. In the examining room I could hear the nurses in the background, whispering: "There's nothing wrong with her neck. It looks perfectly normal. What's the matter with her?"

I was severely embarrassed... and severely depressed.

Denae

Not so long ago, I asked a friend of mine who had just returned from weeks of volunteer service at a leper hospital in Korea to describe his experience. "Pil Sung, what are they like?" I asked. "Tell me; you've spent so much time with them. What do they look like?"

I tried to imagine the appearances of these final stage lepers missing their noses, ears, hands and sometimes feet – the appalling sight of their disease-ravaged bodies. My friend paused only briefly, then responded softly, "They look like angels – that's what they look like."

# WHAT'S IN A NAME?

Dad and his mother, Anna

Be it pseudonym, alias, epithet, nickname, or sobriquet – everything it seems must have a name. And like that black-feathered bird implacably perched upon Poe's chamber door, who recalled with such satisfaction those many centuries ago when he was named Raven instead of Crow, we nine Veselits children, too, were pleased with the names delivered us at birth: Elaine, Diane, Denae, Karen, Keith, Gail, Gwen, Charles, Curt.

With a mother named Rose, naturally we were attracted by song titles or literary passages bearing this nomen. We read with interest the distinctly unflower-like Gertrude Stein's observation, "A rose is a rose is a rose ...," her 20th-century reiteration of Shakespeare's "...that which we call a rose by any other name would smell as sweet."Although, it did seem faintly ironic that the decidedly unfashionable and portly – if not formidable – Ms. Stein, so well known for her "rose prose," should reside at such an eminently fashionable Paris address as 27 rue de *Fleurus*.

If there is one thing we can say with certainty about dad, it is that no fact relating to his life could be relied upon as being accurate – beginning with his name. One's surname, the family name, possesses an inherent stability, a permanence which we take for granted. Usually, only marriage or adoption has the authority to change or revoke the sanctity of its permanence.

Blame for the various transmutations of dad's name must initially lie with his status as an immigrant, coming as he did in 1921 as a 3-year old with his mother by ship from Czechoslovakia to America (preceded by his father and uncles). They, along with thousands of other birds of passage, were subjected to selection or deselection procedures at Ellis Island: the sick and infirm of mind to the left – mandatory return to the country of origin – the hale and stout of heart to the right.

But, oh no, not so fast. One last requirement before those gates swing open to the Land of Milk and Honey. Is your name difficult to spell? Too long? Hard to pronounce?" The Ellis Island wardens had instructions to simplify, to assimilate. What goes well with Anderson, Johnson, Smith and Stuart? Certainly not Worczisinsky or Smetanyvitch. So at age 3, Frantisek Jozef Veszelits became Frank Wezelitz, and the golden gates swung open to welcome him.

In 1940, dad, with his movie-star good looks (jet black hair and Paul Newman blue eyes) enlisted in the military, signing in as Frank Joseph Weselitz Jr., a name change from his earlier "Franz Josef" years – a reflection of his Czech pride in the glory decades of the Austro-Hungarian Empire. He cut a dashing figure: very bohemian, very un-Midwest and very attractive to mom, whom he wed in 1948. His scrawling signature on their marriage certificate then identified him as Frank J. Veselits, the name he would keep until the day he died in 2006.

His younger brother, Emil, equally handsome but with wavy blond hair, grew up as Emil Wezelits. Now a Canadian citizen, he is Emil Veselic. Curiously, among his personal papers, he has two birth certificates, both officially stamped. He can offer no explanation for the spare, nor why each carries a different birth date. One time he shared with us that his relatives in Torrington, Connecticut, where he and dad were raised, variously used Vosolich and Veselich as family names. What is even more curious is that through these many decades and transmutations of names and spellings, not one of the relatives, including dad, ever made formal application to the federal legal system for an authorized name change.

As a postscript, we must add that dad always cited his birthday as Jan. 31, 1918. Should we have been surprised then when, going through his papers after his death, to discover on his passport, the date of birth, Feb. 1, 1918?

Denae

Dad was usually "daddy" until our teen years when, seditiously, we referred to him as "Frankly" (as in Rhett Butler's infamous, "Frankly, my dear, I don't give a damn"). "Francois" was another epithet we used during the 15- year stretch as adults when we had no communication with him. I remember one afternoon when Karen and I were guests at Diane's therapy session, and her therapist asked us, "Why do you call your father Francois?"

"Well," I explained, "it's a way of distancing ourselves from him. How *do* you disassociate from a father who does not act like a father? One day I just decided he was dead, and the person who lived at his address and who looked just like him could be called Francois – a man who used to be my father."

It did seem a paradox that dad could be so villainous in his parenting, considering that as a child he had lost his mother to tuberculosis and his father to alcoholism at age 18. We knew he felt the pain of their loss his entire life. In a gender reversal of the Cinderella story, dad at 12 was cast out by his father's second wife into Torrington's Slavic pool of poor relatives, none of whom wanted the care and expense of an extra child. Most of them were shift workers in the town's factories and mines, who drank too much at the Slovak Club and joined the military before they were drafted to escape their dead-end futures.

To add to dad's feeling of rejection, Emil at six was allowed to remain in the family home for a few more years in the company of his newly arrived half brother Eddie. But eventually he too was cast out to find what shelter he could among the blue-collar factory workers bearing his last name.

We did not learn these details until well into adulthood. Our father was very secretive about any references to his past. However, the one story he did tell over and over related to his mother's death – a haunting description worthy of some Gothic opera.

"I was three years old, maybe four," he would begin, his eyes closed, his head inclined toward some distant memory. "It was late at night. I stood crying in the doorway of my mother's bedroom, looking at her as she lay so pale and still in her nightgown, her head resting against the pillow. Fearfully, I watched as a white cloud entered through the window and moved slowly, slowly across the darkness of her room, finally settling above the foot of her bed. And that's when she died."

His voice would always choke in sorrow upon reaching that final image. And I would have dreams, nightmares of white clouds that could come unbidden into quiet bedrooms in the middle of the night and steal away the lives of parents and sleeping children.

Until the day he died at age 88, dad kept tucked away in his personal papers a poem familiar to us all, which he claimed he had written as a young man; the solitary clue to explaining his terrible feelings of abandonment and rejection.

> *If I had a mother and a dad*
> *The love and care that you have had*
> *I would not now so lonely stand*
> *If I had the gift of their helping hand*
>
> *From youth to man you have happily grown*
> *The path of life were taught and shown*
> *Their principles guide you through the years*
> *While I had a life spent in tears*
> *So love and keep them happy lad*
> *For they're your Mother and your Dad.*

Dad was an enigma, an anomaly, a mystery novel with no resolution. And his name for us older girls? "The Intelligentsia" – a droll term, not intended to be complimentary. (Mom referred to us as "the gonna-gonna girls"– a parody of our 'I'm *gonna* do it soon' responses). Other epithets included: lummoxes, numbskulls, ugly mugs and the occasional flunkey, in addition to Cabbage head, which was reserved exclusively for Keith. Where had he acquired such terms? None of our neighbors used them. Imagine my surprise decades later when reading *The Letters of Anton Chekhov,* to find this renowned Russian author referring to the "intelligentsia" (not pejorative) and tagging various other acquaintances as numbskulls, ugly mugs and flunkeys (definitely pejorative).

However, dad's favorite expression for us was "The Cows." Undernourished one and all, when he wanted to rally us en masse, he would call out, "Rose, get those cows in here." At the time, to soothe our egos, we theorized this might be a folksy term used for children in the Slovak community of his youth.

The impact on our developing psyches was interesting. Since "Skinny" was one of my nicknames, and the cracked mirror in our bathroom pronounced me so as well, I had to concur. There was nothing cow-like about me, so that absurd bovine image which dad had conjured up remained for me just that – absurd. No psychic damage done.

On the other hand, I had the feeling that Elaine, Diane, and Karen were not so laissez-faire in their outlook. As teenagers, they were constantly dieting. When babysitting, their first act after the parents left was to search the medicine cabinet for diet pills. Diane suffered from nightmares whereby her normally trim form was transformed into elephantine proportions. She would spend the night trapped in a monstrously blubberous body, unable to move, unable to breathe without gasping. Come morning, with Cisco crowing for us to get up, Diane would find herself awake, but still feeling like a beached whale, requiring substantial effort to debrief so that she could get out of bed and begin getting dressed for school.

Names and nicknames in our household did not stop with family members or pets. Cars, too, as objects of affection or ridicule, were often tagged with distinctive monikers. Every vehicle dad ever owned had at least one memorable defect. More often as not, he acquired them through barter or trade – most of them never registered and most certainly never insured. A green Nash Rambler had a front door and window that did not close and windshield wipers that had to be manually operated by an artful rope and pulley contrivance. Diane inherited that car her first year of college after dad had replaced it with a red Chevy convertible sporting a ripped vinyl top that could not be retracted.

Our all-time classic was a beat-up, dark blue van, a behemoth of a machine, which we dubbed "The Tub." It had been a real bargain, partly because it was so old and partly because all the rear seats had been ripped out, leaving a vat-like basin, hence the name. For family outings, we kids would sit bunched together on the hard floorboards, padded somewhat by a braided throw-rug mom had put down. On the rare occasions we drove into town, we all ducked below the windows, embarrassed that someone we knew might see us.

Front: Gail, Gwen, Mom, Charles, Diane, Keith
Back: Karen, Denae, Elaine

Karen

One of dad's favorite pastimes was to drive us to the top of Mount Spokane on a lazy Sunday afternoon. With his foot pressed down hard on the accelerator, he would move into a sharp curve on the narrow dirt road, his hands in the air – both of them – and a tall brown Budweiser between his thighs. "Look, no hands!" he would chortle. Not until we had careened to the edge of disaster, tree branches snapping against the sides, would he grab the steering wheel and jerk it to the left to prevent us from plunging down the mountainside. This scenario was re-enacted over and over until it almost seemed normal. In resignation, most of us just kept our eyes shut and our bodies flattened to the floor when hills or mountains were included in the itinerary.

Over time, apparently dad decided it was more civilized (and probably more safe) to transport his nine children in a van with seats, so he nailed together a couple of wooden benches which ran its length. He never could figure out how to securely attach them to the metal floor, so when traveling at speeds greater than 40 mph, it was a challenge to remain balanced and upright as we braced ourselves against the walls and ceiling, while the lurching benches behaved more like bumper cars. As Elaine wryly noted, "In those days, if you were driving an old vehicle, it was not called an antique, it was called a junker."

Denae

Dad's love of a bargain reached an extreme the afternoon he pulled into the driveway in a Cadillac, a Cadillac *hearse* – replacement for the Tub, which had finally stopped running. I have never seen a broader grin than when he stepped out of that vehicle, beneath the shady overhang of a sumac tree. You would have thought he had just won the lottery.

"Boy, was I ever lucky today," he beamed into our stricken faces. "This baby is eight years old and only 4,000 miles on it – a great little engine, a good paint job (mortician black), and man oh man, does it have the room! We're going to be riding in real style from now on!" To a man, mom included, we stood unified ten strong in the driveway that day, and REFUSED to ride in that funeral-mobile. What *could* he have been thinking? What in the world would the neighbors say? We would be the laughingstock of Greenacres. No. Absolutely not.

"Take it back," we said. "We would rather walk 15 miles than ride in that ghastly death machine." It was the only time that dad was ever overruled in a family vote.

"Snow-fighter," Charles' 1960s gray hulk of a Buick with its yards and yards of rusting chrome, was a legend in Greenacres. I have an old snapshot of him as a 19-year old, lanky and sandy-haired, wearing a white T-shirt and jeans, leaning against the car like Cool Hand Luke, with the same cocky grin. Since he worked on construction jobs that were out of town, or out of state, the deep, drifting Spokane snow and subzero temperatures often left the construction workers stranded miles from the job site, or sitting in their garages unable to get their cars to start.

But not Snow-fighter. Charles always made it to work, when the other guys would be calling him in desperation for rescue or transport. His fire-breathing, gas-guzzling Buick tank could charge through a 6-foot high snowdrift as easily as a Clydesdale going through a haystack. It was so reliable, in fact, that Charley began to believe it really *was* invincible, that it could go anywhere at anytime. His buddies, both in admiration and in envy, dreamed of owning a car just like Snow-fighter – a car of such outstanding virtues that you never wanted to be parted from it.

Dad's penchant for acquiring unreliable old jalopies was just one of his many idiosyncrasies. Usually, we tried to be good-humored about his excesses and off-beat behaviors; but one holiday in particular brought to the fore a necessary examination of both dad's faults and his virtues.

As the month of April approached with its yellow crocuses, tulips and impending egg-dyeing for the family Easter egg hunt, it served not only as a reminder of the cyclical renewal of life, but also as a warning that we had less than two months to complete our Father's Day card hunt. A not especially anticipated June event, which we observed anyway, fulfilling as it did our desire to celebrate conventions and holidays like everyone else.

For us, with our not-so-perfect father, finding the "perfect" Father's Day card entailed a lengthy and exhaustive search for the perfectly generic Father's Day message. Wishing to avoid hypocrisy or outright lies, it was with heightened difficulty that our quest began in the Hallmark aisles as we carefully lifted card after card seeking the ideal communication. Automatically rejected were any verses bearing such sentiments as:

*Thank you for always making me feel so special.*
*Thank you for never forgetting my birthday.*
*You've always been there for me.*
*I can always count on you.*
*I am so proud that you are my Father.*
*As Fathers go, you're Number One...Tops...the Best.*

Where the average progeny might seek the lavishly worded, sentimental descriptions of their father's virtues, we were seeking the lukewarm – homely testimonials, like:

*Roses are red*
*Violets are blue*
*With you as my Father*
*There's a lot we can do ...*

Such a message, in those days, would have been deemed a prize find in the card department. Eventually, we discovered blank cards with colorful photos of fishing scenes and mountain wildernesses, considerably expanding our repertoire for suitable text, since now we could write our own pallid expressions of praise and gratitude. Keeping in mind, it would have been unutterably simpler to expound upon what we were *not* thankful for.

One year, Gwen was at wit's end over what to inscribe in her card. She had already thanked dad many times for the pony he had given her in the fourth grade (which inexplicably disappeared three months later). In desperation, she finally penned on the backside of a card depicting a man in a canoe on a blue mountain lake:

*Dear Dad, Happy Father's Day. Thank you for*
*giving me life. Love, Gwen.*

By contrast, on those rare occasions when dad gave us a holiday or birthday card, he was unexpectedly formal in attaching his signature, as if showing any form of affection was uncomfortable. One year he mailed out our Christmas cards with *Frank J. Veselits* embossed in gold beneath the text. More commonly, he usually signed off as *FJV.*

When he was 87, the year before his death, I wrote all personal correspondences for him. Because his hands were so crippled by gout and arthritis, the most he could manage in personalizing these letters was an indecipherable scrawl. One morning when I observed the familiar "F" taking shape, I placed my hand over his to stop him. "Say," I prompted, "how about signing *Dad* instead of your name this time. It's a lot shorter."

"Yeah, that's a good idea," he agreed, as I discreetly penciled in *Love* above it, knowing it never would have occurred to him to add the endearment. In those final months, I better understood his love for us; he simply did not know how to convey his feelings.

Denae

Despite the fact that dad had authored *The Parent's Guide to Swear Words*, cursing among the children was strictly verboten in our family. And may I say, it was not a difficult rule to enforce with us older girls, since we thoroughly detested profanity in any form. However, among the younger kids, Gwen, Charles and Curt, there still existed a certain allure to using the occasional curse word. And like children everywhere, the forbidden became the desirable, in direct proportion to the degree it was prohibited.

At 22, I had returned home from a three-week trip to Ethiopia, where I had visited my Peace Corps boyfriend in the tiny village of Wagifo, from the province of Gema Gofu. In retrospect, I am amazed at how resourceful we were in acquiring travel money for our many trips to Europe and other destinations. During our twenties when we were struggling through college on Pell grants and loans, we also worked in gas stations, cleaned houses and waitressed for extra cash. I worked two and a half months as an au pair in Woodbridge, Connecticut, to earn my plane fare to Africa.

After a few days of transitioning from 13th-century Ethiopia to 20th-century Greenacres (the technological gap was surprisingly narrow), I began recounting my adventures of lion-dodging and rhino-sightings to a spellbound 11-year old Curt. Curiously, what seemed to interest him most were the villagers' names. Resonant, melodic, these long-lettered epithets were a cantilena of exotic sounds: *Belayhoon, Kibbedee and Bahylu Abye* – the three Abye brothers – *Asfow, Gowshoo, Berhane, Yackobe, Bekelech, Gizzehein* ... then, *Yeshitela Ishitey*.

"Yeshitela Ishitey," Curt repeated after me, a strange new luminosity widening his spaniel-brown eyes.

"Why, yes," I beamed as he said it several more times with a rapture not merited, it seemed, by this name of such far away origins. Then I got it. Neatly sandwiched in between the sonorous syllables in both words was that forbidden bad-boy profanity, shit. By offering up the name to my younger brother, I had inadvertently legitimized a swear word for him, providing carte blanche usage.

For weeks afterwards, while riding his bicycle, washing the lunch dishes or weeding in the garden, Curt could be heard cantillating to himself, "Ye<u>shit</u>ela I<u>shit</u>ey, Ye<u>shit</u>ela I<u>shit</u>ey…"

When mom entered his room in the morning to awaken him with, "Good morning, Curt, time for school."

"Yeshitela Ishitey."

In the evening, after dinner and television, "It's almost 9 o'clock – time to get ready for bed."

"Yeshitela Ishitey."

Mom could not reprimand him for saying a man's name, nor could anyone else. The joy with which he uttered that African name, even today after more than 40 years, still brings a smile to my heart. How easy it is to call up the image of his wide brown eyes, tousled blond hair and impish grin. "Hey Curt, wanna go to the A&W for a root beer?"

"Yeshitela Ishitey."

# THE GREAT OUTDOORS

Curt and Charles

*When we hear his call we hear no mere bird. We hear the trumpet in the orchestra of evolution. He is the symbol of our untamable past, of that incredible sweep of millennia which underlies and conditions the daily affairs of birds and men.*

–Aldo Leopold, *Marshland Elegy*


Dad was the original nature boy. He loved the majesty and freedom of wilderness areas. Alaska was his dream landscape. Reflecting back on his experiences, he rhapsodized to us, "The herring run used to come into Seward Bay so thick you could *walk* across them. I mean, there were *mill-l-l-llions* of them. You could take a net and scoop up fifty pounds of them; that's how wild it was. Paradise, real paradise."

Robert Service was one of his favorite authors. In fact, his poem "The Men That Didn't Fit In" describes dad to a tee:

> *There's a race of men who don't fit in,*
> *A race that can't stay still;*
> *So they break the hearts of kith and kin*
> *As they roam the world at will.*
> *They range the field and they rove the flood,*
> *And they climb the mountain's crest.*
> *Theirs is the curse of the gypsy blood*
> *And they don't know how to rest.*

Denae

The months dad spent in Alaska as a recruit in training for the paratroopers during the early 1940s were among the happiest of his adult life. No doubt his reasons for enlisting had less to do with patriotism or defending the homeland than with advancing his art career by painting wildlife murals on military buildings and jumping, Errol Flynn-like, out of airplanes.

He once described to me in chilling detail (on a night when I had expected to hear *Treasure Island)* the events of a predawn fire-fight: "Soldiers were screaming, the smell of burning flesh was everywhere. Flamethrowers lit the sky around us like torches!" Tears tumbling from his eyes, dad recounted these haunting images and his anguish at having been left behind, the sole survivor of this grisly holocaust. Both transfixed and horrified, these searing pictures were to remain in my impressionable 8-year-old mind for years – until one day it occurred to me that dad had never served in active combat.

His notion of house and home was primarily as a place to eat meals and do laundry. It was the great outdoors where dad felt most alive and comfortable, instilling in all his children that same zest and passion for nature, which we gratefully carry with us to this day. The nine little apples did not fall far from the tree; his gypsy blood and spirit flowed with equal gusto through our veins.

And in the spirit of equality, dad never made any gender distinction among his six daughters and three sons. We wielded handsaws and axes with the same facility and strength as our brothers. Huck Finns one and all, we helped dad chop wood, snare wild rabbits and dig latrines. We also camped without tents, captured fireflies in glass jars and made our own horseradish sauce.

As teenagers we spent our summers swimming to and fro across the rapids in the Spokane River. However, a more dangerous sport was swimming in the above-ground irrigation canals that crisscrossed the Spokane Valley like the aqueducts of ancient Rome. These concrete-walled ditches were hinged with metal bars every mile or so to trap debris such as tree branches or discarded clothing. All too often in the summer months, delinquent bullies would raise these heavy appendages and forcibly push swimmers behind them, causing near and occasional drownings.

Food foraging was a large and necessary part of our outdoor adventures. And dad was our intrepid guide to nature's bounty. He was a firm believer in field-gathered herbs and folksy home remedies at a time when salt, pepper and catsup were the only known table condiments. When I heard Simon and Garfunkel singing of "Parsley, Sage, Rosemary and Thyme," I thought they were referring to old girl-friends. As antidotes to colds and fever, dad treated us with mustard packs, milk poultices, as well as concoctions of honey, lemon, apple cider vinegar and blackstrap molasses. We always found them to be remarkably effective.

Under his direction we hunted for woodsy patches of edible fungi, like button-tops, cremini, fat porcinis, apricot-scented chanterelles, and the sinister-looking morels. From the overgrown banks along streams we would collect bags of peppery green watercress. In marshy areas we looked for fiddlehead ferns, and in grassy fields we would pull up bunches of pungent wild garlic.

Occasionally, dad – with his penchant for the unconventional – would stray from the known mushroom species and gather random specimens with unusual color patterns or odd shapes. We just assumed that eventually one or all of us would be poisoned to death. But dad, ever the optimist, would dismiss our fears by pointing out his fail-safe method for detecting the toxic varieties:

"It's not going to kill you; I know what I'm doing," he would reassure us from the kitchen stove. "If you're not really sure, all you have to do is drop a silver dime into a pot of boiling water along with the mushrooms. If the dime turns green, throw out the mushrooms." (Don't attempt this today. Dimes aren't made of genuine silver anymore, so it won't work).

Much as most of us loved hunting these elusive fungi, Elaine remembers *hating* them: "Those slimy mushrooms that grew under the pine needles. Dad would put them in everything – soups, spaghetti, salad, casseroles. At the table I would close my eyes and hold my nose. It was like eating the mucous trail behind a snail." (How ironic that as we were collectively cringing from such species as the blackish, pockmarked morels, French chefs were celebrating them as haute cuisine – making of them one of their most grand and opulent dishes: *Morchella Elata*, stuffed with foie gras and sautéed in butter and cognac)!

Nevertheless, what most attracted us, beyond mushroom collecting, were the open dump sites bordering these areas. Like sailors seduced by the Lorelei, we were beguiled by these debris-laden oases – fingers tingling to unearth the treasures which could be ours.

"Scrounging" was dad's word for it. What we lacked in domestic furnishings, whether teapots, bedsheets, nail clippers, or eggbeaters, could be procured at the dumps with minimal effort. As zealous as archaeologists on a dig, we scoured the vast terrain of these landfills. We were amazed to discover a dentist's drill, part of a nun's habit, a Victrola horn, Ouija board, *see-through* (!) nightgowns and a man's black toupee.

No detail of these discarded artifacts escaped our attentions. We even examined with inordinate interest the colorful labels on tin cans and glass bottles to discern what it was that other people were eating. Anchovy paste was a particularly illuminating find, as were Altoid breath mints, Artichoke Hearts and *Extra-Virgin* olive oil.

This passion for scavenging landfills has been equaled by only one other person in my acquaintance, my friend Clara, an artist and art restorer. As a young girl, she hunted the Montana dump sites near her home looking for hand-chiseled wooden legs – no, not chair legs, but actual prosthetics made for a female classmate who had been born with only one leg. The town millwright shaped and sanded these substitutes made from fir, pine, sometimes spruce, and equipped with adjustable leather straps to accommodate her growing body. When outgrown, the old leg would be tossed away along with rusty washtubs, worn saddles and broken dishes.

Each time Clara passed her friend in the hallway at school or sat behind her during an exam, she took the opportunity to study every detail of the leg which did not quite match the other – not in color, shape, nor in texture. She longed to one day free it from its leather harness and stroke its unnatural flesh to satiate her curiosity. But in the meantime, she continued to search obsessively through dirt and trash for these carved planks.

Clara's dream was to someday curate an entire room lined with these wooden limbs, arranged chronologically shortest to longest, marking the years of her friend's growth. Even today, decades later, living as she does in Spokane, hundreds of miles from those Montana scrap yards, from time to time the embers of her youthful obsession re-kindle, and Clara finds herself once again plotting future excavations to exhume those wooden bones.


Circumstances were not quite so dire at home when as older teen-agers we more leisurely roamed the culling fields, having returned year after year by way of our mushroom gathering expeditions. But now, more single-minded of purpose, Elaine, Diane, Karen and I quickly detoured to our favorite landfill, seeking to unearth our latest passion: old letters! We dreamed of them, were greedy for them, even lusted after them. How could we not? when their long dormant, often secret, furtive passages revealed to us a strange and luminous world filled with exotic descriptions of Calcutta and Dar es Salaam, illegitimate births, deaths, criminal acts… lovers' trysts and elopements. Each let-ter rescued from the moldering dirt beneath rusty coffee cans, purpling glass whiskey bottles, broken saws and car tires – or pulled out from lock-sprung suitcases and water-stained diaries – kept our adrenaline surging and imaginations flying.

Yes, there was magic in those words from dad: "Let's go mush-room hunting!" Aladdin's cave awaited. Yet, eager as we were for these drama-laden missives, the one we sought most avidly, super-seding all others in desirability, was the love letter, or *billet-doux*, as it were. Like French pigs snuffling out prized truffles, our appetites for personal correspondence were insatiable; all the more because we knew so little about intimacies between adults. Our sole encounter with a romantic moment was the time dad kissed mom on the cheek for her birthday and danced around the living room with her – while

Mario Lanza sang "Only a Rose" on the record player.

Not yet familiar with Jane Eyre, Anais Nin, Lady Chatterley or The French Lieutenant's Woman, still we knew these women must exist, and find them we would, from whatever source presented itself. So our inadvertent discovery of love letters considerably broadened our knowledge of human nature. Sentimental, confidential, erotic – these discarded missives afforded us clandestine glimpses into other people's lives, three-penny operas by which to sort out adult behaviors and relationships.

Voyeurs one and all, we knew no shame as we collected with racing pulses these fragments of stationery in pinks, lavenders and plain whites:

*Hey Lover Boy, I still can't believe you put that red nightie in my box of chocolates. ... What about next Saturday night for a drive-in movie?*
*Your best girl, Mavis*

*Dear Stephanie, I'm all busted up from the rodeo last week. Matter of fact, I'm in the Yakima hospital... Dam bull neutered me. I don't imagine you'd want me this way, so the weddings off... go ahead and keep the ring.* *Sincerely, John*

*Dear Brian, You take my breath away... the electricity actually jumps when we're together! You're definitely a double woof-woof – a perfect muscle bear... Let's meet next week at the Truffles Pub.*
*Love, Roy*

Time, however, was not our friend in this surreptitious activity, because it did not take mom and dad long to fill their paper bags with mushrooms. A sense of urgency and secrecy permeated our wanton transgressions in the culling fields. We certainly could not take the letters home. Perilous thought. Punishment for even reading them in the first place would be swift and without mercy, so we committed them to memory with a rapidity and accuracy which amazed even us. Our minds recorded them like spy cameras. We could hardly wait for the time after supper when, safely upstairs in the privacy of our bedrooms, we could share them with each other, reciting the lines with perfect recall – every single lurid, delectable detail.

Denae

It seems to me, now decades removed from childhood, safe as can be in my apartment study room, my vision has improved dramatically. Within the framework of those turbulent years, I realize there was an Indoor/Outdoor schism that dictated both our emotional and physical dispositions, depending on where we were.

"Indoors," meaning the time sequestered inside our house – for meals, homework or sleeping – could easily be compared to the experience of Charlotte Perkins Gilman's infamous yellow wallpapered room. Isolating, claustrophobic, psychically and physically destructive – the hours spent inside our various homes were often fit for neither child nor beast. No one had explained that our father was mentally ill, or that his drinking and stormy outbursts stemmed in part from his inability to get a decent job. As a 23-year old enlistee at Camp McCoy in Wisconsin, he was diagnosed as a paranoid-schizophrenic – unsuitable for military service. Yet, inexplicably, he was passed through.

Not surprisingly then, unable to cope with the stress of soldiering while in Alaska he went AWOL, thus earning himself a dishonorable discharge. A fatal disclosure on any job application, which, even if omitted, would eventually show up on a random background check. So, jobless and in perpetual hiding from the military (whom he assumed was in constant pursuit), he spent his days and nights trying to calm his anxiety and bitterness.

Like a caged animal, he paced, skulked, brooded, snarled and then erupted into violence. We too, along with our mother, shared that same fearsome cage which trapped him, trapped us all. But our movements, conversely, were defensive, evasive as we sidestepped him in counterpoint, seeking a refuge, a sanctuary that did not exist. We lived hourly as creatures of the night in that dark and terrible jungle which Blake so aptly described in his **"Tyger! Tyger! burning bright … In what distant deep or skies Burnt the fire of thine eyes? … Did he who made the lamb make thee?"**

"Outdoors," on the other hand, engendered freedom and a reprieve from the secrecy, rules, dramas and storms that comprised indoor life. Being outside meant fishing trips, woodsy weekend camping expeditions, canoeing and trail hiking in national forests. "Bad" things rarely happened when we were out in nature. There we could count on a harmony and safety that did not exist at home. Nature disdained secrets. Crimes against wives and children were not allowed here. Clearly, the omniscient, blazing sun forbade it, as did the towering evergreen trees, rushing mountain streams and dense flocks of migrating wild geese. What a difference a door makes.

Dad

When the outdoors crooked a beckoning finger, dad would rally, rambunctious and jolly, wearing his high-water jeans, rolled above his ankles. Like him, we too would be wearing the same spirit of adventure. "Let's go fishing!" The call of the wild was in the air as we rushed to follow dad, now Indiana Jones, gathering the necessary accoutrements. Off we would blaze in our wood-paneled Nash Rambler station wagon, all the windows rolled down. Arms, heads and fishing poles poked out in jumbled disorder; excited bits of conversation, whoops and shouts trailing the car like puffy clouds of dust.

I recall my amazement not long ago when a fishing-addicted friend, alluded to "catch and release," and then had to explain it to me. I thought he was making it up. Like many other poor households, we were dependent on freshly caught fish to supplement the food supply. No one that we knew in the '50s or '60s ever tossed back perfectly good fish. If one was too small, it was fried, cornmeal-coated like all the others, and served to one of the little kids.

Equally mystifying to me was the afternoon I observed this same friend "waxing" his fishing pants as they stood in place on his lawn, looking every bit like a man amputated from the waist up. (Apparently the waxing ensured waterproofing from wading in rivers and lakes.) But what intrigued me most about his passion for fishing was the amazing collection of colorful antique lures displayed prominently on his walls. I imagined them instead as ornaments hanging from a Christmas tree, rather than being pulled all bloodied from some poor fish's throat.

As children, our fishing gear was pretty basic. Each of us was equipped with a straight-as-you-could-find limb, preferably a half-inch in diameter, snapped off some tree. Add to that a 10-pound nylon test line tied to the pole, with a few bent nails for sinker weights. All that remained was to attach a red and white plastic bobber (my favorite fishing accessory) and a freshly dug Greenacres worm wriggling from the hook. And there we would be on a hot July afternoon, five or six of us jammed shoulder-to-shoulder, hip-to-hip in our green, flat-bottomed, paint-peeling rowboat, with dad pushing us away from the dock.

"You're sitting on my hand." "Ow! Your hook is sticking me in the leg." "That's not your fishing pole, it's mine."

"Yours broke when you leaned over to help Charles with his worm." "Could you just move over? You've got blood dripping from your finger, and I don't want it on me!"

It took a while for everyone to get situated as we rowed toward the center of the lake. Invariably, there would be a leak or two at the boat's bottom, and the person whose feet were closest was usually the one to ladle out the water at regular intervals using dad's spittoon can. Once we were settled and lines had been dropped into the water, the rules were simple and unequivocal: Never stand up. Be quiet. Watch your bobber.

The excitement of the hunt beat fiercely in our competitive little hearts. Each wanted to be the first to land a fish. And the species most likely to be hooked with our primitive gear were crappies, blue gills, perch, catfish and trout. We loved them all. That some of them were classified as better or worse than others in a hierarchical caste system imposed by elitist *a-fishionados* would have greatly surprised us. What did we know of "bottom-feeders," "caviar-yielders" or "game fish?" There was no snobbery in our discernment. We loved without judgment anything with a tail and fin which chose to bite on our hooks.

As the sultry afternoon hours dragged by, the little kids – Keith, Gail, Gwen and Charles – no longer flicked off the biting horseflies. Faces red-flushed and blond heads hot to the touch, periodically one of them would soundlessly lurch forward or topple backward, and an older arm would swoop out in rescue to nest them back into place – all the while keeping eyes alert to the prize. The six or seven red and white bobbers orbiting our boat were key to the leviathan kingdom below; our collective gaze locked on them like hounds to a fox. Our bodies were poised, tense, alert, with not a hint of breeze to break the monotonous oppression of heat and silence. Only the occasional darting of a blue-tailed dragonfly rendered any distinction between the implacable blue of sky and water. Our bobbers sat upon the surface still as tombstones.

The hotter it got, the more fiercely we stared at them, willing them to move, willing them to plunge beneath that unyielding, inviolable cerulean calm. Our brain cells began to melt; plasma coalesced. Mirages formed, changing resting turtles on logs into desert dunes and sway-backed camels. Palm trees appeared, then oozed, lava-like over driftwood, transmogrifying into history maps and Dead Sea scrolls.

Evolutionary forces digressed, reversing into a backward orientation in that slowly sinking fishing scow, as molecular breakdown fore-stalled and clogged our motor skills and brain function.

Then, without warning, from the abyss of mind-numbing inertia, a flash of red and white broke the spell; a bobber had been swallowed by the liquid blue. All six poles jerked up simultaneously, flinging water, lines, sinkers, left and right – pelting faces and appendages in circus-like pandemonium. No one had any idea *whose* line held the biting fish, until from above the melee, someone yelled, "I got it!" and a sleek little quarter-pound blue gill would be pulled over the side, dripping wet and fighting mad.

Charles, Curt, Gail

Since dad was both fearless and reckless in his approach to na-ture, he expected us, as his children, to be equally brash and undaunt-ed by any predicament that might arise. So, not surprisingly, risky business went hand-in-glove with these escapades. We were often exposed to dangerous situations with no advance warning or preparation. Barefoot or in worn sneakers, we scaled sheer rock cliffs and were encouraged to swim across fractious river currents to test our nerve and physical prowess. During firewood-gathering expeditions, Keith and we older girls would float driftwood and large logs downstream to wherever dad had parked the car. Once the logs were beached, we would proceed to cut them with old logging saws into foot and a half lengths to bring home for chopping. Every one of us girls as teenagers could wield an axe with the authority of a seasoned woodsman. Considering that none of us weighed more than 115 pounds, we were amazingly tough and resilient.

As a recreational pastime, one would assume swimming to be innocuous and hazard-free. Apparently, not for us. One August afternoon at Newman Lake, Diane at 15, found herself swimming in a thicket of snakes when she happened to get separated from the rest of the family who were splashing around much closer to shore. A strong swimmer, she had been enjoying the solitude of being out by herself near the middle of the lake. What she didn't know was that due to a warmer early spring, the lake was clogged with water lily roots, sea grasses and algae which unfortunately had spawned dense populations of rats and other aquatic species – favored fare for water snakes.

Unsuspecting then, floating on her back like an overturned turtle, Diane lazily dipped her hands into the sun-warmed water to keep moving. A series of odd-shaped ripples attracted her attention. Peering more closely, she was horrified to see surrounding her dozens of undulating black water snakes, like one of those luridly illustrated scenes from a horror comic book. Fighting down panic, she forced in a few deep breaths; then slitting her eyes to shut out the grotesque sight, she charged through the water like a hydroplane until reaching the safety of shore. Free-spiritedness clearly had its downside.

Poor Charles as a young teenager experienced a worst-case scenario when swimming one summer with friends at Liberty Lake in a secluded spot known as "the lagoon." A broken-down wooden dock extended out from the bank into 8-foot-deep water, cloudy with silt and rockweed. Diving off the end of the pier, Charles was a blur of red trunks and tanned lanky limbs, navigating the sandy bottom, looking for quarters or half-dollars that might have fallen from a swimmer's torn pocket.

A shirt-clad object caught his eye almost immediately. Swimming closer to investigate, he realized it was a human body. Worse yet, he recognized the features! Staring up at him was the bloated face of a 9-year old boy who had lived in our neighborhood. So appalling and frightening was the discovery, Charles actually started screaming under water "Oh my God! Oh no!" as he propelled himself up and out of the water like a torpedo – crashing seconds later onto the dock in a state of utter shock.

The wailing of an ambulance siren overlaid the scene along with the cries and whispers of the huddled teenage swimmers. A police investigation determined much later that the boy had been walking alone on the slippery dock and had fallen, unseen, over the side. Because he was such a poor swimmer, the investigators determined that the deep water had apparently overwhelmed his frantic struggles. So traumatic was the discovery for Charles, he would not swim again for months, and never again went near the silty waters of the lagoon. Who would guess that diving off a dock could be so fraught with peril?

Denae

Another swimming incident culminated in a much happier ending. Dad and mom had dropped Diane, Curt and myself off at Sandy Beach resort at the northern end of Liberty Lake. Once settled, we listened appreciatively to Little Richard's "Good Golly Miss Molly" and other '60s tunes blaring from portable radios on the hot, crowded sand. Later in the afternoon, I watched my tanned, muscular twin in her blue bikini coach little 7-year-old Curt in diving techniques from the floating dock, situated about 50 yards offshore. Backward flips, somersaults, jack knives – it amazed me how strong and athletic Curt was in replicating Diane's dives and swimming efforts. Finally tiring, both their faces flushed red and grinning, they climbed out of the water, pushing aside empty bottles of Orange Crush and Coca-Cola to join me on the green and white striped blanket, happy to rest and dry off.

In the distance, I detected a swimmer making odd flailing movements with his arms. Dismayed, I called loudly to Diane, pointing in his direction, hoping to alert nearby sunbathers as well. "Doesn't it look like that man is in trouble?" Casually, a few people looked up, then resumed their conversations. More alarmed, I added, "Look! He's bobbing up and down . . . I think he's drowning!"

Diane jumped up yelling, "I'm going after him!" Simultaneously, Curt bounded up and yelled, "I'm going too!"

"Oh no, Curt, you're way too young – not a strong enough swimmer. Please stay here with me!" But he was already diving into the lake behind Diane, the sudsy foam splaying everywhere as their arms and legs pounded the water.

For a moment, I considered running behind them to help. But I was much too poor a swimmer; I'd never reach the man in time. So I sat there spellbound, hardly breathing, as the far-off swimmer went under two more times before they reached him. Diane recalls hearing him say "help" only once, faintly, as she lifted his head and shoulder to begin the swim back. Dog-paddling alongside, Curt lifted the man's opposite arm and shoulder to relieve Diane from some of his weight.

After a few long minutes, they were just yards from shore with the now unconscious youth when several watching men jumped up from their beach towels to carry him the rest of the way onto the hot sand. Paramedics had arrived and were pulling oxygen equipment and a heavy stretcher from their truck.

By now, the entire beach of bathers – dozens of them – were entirely focused on the supercharged rescue efforts of the paramedics. At the same time, panting with exhaustion, water streaming from their heads and arms, Curt and Diane dropped wearily onto the blanket to watch. Radios had been snapped off and all conversation ceased, with the only sounds the tense remarks of the rescue group.

Finally catching her breath, Diane leaned over and whispered to Curt, "Let's not identify ourselves to the man or the ambulance guys … he'd feel indebted to us for the rest of his life and wouldn't know how to thank us." Wide-eyed and in a state of shock himself, Curt nodded his head, keeping his attention on the resuscitation drama.

Gazing at my twin and younger brother sitting next to me, tears squishing out from beneath my eyelids, I could hardly contain the pride I felt for their incredible bravery. Little Curty, barely 60 pounds soaking wet, had assisted in the rescue – our youngest brother, who had been born April 29, on Diane's and my birthday. Together, the three of us had actually saved a man's life – a defining, sobering moment that was simply indescribable.

The next day we read in the *Valley Herald* about the near drowning at Liberty Lake. Discharged from the hospital that evening, the teenager expressed his gratitude for his "unidentified rescuers." Looking at each other from above the pages, neither Curt, Diane, nor I said a word; we just nodded knowingly and smiled.

Gail

Boredom can be a dangerous state of mind for four young children craving excitement on a hot summer day. So there we were at daddy's small motel apartment on Sunset Highway for our weekend visit. I remember the day as being unbearably hot, the sun burning, scorching us as though it wanted to ignite the whole world. Such unrelenting heat provoked an urgency, a desperation to escape.

Younger brother Charles, age nine, began sketching out an idea which immediately caught our interest. "There's a railroad trestle over the highway that you guys don't know about. I walked over it all by myself last week when we were at daddy's." Proudly, he continued, "You won't believe how scary it is! Between the empty spaces of the railroad ties you can look down and see the cars zooming by. No safety rails, either. If you tripped, you'd go right over the edge, and there you'd be. . . splattered all over the highway."

Gratified by our collective expressions of awe and horror, Charles concluded with, "I bet none of you would dare do it – you'd be way too scared!"

Gail, Gwen, Charles, Curt.

His challenge was irresistible. Of course we would do it. Since daddy was away at the tavern and wouldn't be back for hours, this was precisely the diversion we were looking for. We began the long climb up the steep slope, which abutted the summit of the overpass. I must admit to a creeping feeling of apprehension, as I had no idea the trestle was so high. It was perhaps a 125-foot drop to the highway below and a 300-foot horizontal stretch over empty space until reaching solid ground on the other side. Not only did the jaw-dropping height unnerve me, I also realized that as the oldest, at 13, it was my obligation to keep Charles, 9, Gwen, 10, and Curt, 6, safe. The potential consequences were beginning to set off alarm bells. But the excitement of the moment overruled my usual good judgment. If I called off our fun, the kids would be so disappointed. Besides, how could I stop them when, perversely, despite all my misgivings, I was just as eager to test myself against the dangers of the challenge.

By this time, Charles and Gwen had already crossed the trestle and were laughing, jumping up and down on the other side. Beckoning, they yelled for me to hurry across with Curt. If only they knew how terrified I was – but there was no turning back now. Repositioning my grip on his hand, I glanced down at the speeding cars, nearly convulsing with dizziness and nausea. *What if I freeze right in the middle of the overpass?* Sensing my panic, Curt's face was now white as a sheet and his hand clammy; he began trembling. "Don't look down, Curty; we'll be across pretty soon. We're almost there," I whispered.

After what seemed like hours, we reached Gwen and Charles. Holding back tears, I still couldn't relax, because I knew I'd have to re-cross the wretched trestle to get back to daddy's motel. My voice was tense and grim as I motioned for everyone to start back. They were reluctant to end our adventure, and could not understand that the game had changed. "Hurry up! We need to get back. You two go ahead; Curt and I will follow."

Watching their fearless crossing, my spirits lifted with the light breeze as it picked up strands of their blond hair, tossing them this way and that. Bare arms and legs tanned from being outdoors, Gwen's shoulder bumped Charles as she kept to his side for morale. Pretty soon they would be safe. Now all I had to worry about was Curt.

We began by walking very slowly, nervous about losing our balance, eyes intent on each railroad tie, trying to avoid dropping our vision to the cars below. I began to relax. *What was I so worried about?*

*Little nervous Nellie ... everything was turning out just fine.*

Then I heard the train whistle behind me. Not indistinct, as in a long ways off, but shrill and loud, as if – turning quickly, I saw it – big and black, bearing down on us. For a second I froze and could neither think nor move. *What should I do?* My worst fear right behind us and all four of us still on the tracks!

By some miracle words came to me and I yelled. "Run! As fast as you can! Don't look back!!"

Gwen and Charles were so far ahead, I was pretty sure they would make the other side, as long as they didn't stumble or panic. Curty, however, was terrorized on the tracks. Trying the best I could to shut out his screams while grasping his hand, I began dragging, half carrying him, as fast as I could run; the train whistle – as frantic as I – was blowing every few seconds at my back. With sickening clarity, I knew it could not brake in time to save us.

Only a matter of seconds now, we were almost across. Lifting my head, I could see Charles and Gwen had made it; their bulging, terror-struck eyes were unforgettable as they watched the train gain on me and Curt. My life did not pass before my eyes in those final seconds; Curt was my only focus. *Please God, save him. He doesn't deserve this. . . Take me, if someone has to die.* Only a few more feet. With all my strength I lifted Curt and thrust him from the tracks to where Gwen and Charles were. Leaping off behind him, I felt a windy blast as the train screamed by.

All of us lay there in the dirt crying, too dazed and too numb to speak or move. Finally I got up. I had to get away from those horrible tracks where we had all nearly died. We walked back to daddy's together in silence, no longer minding the heat or the boredom. None of us ever told daddy or mom what happened that day.

# WHEN the SAINTS
# GO MARCHING IN

Front: Keith, Gail, Diane    Back: Karen, Elaine, Denae

God bless the Catholic Church. Its Latin Mass and idiosyncratic theologies suited our imaginative temperaments perfectly.
Denae

Until adolescence, we older girls in white cotton anklets and starched knee-length dresses dutifully trailed mom and grandma Hartman to Lutheran Sunday services each week, imprinted by little else than the volume and sincerity of grandma's wobbly, falsetto-pitched rendition of "Rock of Ages," her favorite hymn.

Dad's religious affiliation was less obvious. He looked to the majestic purple mountains and golden fields for his devotional needs. However, to his credit, with the births of the younger kids – Gail, Gwen, and Charles – he was visited by an epiphany advocating family unity.

Tucking the ubiquitous beer bottle out of sight beneath the dining table, he closed the lunch prayer one day with an appeal to mom: "Rose, you and the girls have asked me a hundred times to go to church with you. That Lutheran mumbo-jumbo is just like so much rice soup to me – nothing like those rabble-rousing Latin masses in Torrington that *Chutka* used to take Emil and me to. Those prune-faced nuns and knuckle-breaking priests could shake you up like nobody's business. You got the whole ball of wax from them – sermons you could really sink your teeth into."

Warming to those long ago memories, dad forked his Spam and fried potatoes with gusto. "If you and the girls will convert to Catholicism, then we could all attend church as a family."

Sacre bleu! Dad was going to voluntarily join the ranks of the godly – to become pious and obedient!? I tried to imagine him tamed and reformed, no longer the venom-spewing Rasputin terrorizing our household. It was a stretch. It must have finally occurred to him that he could end up in Hell – forever. Briefly I savored the vision, then reconsidered. Who was I, after all, to be skeptical when lesser men than he had rebounded into sainthood?

So in 1959, the year before little Curty was born, all ten Veselits inscribed their names into the St. Mary's Church registry, filled with hopeful expectations of change. It's not hard to recall that first Sunday mass, climbing the wooden steps, en famille, all the girls' hair smashed flat by the mandatory headscarves, as we braced ourselves against the gusting February wind. Pious in form, if not in thought, we were bowed over like the ice-encrusted pine trees surrounding the modest white clapboard church.

Two black-frocked priests greeted us, their ankle-length, dress-like cassocks draped over black trousers. Each was necklaced with a heavy, wooden-beaded crucifix.

"Welcome, welcome," they sought us out, pumping dad's hand. "Glad to have you among the flock," at the same time directing us toward the two basins of holy water attached to the inside foyer wall. Novices to this ritual, we scooped up overgenerous handfuls of the water to make the sign of the cross – splashing most of it over our coat fronts and sleeves (the stigmata of the uninitiated).

It seemed to me we had regressed in time back to the black forests of Transylvania, finding ourselves like the rustic folk, bearing crosses and garlic amulets as protection against the ebony-clad Draculas and vampires.

The spectacularly black and white costumed nuns seemed especially congruent to this exotic landscape, as did the tiny, dimly lit, wondrously secretive, confessional chambers. Mass was conducted entirely in a foreign tongue, and the priests were given to swinging out great sooty clouds of incense from their chain-dangling brass pots. Oftentimes polluting the air so densely that asthmatics and the elderly, choking, would flee down the side aisles on foot or in wheelchairs, rushing outside to fill their lungs with fresh air. The rest of us, forbearingly, applied hankies or toilet tissue to our burning eyes and noses.

Holy water, too, was hurled from colander-like gold chalices, synchronized to the chiming of the altar boys' bells. Worshippers closest to these water-sloshing ecclesiastics would cast their faces in the opposite direction like a choreographed flock of sheep, hoping to avoid the downpour.

Life-sized painted statuary of the disciples and the Blessed Virgin – who was usually clad in powder blue – lined the walls and hallways. Beneath the hem of Mary's robes, I spied a wily, half-coiled snake – rather an unsubtle reference, I thought, to Eve's committing Original Sin in the Garden of Eden, encouraged by snakey.

These realistically painted holy men and women possessed nowhere near the drama of the larger-than-life, blood-stained Christ hanging heavily from the wooden cross mounted high above the altar. Slumped as he was, burdened by the consciences of a world full of sinners, it seemed structurally impossible for the two slim nails extruding from his palms to bear the considerable weight of his unhappy form. However determinedly I tried to keep my focus on the priest and his Holy Scriptures, I could not entirely deny a few stray glances, rolling my eyes up to Jesus, hoping today would not be the day he slid prematurely from Calvary – crashing onto the matching vases of white chrysanthemums on the altar, or worse yet, onto the defenseless priests and altar boys.

Father Joseph Brunner was the holy man in charge of this conservative 200-family congregation – a prince among priests, if not a study in black himself, right up to the ebony irises of his eyes, soulfully regarding us from their pious depths each time he placed the communion wafer on our tongues or palmed our foreheads in benediction.

Elaine recalls Father Brunner with this description: "His vestments were always rumpled, with holes from pipe tobacco burns buried among the wrinkles. Two or three days growth of charcoal stubble covered his face, looking like a field recently burned. He never seemed altogether clean, probably because his bigger priority was taking care of the needs of his very poor parish."

Father Brunner and St. Mary's Catholic Church were a hugely stabilizing force for our struggling family. Starved as we were for knowledge of the world beyond the terrors and restrictions of home, the church's landscape established boundaries that were constant, predictable, and for the most part, fair – a place like school, where one could relax one's guard. After all, was it not into Father Brunner's trustworthy ears that we whispered our deepest, darkest concerns and sins during confession? Such an act would not be possible without a high level of trust.

So fearful and suspicious was I of my own father that I never confided anything to him of a personal nature, not as a child, nor as an adult. I never voluntarily kissed or hugged him, either. Once when I was ten, he invited me on a hot summer evening to go to the movies with him – alone. The idea so terrified me that I immediately begged off, complaining of a severe stomachache – a believable deception, since I suffered painful intestinal cramping after dinner every night for years, a consequence of his violent mealtime tirades.

Our home operated under the rigidly enforced "Children are to be seen and not heard," or, if you will, in a more contemporary voice: "From the moment I could talk, I was ordered to listen." I marveled that God had given us all larynxes, so little use did we make of them.

At age fourteen, in an unprecedented act of rebellion, I dared to defy this heretofore-inviolable decree. While I stood peeling potatoes for dinner at the kitchen sink, dad had singled me out for ridicule. "Look at her, peel, peel, peel; that's all she's good for; a lazy, good-for-nothing cow like the rest of you … defiant too … I see that look on your face. You'll keep peeling those goddamn potatoes 'til hell freezes over."

His needling and criticizing spiraled out ridiculously, beyond any semblance of logic or truth. He loved to tax us to our absolute limits. Well, I had just reached mine. Flinging the potato peeler into the mountain of brown skins, and without turning around, I spat into the facing window, teeth clenched, "Leave. Me. Alone."

The echo of my words almost knocked me over, so shocked was I to hear them. There would be hell to pay for this little self-indulgent display.

Dad began slapping and kicking me. I must have blacked out, because soon after I was surprised to find myself alone on an upstairs bed. Those two small rooms at the top of the house were the farthest from dad we could get. Since he rarely climbed the stairs to this space, it was regarded by most of us as a kind of sanctuary above the noise and violence of the lower rooms.

Just as the world's highest peaks are revered for their sacredness – their very altitude nudging them closest to God –I suppose, in a small way those two alcoves tucked beneath the roof's slanting eaves were our Macchu Pichu, Mount Fuji, or Kilimanjaro – our safe place to seek God's protection. It was here that one by one family members with the utmost discretion crept up to me to pay their respects – as though I was the open casket at a viewing, awaiting the final comments. "How did you dare?" whispered Diane. "You're the family hero," from Karen. "I just wish I could smack him, he makes me so mad. He's got no right to hit mom or any of us," huffed Elaine, with clenched fists. "Thank you for standing up to him; someone needed to do it."

Ironically, given the constant siege of violence (or threat of) generated by dad, the number one rule in our household commanding absolute obedience was "Honor thy Father and thy Mother." Attached as a caveat was daddy's humorous little sequitur, "And you know what I mean is, do as I say, *not* as I do." Wink, wink. Even he was aware of the obvious contradiction between his actions and his words.

Much as dad might be confident that we were his minions, his chattel, to serve as he saw fit, on occasion his paranoia over the inevitability of old age subverted his usual bravura. At these times, he would line us up in the living room, pull out the family Bible from the red Chinese cabinet (reserved for birth certificates and other special documents), and begin a lecture on "Children's Responsibilities to their Parents."

"Your mother and I brought you into this world and have spent our lives clothing and feeding you. Is it too much to ask that you take care of us when we're too cotton-picking old to blow our own noses?"

It was at this juncture that dad dropped the *we*, invoking instead the narcissistic *I*. "I want you to promise me, on the Holy Bible," thwacking its black leather cover with his open palm for emphasis. "Promise me you will never put me in a nursing home, by God, no matter *how* sick I get."

Clearly his fear of old folk's homes bordered on the psychotic. "As God is your witness, place your hand on this Bible, and *swear* you will never let me die in a goddamn rest home!" The book would be passed to each of us, as one by one we solemnly pledged our loyalty to dad's wishes. At the time Elaine was 15, Diane and I, 12; Karen and Keith, 11 and 8; and Gail and Gwen, 7 and 5.

So painfully binding did I believe these oaths, that over 45 years later when dad was terribly sick for two and a half years – a diaper-clad, bent old man in his eighties – I almost single-handedly kept him out of the long-term nursing facilities which he so feared. In the end he did indeed die at home, a changed and humble man. My siblings and I had kept the promise we had made him those many long years ago as children.

## Mass in My Bedroom
Gwen

As a ten-year-old, I recall sneaking the Sunday Missal home from church so I could say mass in my bedroom by myself. There was something about reciting both the priest's part and the respondent's that was satisfying to me. Maybe it was an attempt to bring God the "right" way into my life.

I remember dad doing his best to instruct us spiritually by reading from the Bible in the evening as we all sat around the dining table. I don't recall much of the content – although I listened carefully – but I do recall dad chuckling when he came to passages about "not drinking too much wine." At those times, he would move his beer bottle under the table to "hide" it, as if God couldn't see it just as well beneath the table. Who knows, maybe that little deceit was the foundation for me becoming so extremely honest – almost to a fault.

With the utmost reverence, again and again I would repeat the words I had heard in Sunday mass once I was back in my bedroom.

Perhaps my actions were a subconscious longing to connect with a father – my own, Father Brunner, a heavenly Father – *any* father.

I gave myself communion using a torn crust of bread from mom's kitchen for the host and a little red Kool-Aid for the wine. I may not have fully understood the sacred significance of "the body and blood of Christ," but somehow I knew I was being fed spiritually.

Funny how God can use just about anything (maybe even everything) to plant the seeds of faith and hope into our lives, from the simplest – a couple of fish, a few loaves of bread, a stolen weekly missal – to the more complicated, like an alcoholic father trying to provide spiritual instruction to his children, to the supernatural – an extraordinary starry night that He gave to Denae.

Denae

Diane recalls in vivid detail our First Confirmation (and concurrently, First Communion) at St. Mary's. "The March of the Freaks," she jeers in mock horror, pointing to a black and white snapshot in the family album depicting us in our vestal virgin finery. Simultaneously, we both cringe at the memory.

Provincial it may be, but the Catholic Church annually sponsors its own fashion spectacle in the "coming out" of its First Communicants – an event showcasing the 7-, 8- and 9-year olds, decked out in white party dresses, veils, fancy shirts, pearls and lacy white gloves.

Since Elaine, Diane, Karen and myself converted to Catholicism as teenagers, by the time of confirmation we were five or six years older, not to mention seven or eight inches *taller* than the other kids. Sunday morning of the big day, lilac-scented breezes lifted our hair and petticoats, as dad insisted we pose in the front yard for pictures. Half an hour later, we found ourselves reluctantly assembling at the back of the church with 25 or 30 other catechumens – Keith and Gail (age appropriate), included.

Standing conspicuously behind them in our bridal whites, we older girls with folded hands prepared for the Grand Promenade down the central aisle, while the congregation stood in rapt attention, walled in by stately vases of white gladiola and trumpeting lilies. Then, unexpectedly, Elaine got the giggles, partly due to the heat and cloying incense, but mostly because she had noticed a yellow, 39 cents tag stuck to the heel of an 8-year-old boy in front of her – betraying the fact that, despite his expensive-looking slacks and sports coat, his shoes had obviously been purchased secondhand, like our own.

"Yes, the Parade of the Freaks," continues Diane. "A fractured version of *Gulliver's Travels,* we towered over the Lilliputians like giants – flowered doilies on our heads, palms pressed together like church steeples – spinsters at the prom. We looked completely ridiculous. How *could* they have put us on display like that?" For once in our lives, dad's description of us as the big cows seemed entirely appropriate.

Elaine

I remember all the times we walked the four miles home from church on Sundays when we had no ride. Dad would drop us off before mass, and go fishing for the rest of the day. After the service, we girls would pull off the hated headscarves, shaking our hair free, while Keith would peel out his yo-yo with the broken string from his back pocket, and we'd all head for the railroad tracks to avoid the stares of the O'Reilly kids and other parishioners likely to be passing by in their cars. Invariably, Karen or Denae – someone – would have stashed in their pocketbook a paper bag and knife to cut dandelion greens. There were always patchy clumps of them growing between the railroad ties or beneath rocks in the open fields. With our bag filled, we knew for sure when we reached home we'd have lunch, even if it was just a big bowl of dandelions.

July and August Sundays, we would feast on apples from the orchards growing alongside the tracks. Standing in the cool purple shade and hidden by the tree branches, with St. Mary's steeple cross still visible behind us, we'd make up for our scanty breakfast by gorging on the fat juicy fruits. As for the Ten Commandments – especially the one about not stealing – we thought nothing of it. It never crossed our minds we were doing anything wrong.

Denae

I recall being utterly intrigued by the entire concept of the confessional – that mysterious, dark Ali Baban porthole to God, which opened only if you knew the magic words. Saint Mary's confessionals were located at the back of the church proper: two sets of three closet-like rooms. The middle room was occupied by the seated priest, awaiting the penitents on either side. You entered by parting a heavy red velvet curtain. Of especial concern was the thickness of the plywood partitions, since each person queuing up for forgiveness – squirming grade-schoolers, restless teens, or anxious adults – wanted to be sure that only Father Brunner's ears would be receiving the unholy details of their crimes.

"Besides, tombs are so tight." That line from Diane's Sun Running poem aptly described for me the confessional. Hardly larger than an upended casket, there was just enough room to kneel as you waited for the priest to slide up the little wood panel. I could smell his after-shave, if he wore any, or the spearmint flavor of Chiclets on his breath. Making the sign of the cross, I would whisper into his ear: "Bless me, Father, for I have sinned."

My recital of transgressions was about as exciting as beach sand – a good time for Father Brunner to think about his annual vacation to Mexico. "I couldn't help it, Father – last Tuesday night I imagined daddy going out to sea on an ice floe,

Diane, Father Brunner, Denae and Curt

with a polar bear right behind him, a *hungry* polar bear," followed by "And the next night I thought about our house being on fire and rescuing everyone but daddy, hoping the house would fall down before I could save him."

With the "biggies" out of the way, I could move on to lesser crimes, like threatening to cut off Diane's eyelashes while she was asleep, or pretending I didn't notice the scarf falling off my hair during Sunday mass.

Hair, both by its presence or absence, occupied untold hours of our attention once we were inculcated in the traditions of Mother Church. Never having seen a bald woman, we were intrigued by the whispered disclosures about the nuns. Much was our curiosity as we sat in catechism class, absorbing every detail of Sister Marie-Therese – turquoise rosary beads draped over her corset-flattened chest. We longed to lift those yards of heavy fabric to discover if she was truly hairless. When she warned us of the bishop's pending visit to test our Bible knowledge, our thoughts were focused instead on detecting a stray, oxygen-starved tendril, betraying a refusal to sacrifice her hair to the church. *Had she actually shaved her head, like Mother Superior Beatrice-Rose? Or was it all coiled into a bun, artfully concealed by the flowing waist-length veiling?*

Suddenly, her words implicated us as well into this complicated theology of women's hair: "Children, we must *never* enter the Sanctus Sanctorum without first covering our hair – whether with a hat or scarf – so offensive is it to our Blessed Lord. It is our way of showing submission and obedience to Him. At its worst..." Sister paused to clutch her dangling crucifix, as though for spiritual bracing. "At its worst, the uncovered hair is a powerful temptation to our fellow man, oftentimes causing the commission of a deadly mortal sin, which as you have learned, children, is an offense grave enough to close the doors of Heaven to your immortal soul."

Gasping at the import of this revelation, I looked across my desk to Karen, sitting implacably one row over. "Vanity, thy name is Karen" was a family joke originating from her obsession with her hair. Wanting to be blonde like Diane, she had once bleached it with straight purex from mom's laundry room. Disastrously over-processed, her hair stretched like overcooked pasta when she tried to comb it. Mercifully,

Diane, who was more skilled in bleaching procedures, helped cut and then re-color Karen's hair back to brown.

Running my eyes up and down her shoulder-length hair, now frizzy with split-ends, I marveled; _This_ *is a source of temptation? Enough to keep a man from Eternal Bliss?* I threaded my fingers pensively through my own short-cropped tangles, then raised my hand to Sister Therese in objection. Not so long ago, I had read Alexander Pope's *The Rape of the Lock* (a 1712 tale of ravished hair) from our home set of *The Illustrated Classics*. Its content was as preposterous and mystifying as Sister's statement. This would be a good time for clarification. However, as I imagined myself saying *"Rape of the... "* out loud in front of the class, I slowly lowered my arm. I couldn't do it.

The question burning on my lips was not to be resolved until many years later as a college student in anthropology. I made it my mission to track down this elusive, phobic reaction to women's hair.

*The Women's Encyclopedia of Myths and Secrets* by Barbara Walker was a rich resource for my inquiry. Its pages revealed that ancient Egyptians believed female hair contained protective powers for the afterlife, such that widows buried clippings of their hair along with their deceased spouses to protect them in death. Comets were believed to be the Great Mother's hair, foreshadowing doom for humanity. Tantric wisdom opined that the loosening of women's locks could unleash cosmic forces of either creation or destruction. Accordingly, Scottish girls in medieval Europe were forbidden to unbind or comb their hair after sundown if their fathers or brothers were away at sea, by way of preventing stormy gales from sinking their ships.

Over time all this collective folklore funneled down to St. Paul's decree that Christian women's heads be covered to prevent their invoking demonic powers harmful to both men and nature. Carrying such measures even further, church fathers compelled nuns to shave their heads upon completion of their vows to deny them the source of any magic powers.

For similar reasons, the millions of women arrested on suspicion of witchcraft during the Middle Ages were forced to have their heads shaved *before* being tortured to guarantee they could not work a spell against their abusers. France's Joan of Arc was condemned to burn at the stake in part because she had dared to cut off her own hair following her arrest. Her inquisitors felt it was *their* prerogative to perform this indignity.

I did often wonder why the witch in fairy tales was always endowed with volumes of flowing black hair (White would be unthinkable – no matter how ancient the hag). This pairing of black, witches and evil is so archetypal that no illustrator, however avant garde, would dare paint her as a blonde or a redhead!

Such preoccupation with hair during catechism class was inestimably heightened on those occasions when Mr. Manfred substituted for an ailing Sister Marie-Therese. Pious, meek, learned in theology, he was as solidly Catholic as the confessional. But it was not for his piety or intellect that we esteemed him. No, it was for his toupee. Hand stitched – we could see the tiny rows of sutures along his part line – its thick bristles of hair lay in diagonals from the part, in crude imitation of a more fashionable cut. We did not fault him, however, for this stylistic atrocity, since he offered himself up to our probing curiosities with such equanimity.

Neither eyebrows nor eyelashes framed Mr. Manfred's soulful brown eyes; black-rimmed glasses concealed these lacks. But children love anomalies. Sitting at our desks in grass-stained sneakers, short-sleeved white blouses and gray woolen skirts, we savored his differences, admired his uniqueness.

During Sunday mass, after a hurried genuflection, I would immediately scan the congregation for the telltale, stiff dark thatch that identified Mr. Manfred. "There he is!" I'd whisper excitedly to Elaine, wedged in the hard wood pew next to me. She'd pass it on to Karen and Diane, our collective gazes attached like laser beams to his cranium as Father Brunner guided the more devout through the *pater nosters* and *mea culpas*.

Critically and with the care of an Inspector Clousseau, we examined for later discussion his "toupee management." Most problematic for him were the excessively windy March and November days, on which we observed its wondrous gravity-defying tilt. At any given moment – what with all the alternate kneeling and standing – the precariously perched coif could easily slide from his head, revealing at long last the splendor of his shiny bald skull.

However, my chronic musings on Mr. Manfred's artificially-forested scalp were interrupted one sunny afternoon in catechism class by the sudden, ominous turn of his discourse. "This afternoon," he began, "we contemplate the possibility of committing our lives to God and to the service of Mother Church by becoming a nun or a priest." He paused to smile admiringly at a seated Sister Beatrice-Rose, her pearl-pale hands folded devoutly upon her lap.

"My dear children" – he looked back to us – "consider yourselves blessed indeed if you hear our Beloved Jesus knocking at the door of your heart. Listen carefully for him, and when you do hear the call, say yes, YES! With all your heart."

I felt like I was going to throw up. *Could this be possible?* Bad as it was at home with dad constantly on the rampage, now the church, which had finally afforded me some respite from the terrors at home, was beginning to look like the enemy, too, attempting to trap me into nun-hood. *Shave my head? Wear black and white the rest of my life? No makeup? No boyfriends – just an endless litany of prayers and rosary beads? Not on your life.*

A fear as profound and disturbing as anything I had experienced at home clouded over my soul. Once again, my very thoughts were at risk. At home, dad could read our minds; now the church, too, verged on trespass. *How does one refuse God? If I heard The Calling, I'd have to say "Yes," wouldn't I?* The possibility of Cosmic retaliation haunted me. It never occurred to me I had a choice. The nuns had warned us about divine retribution, like at Holy Communion: If you tried to swallow the wafer at mass without first properly confessing all your sins, it would turn black on your tongue. And then – even worse

– right there in front of Father Brunner and the whole congregation, a bolt of lightning could come and drop you on the spot!

So now I had to worry about The Calling; day or night, it could come knocking. Nevertheless, I decided – despite jeopardizing Eternity – I was *not* going to reconcile myself to becoming a nun. Instead, I would create as much internal noise and confusion as possible. If I didn't hear the Calling, surely God would not hold me responsible for not claiming it. I began by chanting nonsense mantras; then I memorized long columns of Shakespearian sonnets and Socratic dialogues; spent entire evenings contemplating Zeno's Paradox. I even stopped cleaning the wax out of my ears in case God got tricky and decided to deliver his request externally, the normal way.

Even so, I still beseeched Him every night at prayers, "Please, Heavenly Father, send The Calling to someone else. Linda Stonehocker has a big collection of crosses and rosaries; I'm sure she'd work out a lot better than me."

Overnight, with that dreadful disclosure of Mr. Manfred's, it seemed life had singled me out for overtime in the misery department, until one weekend when Diane shared with me a hair-raisingly similar experience at Marycliff, the all-girls' Catholic high school she and Karen attended.

Sister Charitina, the head nun, had unexpectedly called Diane out of religion class several days earlier. Modestly attired in the school uniform of gray/blue knee-highs and pleated skirt, her white blouse buttoned to the very top, Diane entered the office, drying her wet palms into her skirt folds as she looked up to see facing her, a somber-eyed jury of black-robed sisters.

"Come in, dear," Sister began officiously. "It has come to our attention, through much prayer work with our Beloved Father, that He has designated a special path for you, a blessing given the chosen few. We ask that you consider preparing yourself for the most glorious of all vocations, the life of the sisterhood, a sacred union of you and God the Father." Smiling, she reverently touched the simple gold band encircling her own ring finger.

"No way!" Diane stormed to me in response to the memory. "What in God's name could they be thinking? I bleach my hair and wear my skirts and blouses shorter and tighter than any of the Marycliff girls. My clothes and breath reek of cigarettes; I'm not the slightest bit pious, and I don't even know where the campus chapel is!"

I had to agree. She was definitely *not* nun material. Blonde, perfect figure, her blue eyes so stiffly mascaraed they could catch a falling bird, she would certainly have been my last choice for sisterhood – like expecting Helen of Troy to shave her head and join a convent.

"I'm so afraid they'll try and talk me into it, force me against my will. If they asked dad, he'd probably say 'Yes!' and hand me over."

Diane at 17 did not live at home, but like Karen, roomed and boarded with a family in town, exchanging cooking, cleaning, and babysitting services to pay her Marycliff tuition. Feeling completely vulnerable, she had no parental protection, what with dad at Eastern State Mental Hospital and mom overburdened with the single parenting of the six remaining children at home. No wonder she was panic-stricken.

"So what are you going to do?" I asked, dripping with sympathy.

"I'll probably stop going to most of my classes, turn in my assignments late. And I'll start troweling on the makeup. Sister Margaret *hates* rouge and red lipstick. There is no way I'm going to sign up to be a nun!"

With set jaw and absolute resolve, Diane more than prevailed in her strategies. At graduation no one even noticed her absence. It was just assumed she had dropped out sometime in the school year, maybe to pursue modeling. Her picture wasn't in the yearbook, either – just another Jane Doe who had fallen between the cracks. As for the Marycliff nunnery, alas, it lamented the loss of this vestal virgin, so eminently suited for glory within its membership.

# POOR MAN'S SOUP

Keith, Gail, Gwen, Charles, Dad, Mom, Diane, Karen, Elaine, Curt

Denae

**Sate**: to cram, fill, glut, stuff, gorge. That's what Webster's has to say about this word. I have my own definition. Tomato. On a warm Saturday afternoon in late September, it taught me everything I needed to know about sate.

Not yet a teen, I watched from the kitchen window as daddy pulled up in the driveway and hoisted from the car trunk a wooden crate filled with luscious red tomatoes. Carrying it into the dining room, he set it ever so gently on the table. All nine of us kids gathered around the box inhaling the earthy sweetness, while at the same time eyeballing its contents with a predatory lust.

Since it was canning season, I assumed we would soon be peeling, slicing and boiling the fruits, then stuffing them into Mason quart jars to be lined up on shelves in the lower basement for winter consumption.

"Oh no." Daddy seemed to read my thoughts. "These are for eating. There are lots of green tomatoes in the garden ripening up for canning."

So what is something you get really excited about? I mean *really* excited. The doctor telling you that your brain tumor is really a cyst? Discovering that garage sale painting is an authentic Van Gogh? Well, that's the level of excitement generated by food entering our house.

By the age of eleven, I had never been served seconds, and had certainly never eaten until my stomach could burst. Keith recalls spitting on our food at mealtime – a way of rendering it so unpalatable that nearby hungry fingers would not be inclined to reach over and grab it. More commonly, I ate as fast as possible to ensure that what was on *my* plate ended up in *my* stomach. As for the spitting, even though I don't remember it, Gwen and Karen assure me it is so.

So there we all are, bellies grumbling, mouths salivating at the Babette's Feast in front of us. I knew exactly what was coming next, exactly what mom was going to say: "Not so fast. This has to be spread out over a lot of meals. We've only got a few potatoes left in the bin and we're running low on peanut butter. So, Frank, would you hand me a knife? You kids can each have a quarter-slice of tomato."

Yep, that's what she said, right on cue. I could have wept. The same old parceling out of food. Just enough to wet your whistle, just enough to get your taste buds all stirred up. Such an itty-bitty morsel, too. If you were quiet, you could hear the plop! as it hit the bottom of your empty stomach.

Shoulders hunched, I stared at that voluptuous fruit with something like hatred welling up in my chest. This was nothing short of unadulterated torture. I was beginning to wish daddy had never brought that wretched box of tomatoes home. To have such bounty only inches from my mouth and then to be rationed a couple miserable swallows was just more than I could bear. Turning, defeated, I headed upstairs.

Daddy spoke next. "Oh, come on Rose, just this once let's have at it and eat till we're sick. What do ya say?"

I couldn't believe my ears. Making a sharp left, I returned to the table. Mom nodded her head and smiled. Was it really true? We all turned as one in disbelief, looking to daddy for confirmation. "What are you waiting for? Have at it!!"

Paradise lost – regained. That box of sun-ripened tomatoes became a veritable river, a red landscape of juice, seeds, pulp – on our hands, in our mouths, running down our chins, necks and onto our elbows. Caught up in the orgy of eating, I felt like smearing the redness into my hair, over my eyes and up and down my legs. Maybe I did – I hope so. Because the feeling of abundance was so unprecedented, that if this moment was never to come again, I wanted to experience it fully, to drench myself in it as thoroughly as humanly possible.

The end was the best part. With the wood crate now completely empty – we had even licked the juice off the table – my stomach felt full, loaded, glutted, gorged, SATED. At that moment, daddy had achieved sainthood, and mom too. As for me, I think I passed out from sheer happiness.

Gail

Cooking with mom was a hazardous experience, both physically and emotionally. Because she was incapable of managing her own nervousness, I was, consequently, kept in a chronic state of panic. A truckload of Lorazepam would not calm me.

I knew dad put a lot of pressure on mom, causing her to be a nervous wreck no matter what she was doing. There was simply no way for me to avoid kitchen duty. In the summer months with school out, dad maximized the earning potential of the four big girls, rounding them up at 7 a.m. like a platoon commander, and sending them off to Mr. Hurry's strawberry and raspberry fields, leaving me to fill out the kitchen staff.

During these meal preparations, mom was more like a drill sergeant than a mother. To make matters worse, she had never liked cooking anyway. With the extra aggravation of three small children underfoot, she was impossible to work with. I would be running frantically in 15 different directions as she called out her orders: "Gail, you need to start peeling the potatoes…and don't forget to bring in extra tomatoes from the garden." Followed by, "Are you blind? Can't you see Curt's diaper needs changing? And look! The gravy is boiling over!!"

One harried day, tension was mounting with noon approaching and the kitchen a blast furnace from the oven running at 400 degrees all morning. I was hot and tired, doing my best to keep up with mom's flurry of commands, when suddenly she yelled: "Gail, hurry and take those pies out of the oven before they burn!"

Totally unnerved and in a rush to obey, I yanked open the oven door and grabbed the hot pies with my *bare* hands. Seeing the pain register on my face, mom scowled angrily, "Don't you dare drop those pies after I worked so hard to make them!"

As the hot metal seared my fingers, I ran in what seemed like slow motion, to drop the pies on the counter. I shuddered to look at my hands. White lines ran the length of all my fingers where the flesh had been burned. The pain was beyond belief. As I opened my mouth to scream, mom yelled, "Don't you dare cry! It was your foolishness that caused this. Daddy will be here with the girls any minute, and lunch still isn't ready. So if you're going to snivel, do it in the chicken coop where no one has to listen to you!"

Without making a sound, I ran from the house to the coop. My hands hurt so much I thought I would black out from the pain and fall senseless into the dust and gravel – leaving the hens to peck at what was left of me. Within minutes, I heard mom calling for me to help her finish making the lunch. No sympathy, no mention of salve or a cold cloth. I wanted to disappear, evaporate, never to return again to that hellhole of a kitchen.

This all happened before my tenth birthday, the only consolation being that in a couple years I would be old enough to work beside my older sisters, and Gwen would inherit the wretched job of assisting mom. I reveled in the thought of returning home from berry picking and having lunch served to *me*. Life as a field worker earning a wage seemed far superior to enduring the drudgery of working in the kitchen.

Witness To An Execution

Karen

Gail's story about the chicken coop reminds me of those traumatic times when dad instructed us in the preparation of domestic fowl for the dinner table. Elaine, Diane, Denae and I were all taught how to chop off the heads of our chickens – the progeny of our banty rooster and banty hen, Cisco and Tiny, respectively. Tiny was blind, and Cisco, dad's best friend, had only one leg. However, he more than compensated for the loss by his ferocious disposition; none of us could get near him. Inexplicably, with dad he was meek as a kitten, clinging to his shoulder during routine gardening chores or on the occasional fishing trip down the river.

Dad kept a special stump and sharpened ax in the back yard, ready for the kill at a moment's notice. Once the head had been chopped off, the still twitching lower half of the chicken was dumped into a pot of boiling water to loosen its feathers. Whoever was assigned the plucking detail had to snatch the hot steaming feathers from the skinny, white carcass. Dad performed the final singeing with long wooden matches to rid the poor creature of its few remaining quills.

The stench of boiled, then burnt wet feathers from a still heaving chicken in a bloody pot is a smell and sight not easily forgotten – enough to make you gag at the thought of Chicken Cacciatore. In the meantime, someone had to pick up and discard the severed head with its alert bulging eyes, along with the bloody detached feet.

Alas, barnyard fowl came and went in our household until dad escalated to larger farmyard breeds – a family cow (we used to ride) which, against our protests, he butchered for its beef, and an unfortunate goat named Curly that he milked to death. The horses he brought home – one, a memorable swayback – are another story altogether.

We were never lucky in keeping our beloved pets for very long. Smiley, one of our many stray dogs that was killed by speeding cars on Sprague Avenue, had a face that was permanently frozen into a grin (hence his name). When hungry, he self-fed from an open bag of cheap dog food that mom kept in a corner of the kitchen. He drank from the toilet bowl in the second floor bathroom (along with our youngest brother, Curt, who also didn't know any better) when we forgot to fill his water dish.

Mom and dad heeded no clear-cut boundary between pets and food. Our pet rabbits ended up in two-quart Mason jars one day while we were at school. No one told us when we got them as bunnies that they were being fattened for table fare. So we cuddled, fed, named and tamed them, just as we did our dog, cat and parakeet.

On that dreadful day when we four older girls walked into the kitchen hoping to see cookies on the counter for an afternoon snack, instead to our horror we saw Pinky, Blackie, Whitey, Sparkey, and all the others lined up in a row facing us, with their little paws pressed against the clear glass – headless and furless.

To say we were shocked doesn't even come close to describing our feelings. Completely undone, we all burst into tears. I think mom was a little shaken by our dramatic reaction: "We will never eat our bunnies for dinner, even if we're starving!" we sobbed as we fled upstairs to our bedroom.

When we could, we buried our pets under the sign boards at the back of our property, an area sometimes referred to as the "killing grounds." Here we held simple ceremonies over the cloth-covered remains before burying them in the rocky soil. Occasionally, we would erect a cross made of glued popsicle sticks for family favorites like Smiley. Keith once had the worrisome dilemma of how to bury his dead snake. He couldn't decide if it was more appropriate to lay him out in a straight line or coiled up in a circle.

Neither mom nor dad usually attended these funerals, although when Cisco died dad was so upset he closed the chicken coop forever, saying no rooster could ever replace him. With Cisco gone, Tiny eventually died of loneliness, so we thankfully returned to eating store-bought chicken.

Elaine

We were never quite sure how seriously dad regarded our poverty and chronic food shortages. Amazingly, he often used these occasions as fodder for practical jokes:

"Hey, you want some chocolate cake crumbs?" he'd offer, wide-eyed and teeming with sincerity. In response we'd rush over to him, extending our cupped hands. With no change of expression, he would dump Copenhagen grounds into our palms and chortle with glee that he had duped us.

Sometimes in the evening when he was in the kitchen making supper, he'd call out: "We're having steak tonight! Boy, oh boy, it's going to be quite a feast." Nine hungry mouths would start salivating on cue, and we'd head for the table. Within minutes dad would appear at the doorway like the head waiter at Maxims, holding aloft a hot, steaming plate. "Ta-da!" he would exclaim, lowering it to the table with great flourish. All eyes would lock onto the plate of the lucky person, first to be served. LIVER! smugly reclining in a dark pool of soy sauce. Very funny, dad.

I cannot forget my engagement-party dinner at the Greenacres house when I was 22. Even though I no longer lived there, still, it was the most convenient place for the family to gather, including those still at home – mom, Gail, Keith, Gwen, Charles, and Curt.

My fiancé, Bill, was not altogether impressed with the bill of fare. On such short notice, the best mom could pull together for an entrée was chicken necks camouflaged by a thick sauce of Campbell's cream of mushroom soup. There must have been a salad and, hopefully, some noodles. But all I remember were the skinny chicken necks. Whether because of the meal or in spite of it, our engagement was eventually called off, and I went on to marry, almost two decades later, Richard, the *real* man of my dreams.

Gail

Dad left home when I was 13. A year later my older sisters were gone as well. Elaine was in college, and Diane and Denae were serving as VISTA volunteers in Georgia and Illinois, respectively. Karen was working as a live-in companion to a wealthy Spokane socialite so she could complete her last year of schooling at Marycliff High School.

Feeling more confident in her abilities, mom quit her part-time cleaning jobs, and was hired as a full-time housekeeper by an elderly couple, the Tuningas. She hoped the pay would be sufficient to remove us from the public dole – from our status as deadbeat welfare rats. Nonetheless, making ends meet was a constant struggle, and the end of each month was always a scary time. Ingeniously, Charles as a young teen, devised a plan to ease these end of the month deficits. At the time mom did not have a checking account; she was paid in cash and kept the money in an envelope in her bedroom dresser drawer. Midmonth, without telling her, Charles would take $20 dollars and hide it in his room. Near month's end, mom would be despairing over the empty envelope, at which time Charles would magically produce the $20 and we would all breathe a little easier.

So while mom looked after the Tuningas, I looked after Gwen, Charles, Curt, and sometimes Keith. After a long day at school, my second life as surrogate mother began when I got home. I checked homework, packed school lunches, laid out their clothes for the next day and then began making supper.

Trying to produce a reasonably nourishing meal for our family, now numbering six, was a challenging proposition, primarily due to the scarcity of ingredients. Summer months were best because I had the full bounty of our garden, while the winter months were more problematic. Given our diminished larder and an absentee mother with no sense of menu management, it was left to my 13-year-old ingenuity to conjure up the meal.

Peering into the refrigerator, I could usually find a couple pounds of raw liver – inexpensive and nutrient-rich – reposing in an abyss of white open space. However, no matter how long I cooked it, inevitably the blood from the liver would spill across the plates like the red sea, overflowing the mashed potatoes and gravy. Six year old Curt could not stomach the sight, so I never made him eat it. He usually got a peanut butter sandwich on Liver Night.

Curt

One icy January afternoon I came home from school and as usual found no note specifying what to make for dinner. Eight hungry eyes looked at me, awaiting their meal. Anxiously, I called mom at the Tuninga's and asked for instructions.

"Oh, just look in the freezer and see what you can come up with." Right, like I'm some culinary wizard who can magically pull out a three course dinner from the arctic tundra.

Peering hopefully inside, all I could find, besides ice cubes and bread, were two frozen pigs' feet. Not only were the hooves completely devoid of meat to feed six people but there was also *hair* on them. I couldn't help but visualize what the feet used to be attached to. My stomach turned; I retched, then cried. If it wasn't pigs' feet, it was ox tails, chicken necks, beef kidneys, calf brains, gizzards or cow tongue. We were eating all of the cheap, bottom-of-the barrel organs that no one else wanted. Some days I swear, the inside of our fridge looked more like a coroner's lab with all the containers of decomposing animal parts.

I had met my match. There was no way I could make anything even remotely palatable with these disgusting ingredients. *Imagine little Curt facing half a pig's hoof on his plate when he couldn't even tolerate liver!* Gingerly, I lifted the two feet from the freezer with a pair of salad tongs – I couldn't bear to touch them – and deposited them outside on the compost pile.

For dinner that night I made oatmeal, and no one complained. They were just thankful they weren't eating pigs' feet.


After dinner, and with the dishes washed, I usually spent a good deal of the evening listening to mom unwind from her day. She was now 50 and worn out from hardships, while I was 13—both of us carrying heavy loads, with no relief in sight.

My relationship with mom at this time was both confusing and complicated. It wasn't hard to pity her. She was a woman of few options, and the desperation showed on her face. Still, I resented her for bringing me into her misery. I felt trapped not only by her needs, but also by the needs of the rest of the family. When mom referred to us as "the hungry mouths," I felt guilty for being one of them. However with me as surrogate mother assuming the household chores, I was finally able to lessen my terrible feelings of guilt.

For the rest of junior high and high school, I kept cooking, listening and consoling. When I graduated at 17, I left home, never to return. Finally, *my* life had officially begun.

## Denae

Gail has always been conscientious, almost to a fault. You could always count on her to complete a task to perfection, no matter what she was assigned. However, one of our favorite Gail stories demonstrates the extremes to which she would go to accomplish a goal.

Each afternoon she would hurry home from school to begin prepping for supper. After carefully setting the entrée on the table, she would call Keith, Gwen, Charles, and Curt, and solicitously serve each one. Yet herein lay the perfidy. Despite Gail's efforts, the kids would quickly sit and gobble down their food, anxious to resume whatever activity had preceded the meal. Any hope for polite conversation or culling a random compliment was futile. Each night, more disheartened and with growing objection, Gail would collect and wash the dishes, all the while spinning endless solutions to this seemingly unsolvable problem.

Weeks passed, and the situation only worsened. Gail was at her wit's end. Nothing, it seemed, could slow down the clashing silverware or ungrateful adolescent appetites. Then, mercifully, fate stepped in to intervene, and in that moment she found deliverance.

Vegetable soup was on the menu next evening. Gail hummed victory tunes to herself as she minced and chopped the ingredients. With a triumphant flourish she set the pot on the table and sent out the dinner call. Noisily, the younger kids gathered, settling into their chairs as Gail ladled each a serving of soup. Within seconds, four metal spoons were poised above the steaming bowls like hawks above a hare. In rapt attention, at the very moment of descent, Gail cried out, "Stop!"

116

and four astonished faces turned to her. "Before you begin eating," she continued, "there is something you should know. Just before putting the soup on the table, I dropped twelve sewing needles into it."

Revenge sat sweetly upon her lips as the meal that ensued became the slowest and most carefully masticated supper in all of human history. Needles were separated from hamburger, potatoes and onions with the painstaking care of diamonds from ore. And ever after, the evening meal was eaten with a solemn, measured rhythm – safeguard against any future possibility of being served once again Gail's unforgettable Needle Soup:

> *2 lbs. hamburger*
> *6 carrots*
> *8 potatoes*
> *2 onions*
> *1 jar of canned*
> *tomatoes salt and pepper*
> *12 - #18 sewing needles*

*Brown hamburger in a frying pan. Add diced onions and cook until done. In a large pot add chopped carrots, potatoes, and tomatoes. Boil 10 minutes until vegetables are done. Add browned hamburger, onions, salt, and pepper and simmer for 5 more minutes. Remove from stove and drop in the needles. Serve immediately.*

# SECOND COURSE,
# SAME AS THE FIRST

Keith and Gail

Denae

$W$ho would think a simple can of sauerkraut could bring down an entire household? But it did, and over something as blameless as being hungry – *really* hungry. However, before beginning, I must preface this story with a mitigating consideration, a consideration that questions the veracity of memory, no matter who is telling the story.

Buddhists will say there is no "true story." It's all personal: Truth is perception/Perception is truth. I desperately want to disagree. Story-telling is as ancient as Father Time. Surely there must be some reliability, some stability to individual experience and memory, such that it can be used as a cornerstone for reality as we try to make sense out of our lives and those we bump into around us.

Perhaps a turn from literature to art will cast a more revealing light on this perplexing matter, rebutting the provocative claim that there is no true story – i.e., no "true" painting. If the artist represents the world he sees around him as honestly as possible, should we not then expect to find in his colors and lines a perception of reality which is authentic, reliable – indeed, "true?"

Botticelli paints a nude, "Venus": Windblown, she stands adrift at sea on a large oyster shell.

Marcel Duchamp paints a nude, "Nude Descending Staircase": A vertical series of disturbing, pulsating lines in a chaotic environment.

Picasso paints a nude (pick one, any one): Women's faces resemble African masks, with figures that contain sharp angles and bloated appendages. Breasts and buttocks circumnavigate the canvas, making random stops at places they do not belong.

So, which is the true nude?

This intentionally circuitous route leads me to the story of our family mystery "Who Drank the Sauerkraut Juice?" You see, it is a grave matter to impugn the integrity of a parent's intentions, or actions, which is why truth is so central to this troubling tale, as is the awareness that were my father alive today, his version might be considerably different.

For breakfast I had eaten boiled flour – we called it "gruel." Nothing for lunch at school. So, now on my way home from my 8th grade class, all I could think about was food. Empty belly, empty refrigerator, empty cupboards. The calendar on our wall read November 28 – three days to go until the welfare check arrived. In those days, we all watched the calendar: 29, 30, 31. Most grim were those last few days because our ration of surplus commodities never stretched. "Time to tighten your belts," would be dad's unoriginal comment.

The situation was about as dire as an evening in Peshastin, Washington, where we once lived as migrant farm laborers. The day had passed with not a cracker to split between us, and now it was suppertime. Wordlessly motioning for us older girls, Elaine, Diane, Karen and myself, to sit on the couch, mom handed each of us a magazine. Inside were pictures of hot, tasty food: buttery corn-on-the cob, fried chicken, strawberry shortcake, oozing with whipped cream. Turning the pages slowly, we studied each photo, then exchanged magazines, silently contemplating more mouth-watering images. We didn't have to be told this was to be dinner. Years later as an adult, I cannot forget a conversation with my elderly employer, a sharp-tongued woman of 80. "You know, Denae," she said, "I have never been hungry a day in my life. And it annoys me terribly when people hyperbolate so – claiming they are 'simply star-r-rrrving.'" So divergent were our experiences, she might as well have been from another species – an octopus, perhaps – discoursing with me on the subject of appetites.

"The food problem," as Elaine so succinctly tags it, had me *rumen*-ating on a solution as I entered the kitchen – a girl on a mission. Somewhere behind all those yellow-painted, wooden-knobbed cabinets had to be an overlooked can of food or crust of bread. Standing up on a chair to reach the highest cupboards, my tucked blouse pulled out from my skirt in the act of stretching as my fingers groped blindly along the dusty shelves – through spider webs, dead flies and other unidentifiable remains – until I touched pay dirt, a long-forgotten can of sauerkraut.

Alone for the moment, I needed to act quickly. With no can opener in sight, I grabbed a paring knife and hacked a jagged gash across the tin top, folding it back for inspection. My dilemma now was: should I gulp down the entire contents, eat a small portion or just drink the liquid? Hanging in the balance was dinner for the rest of the family; the greater my gain, the greater their loss. In the spirit of compromise, I guzzled the sour juice like a parched Bedouin at the waterhole. Then, folding back the tin, I carefully returned the can to its place for the cook to find. Exit Denae.

Act II, Scene 1. Enter daddy. Or shall I say, enter Hurricane Frank, Category 4. "Goddamn son of a bitch, get your fat asses in this god-damn kitchen! I'm going to get to the bottom of this if it's the last thing I do!"

Leather belt swinging ominously in one hand, can of sauerkraut in the other, blue eyes blazing, he glared into each of our ashen faces, scorching us red with the intensity of his rage. "Which one of you overstuffed cows opened this can and drank the f___ing sauerkraut juice? If I don't get an answer soon, I'm going to beat the living bejee-sus out of all of you!"

The stage was set for slaughter, and I don't mean quick death, either. We're talking major torture, "the death of a thousand cuts." Swooning in terror, the little kids stayed upright only because we older girls were supporting them with our hands and knees.

*Give me a burning house to run into. Drop me into a pit of rattle-snakes or bury me in hot sand and leave me for the ants.* Daddy's fury was so alarming my tongue was virtually locked to my jaw.

Psychologists will say that until 18, a child has an incomplete sense of morality or conscience. I would like to strenuously rebut that bit of pedantry. At 13, with life passing before my eyes, I certainly grasped the moral implication of the situation – it was like an electric shock running through me! By covertly drinking the juice, I had put the whole family at risk. All would be punished until someone confessed. Sure, I was the guilty party, but what about the punishment fitting the crime? If I confessed, daddy's wrath would probably land me in the hospital... or the morgue. If I didn't confess, everyone would still suffer, but to a lesser degree. And what was my crime? I had drunk a miserable six ounces of sauerkraut juice because I was '*simply star-r-rrrving.*'

How long could I remain silent? I decided to wait daddy out, but if he started beating everyone in earnest, I would have to own up.

Innocence can sometimes find a voice even when immured within the deepest of fears. "But daddy," I heard Karen whisper timidly, "I'm not strong enough to cut through that can. Look, I'll show you. I don't think the rest of the little kids could, either."

Grimly, daddy opened a kitchen drawer, pulled out a paring knife and flipped over the sauerkraut can. "Alright," he said, shoving it at her. "Start cutting."

Karen's ineffectual scratching against the metal made it more than clear that her 11-year-old strength was no match for the can, which ruled out all the younger kids, as well, thus narrowing the list of suspects to three: Elaine, Diane and myself, each to be handed the knife in turn.

Since successfully cutting the tin would guarantee conviction, none of us, innocent or guilty, was overly eager to lacerate its surface. However, since all three of us weekly chopped firewood with an axe, there was no point in pretending we couldn't open a tin can with a paring knife. Given these factors, by test's end, we were still at impasse with no apparent "winner," so daddy returned to his "Lying bastard kids" homily with renewed rage, as though Karen's practical little experiment had never taken place.

Meanwhile, by some miracle, mom had located a few old, wrinkled potatoes to serve with the dab of sauerkraut, so daddy ordered us all to the table. Now at a Category 5, he was flinging his belt and discharging expletives in staccato bursts like a Gatling gun, while we kids, like players in a game of dodge ball, ducked, turned and tilted to avoid the lash of his heavy belt buckle. Who, in god's name, could think of eating in the midst of such an uproar?

"Since you don't want to eat," daddy remarked impatiently, noticing no one had so much as lifted a fork, "line up against that goddamn wall and strip down to your underwear. You can stand there all night until someone speaks up!"

Motioning us to file past him, one by one, to reach the next room, we felt like unwilling contestants in some bizarre beauty contest, shrinking from the ferocity of his gaze. Those few steps seemed like miles before we were safely beyond him. Then, like soldiers awaiting execution, we pressed ourselves in line against the living room wall.

Mute and inert, we nine kids stood there, perfectly visible to anyone standing beyond the uncurtained windows while the glare of headlights from passing cars splashed our bare skin and white underwear with eerie lights and shadows, like a scene in an Alfred Hitchcock movie.

"Rose!" daddy thundered unexpectedly. "Call up Naomi Harper and invite her over for a beer. Let the neighbors know what sons of bitches these lying kids are!"

Great. Now the whole world would know about our crazy family. Tugging our skimpy undershirts down as far as possible to protect our modesty (poor Elaine was wearing a bra, so was more exposed), we prepared for the inevitable as we listened nervously for Mrs. Harper's knock. Our one consolation being we weren't naked – not for the moment, anyway. Out of my peripheral vision I could see the little kids – Keith, Gail, Gwen and Charles – swaying, their eyelids drooping as they tried to stay upright beneath daddy's bitter scowl, while the long hours ticked slowly by.

Elaine

Standing there against the wall, my thoughts were chaotic: *Was it me who drank the sauerkraut juice? I don't remember doing it… Maybe I did. I could have done it… Yes, I'll bet I did.* The question became a mantra repeated over and over as I wrestled with my conscience, wondering if I should speak out and declare my guilt.

Guilt by association. Guilt by action. Guilt by omission. No matter who had committed the crime, we were, all of us, always guilty. There was no "presumption of innocence," such that, after a while, any memory of innocence – the very integrity of memory, itself – was lost to us, buried beneath the subversive rubble of dad's willfulness. Ours was a very democratic household. We were all equals under dad's law – equally guilty.

Denae

Outwardly feigning an innocence that was such a despicable lie, I mentally denounced myself with every vile name I could think of – *Judas, Coward, Yellow Belly, Chicken Liver.* Everyone was crying and marked with red welts because of me. Would the night ever end?

Still, given the quixotic nature of my reality, a disturbing notion came creeping into my mind. *Could I really have done this terrible thing? Maybe it was dad, not me, who drank the juice.* When he was drunk there was so much he did not remember. *Maybe I just imagined cutting open the sauerkraut can...? No, no, I'm sure it was me; of course, it had to be me.*

Mrs. Harper never did come knocking at our door. Mom had held the receiver button down during the call. So, about 2 a.m. daddy discharged us to our rooms. I heard Elaine, in exit, invoke Shakespeare under her breath: " Much ado about nothing." And Lily liver, aka Denae, never told anyone she was the culprit. It has remained the family mystery for more than 40 years.

Diane

Only a few weeks had passed since the drama of the sauerkraut incident, when it seemed that something similar was about to happen all over again.

Dad took a lot of pride in the yard, flowers and trees surrounding our home. We were constantly grooming them, pruning, transplanting, watering, so that in some respects our half acre property looked more like a park—at least we thought so. The flowering locust trees, shady elms and fragrant lilacs bordering the front and sides were greatly admired by all of us—and not just for their beauty, either, but because they provided camouflage—a means of disguising the swaybacked roof, cracked windows and mismatched siding of our house.

On that particular day, most of us kids were sitting studiously at the dining table absorbed in our homework, when dad came growling in to the room.

"Which one of you sons of bitches broke off the tree branch next to the kitchen door?" Glaring at each of us, he continued, "You can bet your sweet life I'm going to get to the bottom of this!" Then flipping off the cap to his beer bottle, he stomped off outside.

My body went rigid at his words, my jaw clenched. *No, no; it's* *not going to happen again,* I thought. *This time is going to be different.* Because I *knew* who had broken the branch. I had seen it happen.

It was do or die time—my moment at the crossroads. *I'm going to stand up to him. I don't care if he beats me to a pulp—or even if he kills me. He can do anything he wants. But I'm not going to be bullied ever again. I am not going to live in fear the rest of my life. I refuse to.*

Resolutely, I stood up from the table and went outside to find dad pacing on the front sidewalk staring at the broken tree limb. This is it, I thought, as I stood next to him. Taking a deep breath to calm myself, I looked right into his eyes. "*You* did it. I saw you."

I braced myself for the first smashing blow. Nothing happened. He just walked away.

Gail

Much of my anxiety and trauma as a child centered around food problems. Because dad was unemployed and mom worked part-time cleaning homes, we were eligible for surplus commodities, precursor to food stamps. Like the dreary photos of bread lines during the Depression, once a month we would be at the "food depots," collecting our allotment. It was a day I dreaded, always feeling ashamed to be standing in line, nervous that someone I knew would see me with the other poor people waiting for their handouts. I criticized myself, thinking: *If you can't even provide your* own *food, what good are you? A nothing-burger, that's what— just another drain on the system.*

Guilt and humiliation gnawed at me. The indelible mark of poverty seemed to brand us as clearly as Hester Prynne's scarlet letter. I resented mom and dad for bringing children into this world they couldn't adequately feed, and spent many hours contemplating such inequities. Life was a very serious business and, consequently, I was a very serious 13-year old.

After the long wait, it was a relief to finally reach the front: paperwork needed to be checked off, food items counted – there was no quick way to collect the goods and make a fast getaway. Since the packaging was black and white, stamped boldly with "USDA SURPLUS COMMODITY," there was no disguising where our groceries came from. If only I could transfer the tinned contents into empty Campbell's soup cans – our standard for culinary excellence.

The commodities we received: flour, sugar, corn meal, rice, powdered eggs, powdered milk, lard, peanut butter, spam and canned beef was food at its basest level. No amount of skill or alchemy could produce a meal that was anything other than sustenance, a means to fill an empty stomach.

We tried to be creative, but it was impossible. I tried to scramble the powdered eggs, but they weren't suitable for anything except baking. As an experiment, I once dropped a plate of these eggs into Smiley's bowl, but he wouldn't touch them. When added to water, the powdered milk became so lumpy that even a jackhammer couldn't break up those stubborn clumps. So, before drinking, we employed a series of complex straining techniques to filter out the clots.

Canned beef was my least favorite. When you opened the tin it smelled just like dog food and was encased in oozing jelly. As it slid into the frying pan, I would add flour and water to make gravy for serving over rice. I always felt this was meat that had not quite "turned" – meat not good enough to be sold in grocery stores. Teetering between barely edible and rancid, it was distributed to the surplus commodity recipients, eventually making its way to our table. I knew my theory was correct, because more than once I found half-used cans of this meat in our fridge swarming with maggots. Thankfully, when it got to this point, we were permitted to throw it out.

The summer garden was the center of our culinary universe. On our half acre we grew every imaginable vegetable. We made our own compost, supplemented with local cow manure. Our gardening methods were purely organic, more out of necessity than conscience since we had no extra money for pesticides or herbicide. However, there was no shortage in our work force, since all nine kids were working in the garden from the time we could walk. Standing between the rows with salt shaker in hand, we could eat to our hearts' content.

Irrigation came from a city-run system that allowed each family four hours of water twice a week. Once the spigot was turned on, it was like trying to channel the Columbia River into our back yard. Since the scheduled times varied from week to week, the gushing water could come as late as midnight, or as early as 4 in the morning. Times were not negotiable. So there we would be with hoes and flashlights, up to our knees in water, trying to keep the raging torrent contained as it swiftly spilled its way throughout the rows feeding into the garden. None of us could sleep afterward, because we would be so over stimulated from the effort of guiding hundreds of gallons of water to its destination.

Denae

Not for food alone was our garden so central to childhood. It also served as camouflage or backdrop for many a covert activity or unexpected confidence. Every teen in Greenacres was privy to the dark night Curt and Charles planted two small cannabis in the middle of mom's tomato patch. Thinking they were 'volunteers' of some latent heritage species, mom faithfully tended them for weeks, eagerly anticipating the yet-to-form fruits. Come September, the now towering, colossally branched shrubs were the showpiece of the garden, yet oddly, still bereft of fruit – an anomaly which mom reconciled as an oversight of the bees during pollination. Inexplicably, these prize tomato plants disappeared as abruptly as they had arrived. Not so much as a stray root remained to suggest they were ever anything more than an inspired mirage.

It was also in the garden that the naivete of my adolescence was severely jolted one hot July afternoon when Karen at 11 and I were listlessly weeding around the rutabagas and sweet peas. Resting her sunburnt chin for a moment against the wooden handle of her hoe, her bare feet half buried in the black dirt, Karen paused in reflection.

"I can't wait until I'm 21," she declared in her usual pert manner.

"Why is that?" I enquired.

"Because then I can drink a dry martini."

Caught off guard, my usually creative mind was flummoxed by her answer. *Dry martini?* So alien were the words to my frame of reference the most I could conceive by way of imagery was a dry river bed. As for martini, cognitively, there was simply no place to put it.

Mute, with reluctant admiration, I stared at my younger sis, knowing I had been majorly upstaged. And there was not a thing I could do about it, except return to hoeing around the rutabagas.

Gail

My attachment to the garden started at an early age when mom taught me to plant, thin and cultivate. It was one of the few times I felt at one with her, a means of acquiring the attention I so desperately needed – although unfortunately her maternal instincts were more apparent in the way she cared for plants than in the way she cared for her children.

For mom, the garden was a mental health clinic of sorts. Many evenings after work she would retreat there and stay until dark. Around 10 pm, she would slip into the house – dirty, sweaty, tired, but also with a certain calm, as though the garden had replenished her spirit. On those days when dad was drinking and belligerent, mom would flee to the garden and hoe furiously, taking out her frustrations on the endless snarl of weeds. In her world, where there was no money for psychotherapy, she found in our garden a way to exorcise her demons... painstakingly, one weed at a time.

Denae

Poor Gail. Even as a married adult well into her forties, she still could not entirely escape the perfidies of the culinary domain.

Keith's wife, Judy, had been in the hospital recovering from the birth of their third child, Alicia, when Gail drove up from Portland, Oregon, for a few days of sisterly household support – cooking, cleaning, laundering until Judy could return home with the baby.

Conscious of the approaching dinner hour, Gail pulled out a wrapped parcel of meat from the freezer to thaw on the kitchen counter, then proceeded to snap garden beans into a wooden bowl.

"Hi, sis! What's for dinner?" greeted Keith, reaching for some ice water after a long hot day of construction work.

"Oh, something I pulled out of the freezer," responded Gail, nodding toward the brown-wrapped package.

"Aaaggghhh!" shrieked Keith, reaching for the little bundle. "That's not meat – that's Judy's placenta!"

After taking a few minutes to calm himself, not wishing to consider how narrowly he had missed dining on his wife's giblets, he explained: "Yesterday, Judy asked me to put her afterbirth in the freezer until she returned home. Then we were going to bury it together, with a little ceremony under the apple tree in the back yard. According to Judy's best friend, it's a folk tradition which supposedly brings good luck and health to the baby. Since Alicia has been so sick, we're willing to try *anything* that might give her an extra boost."

Gail, not yet recovered from her own near brush with cannibalism, was still bereft of vocal cord function as Keith finished with: "So, whatever you do – I'm sure you'll be calling Karen and the other sisters about this – just don't *ever* tell Judy that we almost ate her placenta for dinner."

# CRIME & PUNISHMENT

Keith, Curt, Gwen, Charles (sitting)

*...because I am happy & dance & sing, they think they*
*have done me no injury,*

–William Blake

Like Ernest Hemingway, who began his faux memoir *A Moveable Feast* by describing a sewer-clogged Paris in the 1920s, it seems appropriate to invoke the subject of sewage, both above and below the ground, as we reminisce about punishments in our Little Shop of Horrors household.

Perhaps Ernest was not being so much earnest as he was being metaphoric when he alluded to the City of Light as being plugged up. Critics posited snidely that mayhaps it was his *own* condition he was writing about, whether literary or physical. That said, all seemed to agree that it was indeed an odd way to begin a book.

In our case, I assure you, the sewage was not of the metaphoric kind; it was substantively the kind that calls for the Roto-Rooter man. In Greenacres, as well as the dozen other houses we lived in – at least those that had indoor plumbing – the overflowing or plugging of the sewer was a constant problem, one which dad seemed utterly incapable of fixing. Granted, one could easily point to his nine offspring to attach blame, but in our defense, long after dad had separated from mom, living out his years alone, unmanageable sewage at his residence could be anticipated with the regularity of the sun coming up each morning.

Diane recalls a humid summer day in August – sweet peas and honeysuckle in bloom, agreeably scenting the air while tiny plume-crested quail daintily threaded their way through the back yard. Lazily, she lounged on a hammock, stretched between two shady cottonwoods, watching the overhead clouds shift in shape as they too drifted lazily by.

"Hey, Diane, give me a hand over here. I've got to dig up that damned sewer again," called out dad, unexpectedly rounding the corner of the house, wearing faded, rolled-up jeans and carrying two shovels.

Looking around for reinforcements but seeing none, Diane reluctantly climbed out of the hammock, choosing to wait a few moments while he made some progress on the hole. As she watched, a hummingbird landed briefly on the mound of black earth piling up on the grass. Dad was now waist deep in the widening pit, his shirt tied round his waist while his sun-burned chest and shoulders glistened with sweat.

"There it is – a broken pipe!" he shouted, as the shovel clacked against something solid, releasing the unmistakable stench of human excrement. Flopping over the bank like a fish out of water, he began retching into the dirt. Still gagging, he thrust the shovel at Diane, a mere 14-year-old. "You're going to have to finish the job. The smell is too much for me. I just can't stop puking."

Denae

Unfortunately for us, the sewage was not always underground. For years it sat around our bathroom and bedrooms in plastic buckets filled with purex water, holding tanks for soiled baby diapers – the cotton, washable kind that came with inch-long, finger-stabbing safety pins. They were stained with every imaginable shade of yellow and brown – colors even the 100-pack Crayola boxes do not contain – from the palest straw to malaria yellow, chartreuse, jaundiced amber and sedgy sepia, to a nasty liver brown. "Nappies," the British call them – so civilized and ever-so-white, like their linen tablecloths and starched frilly servant aprons.

With nine children ranging from 13-year-old Elaine to Curt the infant, we're talking a lot of years of baby diapers. The only thing worse than the sight and smell of those stagnating little swamp ponds was knowing "someone" eventually had to scrub and rinse them (mom had banished them from the washing machine for sanitary reasons) and then hang them on the clothesline to dry. No plastic or rubber gloves to slip on for protection in those days. Nope, the dirty deed had to be done with bare, naked hands plunged into the cold sewage water.

Having washed them hundreds of times, mom was more than happy to pass off this unwelcome chore as punishment to any one of us for the tiniest infraction: an unacceptable edgy tone of voice, being two minutes late to lunch, or wearing mascara to school. I cringe to think of the number of times mom's hands went from washing baby diapers in those plastic buckets to peeling potatoes at the kitchen sink — a minor miracle that "E-coli soup" did not hospitalize at least one of us in all those years.

Who could blame her for farming out this task? Mom always did more than her share of the dirty jobs, working long after supper to keep our family and home functioning. At meals, she always ate the least, passing up meat or potatoes with "I'm not really hungry" to give the rest of us a couple of extra mouthfuls. Underweight all of the 18 years I lived at home, mom's sacrifices for our well-being made us considerably more amenable to being sentenced to "diaper duty" (both on and off the baby). It was a punishment as common as scouring the bathroom sink.

Among a diverse assortment of disciplinary measures, we were often subjected to dad's version of solitary confinement, when he would exile us to the outhouse. (Until I was 11 and we moved to the Greenacres house, all of our residences lacked indoor plumbing). More often than not this banishment was a summertime sentence when bees and horseflies were dropping from the sky, littering the ground – exhausted like us from the 100-degree heat. Sentencing was swift and irreversible. "Get up there to the outhouse, you lazy lummox. The damn door better be closed! I'll tell you when I'm good and ready for you to come out!"

Once sequestered inside the dark, mind-numbingly hot space, there was nowhere to look except into the lidless, wooden-edged pit dropping into a sludgy nightmare sea below – the Black Hole of Calcutta. Above your head, flies buzzed and spiders copulated – or feasted on trapped prey in the creepy corner cobwebs. When it was a balmy 98 degrees outside, it could easily be 110 degrees inside, as one swooned from the stench and heat, praying to God to remain conscious to avoid slipping silently, ingloriously into the gaping jaws of that giant swill-hole.

When I was eleven, we lived in an old farmhouse in the foothills above Spokane. There, salmonberry bushes and wild pink roses crowded the edges of the narrow dirt path which meandered about 25 yards from the house to the outhouse. We could always count on seeing a cardinal, goldfinch or squawking magpie in the canopy of white birch branches overhead, while a green and black garter snake might be disappearing into the tangle of underbrush below.

The calming serenity of the scene was spoiled one morning when I heard mom's voice criticizing me for neglecting to wash the breakfast dishes. Tossing a soiled diaper midpath into the dirt, she called out, "March yourself over here and put your nose to that diaper. Maybe it'll teach you to remember when I ask you to do something. And don't you dare move until I say so!"

Off she stalked to finish the laundry while I tried to recall what I could of dad's lecture last night on "mind over matter," a favorite subject of his. The challenge was to suspend sight and smell, with that dreadful little bundle of excrement a gnat's length from my nose. It was so humiliating to be crouched in this position – for who knew how long? I had to morph into another plane of being. Once there, I could go bicycling or inner tube on the Spokane River – anything I wanted until mom called to end the punishment.

Not all disciplines, however, centered around fecal matter, or "number two" as we were wont to call it. More common was the "cold shoulder" or "silent treatment" coming from dad who would ignore the offending party so absolutely that he or she might as well have been invisible. For the duration of this limbo state, neither mom nor siblings were allowed to address or interact in any way with that person. He would criticize in excruciating detail our physical appearance, character flaws, past crimes, flooding us with a tsunami of degrading expletives. When the ordeal became too much, rather than cry uncle, we usually just cried, which invariably ended the punishment.

The preferred venue for this sport was mealtime, which afforded dad multiple targets as well as a captive audience. Sitting among us wishing for invisibility, Diane often laid her face down, hands covering her head, after dad had lampooned her to the point of tears. So motionless would she lie, it was as though a shaft was pinning her to the table.

"There she goes again with her crocodile tears," he would jeer, briefly pausing to spit tobacco juice into his cuspidor. "Don't we all feel so sorry for her with her big, fat, phony cry-baby tears."

I have to admit that I was utterly intrigued by this description of Diane's tears. Much as we had all cried from time to time in front of dad during punishments, only Diane it seemed was singled out as producing the extraordinary and exotic crocodile tears. What was it about her tears that merited this distinction? And why not alligator, tiger, hippo or rhinoceros tears? Apparently, the size of the tears was not the determining factor, because there were certainly many animals larger than a crocodile, or so I reasoned.

Inventive as dad normally was, in this particular matter I found him vaguely disappointing, so unoriginal in his unfailing consistency to cite the crocodile. Never having seen the expression in print or having heard anyone else use it, I assumed it had no logical foundation, just another of dad's linguistic anomalies.

However, being the little scholar that I was, I checked out *Colliers* and *Britannica* encyclopedias from the school library. In no time at all I could have conducted seminars, so expert did I become in matters of crocodile habitat, mating behaviors, food preferences and the like, but nary a word about those infamous tears.

Compulsively, I stalked Diane with the zeal of a forensic pathologist. And truth be told, I was more than a little jealous that my own perfectly good tears had never been accorded this distinction. Was there something in her demeanor? A biological irregularity which merited his comments? Surely if I persisted, I could eventually produce an answer to this phenomenon. Then, when my time for punishment arrived, I too could generate these special droplets and hear gratifyingly, dad's comment, "Oh, look at those crocodile tears."

Childhood passed with my fascination intact, albeit still uninformed, until sometime in my forties when skimming a Reader's Digest article, the words "crocodile tears" appeared on the page. My gaze locked on that text like Sir Alexander Fleming first sighting penicillin under the microscope. There it was! the answer to the mystery: a digestive behavior peculiar to the croc species. In the act of swallowing its prey (usually still alive and struggling), the reptiles' tear glands release large water droplets – an irony of nature suggesting remorse, yet entirely unrelated to the pain or discomfort of the croc or its victim, thus the expression, impugning an emotional display of sorrow or remorse.

One question was answered, but in so doing raised another. Why had dad so often challenged the integrity of Diane's tears, insinuating by his comment that they were false? Unanswerable, enigmatic, like much of his behavior. We didn't have to travel all the way to Egypt to see the Sphinx; we could find it anytime we wanted, right in our own living room.

Diane was on the receiving end of one particularly memorable punishment, for which she concurs, she *was* partly to blame. Borrowing clothes from school chums was strictly taboo, so we resigned ourselves to our wallflower wardrobes, which occasionally were spiced up by a cast-off blouse or sweater from the daughters of a wealthy family that mom cleaned house for.

"Au contraire" was Diane's response to dad's clothing dictum – determined to be as fine, and au courant as her resourcefulness would permit. Hadn't dad often preached among his platitudes, "You can accomplish anything you set your minds to; it's just a matter of hard work, imagination and persistence." Diane had all three – in spades.

For her, Oleta Maye was the key to unlocking a haute couture wardrobe, at least by Greenacres standards. Her family had money, lots of it, and Oleta loved clothes. She bought only designer labels. So, Diane made it her mission to befriend and bewitch Oleta, the be-witching part particularly key since Diane had nothing of equal value for compensation.

Apparently, their blossoming friendship squared the transaction for Oleta. Since she was pear-like in figure and not unlike a pleas-ant-faced marmot in countenance, her social standing could only be enhanced by walking the hallways with a student as beautiful and smart as Diane.

Because Oleta lived across town, the clothes-borrowing necessi-tated her older brother's involvement as well, acting as chauffeur for the garments. The arrangement was to drive along Sprague Avenue and toss the shopping bag of clothing at the designated target, an old wagon wheel leaning against the crab apple tree in our front yard. "Do *not* stop the car!" was Diane's explicit final instruction. "It might at-tract dad's attention, especially if he is outside."

Watching from an upstairs bedroom window, she would ascer-tain when the coast was clear, then dash downstairs to pick up the contraband, leaving in its place another bag filled with blouses and dresses from last week's exchange, to be collected later by Oleta and her brother.

Surprisingly, Diane's deception worked perfectly for months. In so doing, she became a fashion legend in the hallways and classrooms of Central Valley High School. What she wore one week was certain to be copied with varying degrees of success by the popular girls the next week. Closely observed were her skirt lengths, color choices and the imaginative knotting of her neck scarves. One week she surprised and delighted the fashionistas by wearing her button-down sweater backward. It became a fashion must for weeks.

Alas, despite her success, time was running out in Diane's hour-glass. That day came one windy autumn afternoon when clumps of red and orange leaves were being spun like dust devils at dad's feet as he made the rounds of the yard with Cisco perched high on his shoulder. Together they were assessing which beds were most in need of raking, when their attention was diverted by a speeding car and large airborne object. Hurrying to the wagon wheel where it had landed, dad pulled out the contents in disbelief. Moving so fast that poor Cisco was dislodged, he came roaring through the kitchen door like a bear caught in a poacher's trap.

"What in holy hell is going on here? Are we so goddamn poor that people have to drop off bags of clothing in our driveway like charity food baskets?"

Since Diane was standing there conspicuous in Gucci while the rest of us were outfitted in recycled Salvation Army, it did not overly tax dad's deductive powers to guess the culprit. She received the full blast of his censure.

"Bloody mother of god... What the others wear isn't good enough for you, Miss High and Mighty?" Yanking open the door to the wood stove, he finished with, "I'll show you where this is going right now!" and stuffed the clothes into the red-hot flames. Cremation occurred within seconds.

Diane was appalled. What could she tell Oleta? Worse yet, the doors to her sumptuous wardrobe would now be slammed shut to future loans. Pretty clothes were her escape ticket from our poverty. In them she could fabricate a different persona, become that solid, middle-class student she so aspired to. A harmless pretense, but absolutely essential to protecting her fragile mental health.

Glancing toward the raptly silent Elaine, Denae and Karen, unfashionable as ever in plain white blouses and worn capris, Diane concluded mentally, *Never! Not for me those dowdy rags*. Lifting her head away from dad's ranting and the acrid smell of burnt angora, she paused as if straining to hear some distant voice. *Camille, yes Camille . . . She will do quite nicely.*

Once again, Diane was back in her make-believe world, imagining herself attired in the lavender-blue blouse and skirt Camille had worn to cheerleading tryouts last week.. *Best to find a new location, maybe somewhere at school. Yes, everything will be quite all right.*

Gail

Much as we counted on the outdoors and nature as a place of refuge and safety, even the most public recreational areas did not deter dad from exercising his parental rights if he felt his authority had been breached.

Daddy was taking us all to the city park. When the car stopped, I ran to the swing set, hoping to grab one before they were all taken. I loved to swing, so as soon as I was squarely on the seat, I tried to get going, kicking my legs. But they were just too short to reach the ground, so I sat there idle, like a pendulum without momentum. While pondering what to do, a friendly looking man approached the swings with his little girl – blonde like me, with a pink ribbon around her ponytail – and started pushing her. Noticing my inertia, he asked, "Would you like a push?" Of course I replied with a hearty "Yes, please!" How else would any 6-year-old respond?

For ten glorious minutes he pushed me back and forth, higher and higher until I could touch the sun with my big toe. It was so exhilarating, just basking in the moment – when things came to an abrupt halt. Daddy grabbed the chains of my swing so suddenly I almost fell off the seat. With a threatening look, he jerked me up and dragged me to our car. The man and his daughter stared after us in disbelief.

By this time the rest of the family was hastily piling in, preparing to leave. "Sit right there, damnit." Daddy thundered, pointing to a grassy patch near the curb.

*Why wasn't I supposed to get into the car, too? Why was he so mad at me?*

With all the doors closed, daddy started the engine and drove away. Raising my head, but afraid to move, it took a few moments to register what was happening – daddy was leaving me! My survival instincts kicked in, and I jumped up. Running and running, I tried to catch up with the speeding car. Finally exhausted, I fell down in the dirt, crying, "He's never coming back for me" –too young to understand what I had done to deserve such an extreme punishment.

Another ten minutes went by, which seemed like hours; then I saw our car in the distance slowly turn around to return. A door was opened, and I got in. No words were exchanged. I felt like a leper, not to be acknowledged for fear of contamination.

When we got home I thought my ordeal was over, until daddy motioned to me. "We need to have a little talk." Reluctantly I followed him out to the wood shed, knowing I was in big trouble, but still not sure why. Yanking the door open, he shoved me into the semi-darkness and yelled, "You know you are *never* to speak to strangers, yet you talked to that man at the park!"

"But daddy," I objected, "He was so nice, and he pushed me on the swings just like his own little girl." Slowly he unbuckled his belt, then cracked it against his bare hand. "I guess you haven't learned your lesson yet," and began hitting me over and over for what seemed like an eternity.

The damage done to my psyche that afternoon was far worse than the black and blue bruises covering my back, arms and legs. Some essential part of me had gone numb, and I retreated into a very dark and silent place. Speaking to anyone after my terrible ordeal was so traumatizing that for a time I limited any necessary conversation to family members only.

What, I have often wondered, would have become of me had Jenny not come into my life in this time of such crisis? It's hard to imagine feeling lonely and isolated in a family of 11, but that was my reality. We lived a sequestered life, every move scrutinized and controlled. Daddy never allowed us to have friends for fear his abuses would be revealed. No one was to be trusted, so Jenny was borne out of my desperate need for a confidante.

She was the same age as me, but more mature, an old soul, wise beyond her years. Where I was Nordic in appearance, being blonde and blue-eyed, Jenny was Celtic looking with reddish-brown curls and freckles. She was kind, loving and always there when I needed her. I talked freely to her, sharing my most intimate thoughts and feelings, without any self-consciousness. She shared my joys and my disappointments. When I cried, she cried; when I laughed, she laughed. We were in complete synchronicity. She advised, encouraged, and reassured me. When we played games, she always let me win. She gave me confidence, but more importantly, she gave me hope. She was selfless, as if her only purpose was to be with me during this tumultuous time. I really do not know how I would have survived the perils of childhood without her.

Our relationship lasted many years. Gradually, as my confidence grew and I was able to relate more with my peers, Jenny's existence faded and finally disappeared. I missed her, but instinctively knew she would return if I ever needed her again. As for the inevitable question: Did she ever really exist? Well, she did for me, and I will always be grateful for the comfort and companionship she gave so lovingly and so generously.

Denae

Not every punishment was drama-charged. As a disciplinarian, mom was usually more benign than dad, although on occasion she too could wield the belt with impressive ferocity. At 14, one laundry day I was late in carrying our clothes down to the basement where mom was already surrounded by color-coded hills of laundry – blacks, reds, all whites. Our freestanding, potbellied relic of a washing machine with its four stubby wooden legs and hand-operated wringer was off-balanced as usual from overloading – shaking and shimmying like a fat lady doing the bebop in a juke-joint.

"What are you looking at? Late as usual. Do you think I've got all day to wait for you?" Mom's words jarred me back to reality just as I was on the verge of snapping my fingers to the boogie beat. Apparently my body language was too expressive as I dumped the socks and pajamas to the concrete floor in one jerky motion. I knew better. Like the servants in the Big House, it was wiser to bob and nod than to eye roll, clench your jaw or go rigor mort in response. Too late. Too late.

"You think you're so smart, above helping out with something so menial as the laundry." Jabbing her finger to my chest, mom went on, "For your attitude you can just stand there and say 100 times, 'I promise to be a human being when I grow up.'"

Not wishing to have the number boosted to 200 for a delay, I began the recitation immediately. And just as immediate was my resolve to sabotage the punishment. Mild as it was, it still felt undeserved. How to rebel and still be respectful? I did love mom, even when she was being petty and unfair. Most of the time I felt sorry for her because she was as much a victim of dad's tyranny as we were. Somehow it seemed worse for her since she was an adult and suffered the added humiliation of having all her children witness her abuse. As victims, the most we could aspire to was a little creative, passive resistance – a way to feel empowered and to distance ourselves, however slightly, from the abuse.

In just such a subversive spirit while reciting my irritating little sentence, I mused thoughtfully, *What sounds like being...? Bean, of course!* Ever so prudently then, lowering my voice, I slurred "being" into "bean." Following two more nuanced repetitions, as naturally as a guppy morphs into a fish, my recitation became, "I promise to be a human bean when I grow up."

So sublime was the transition mom did not notice as she continued sorting the clothes. Confidently now, a tad louder, the seditious substitution rolled off my tongue – 33 and still counting – as I was transported wholly beyond the human race, now occupying space as a member of the legume family, imagining myself a 5-foot, 5-inch-tall green bean. Walking, talking, swimming at Sandy Beach, our favorite spot at the Spokane River, I could even visualize my newly elongated self sitting at the dining table with dad, mom and all the kids: "Pass the salt, please."

It was hugely satisfying and entertaining to be so subversive, undetected by mom listening only a couple of feet away, oblivious to my triumph. And the "fat lady" was still gamely tossing her chest and hips, keeping time to the fitful chugging of the overtaxed motor.

To this day, at those moments when I begin to feel powerless and losing control, I think back to that magically transformed sentence and begin chanting it – re-creating once again my sense of joyfulness, my ascendancy, my Unbearable Lightness of Being – the unbearable lightness of being a human bean . . . when I grow up.

Gail

Gwen and I shared the same bed and, unfortunately for her, also the same size and style of pajamas. As a 10-year-old, I once woke up in the middle of the night to discover I had wet the bed. Knowing I would be punished, since I was much too old for such accidents, I had to think of something fast.

Gwen, three years younger, was a deep sleeper. Being careful not to wake her, I gently lifted away the blankets and removed her pajama bottoms, replacing them with my wet ones. Seconds later, I lay back down beside her, now safely wrapped in dry nightwear. Come morning, I knew she wouldn't get into trouble, but for me, it would have been unforgivable.

Daddy was big on punishment, and always seemed to relish being the dispenser of justice. Yet, one night, contrarily, he decided to hand off this role to the older girls, by way of teaching them a lesson about bickering and fighting.

"Make two lines: little kids in front, big ones behind," he ordered. "And make it snappy!" Subsequently, Diane was behind me; Elaine behind 3-yr old Charles; and Denae and Karen behind Keith and 5-yr old Gwen.

"I want you cows to kick the one in front as hard as you can.. Come on; start kicking!"

He couldn't be serious. Not moving, we stared in disbelief. Then Diane gave me a half-hearted kick. Karen and Denae followed suit.

Furious at their lack of force, daddy yelled even louder. "When I say kick, goddamit I mean kick! You wanna fight so much, well here's your chance. Kick 'em good and hard!"

We little kids tensed for the beating. He-Who-Must-Be-Obeyed was waiting to be obeyed. But Elaine was not about to, not this time.

It was one of the few occasions I saw her stand up and defy him. "No, I'm not going to kick little Charles and hurt him."

Daddy was livid at her refusal and pushed her outside into the darkness, thus ending the abuse for the rest of us. I was always afraid to ask Elaine what happened to her that night. But I always remembered her courage, and hoped that she received some special grace for so selflessly defending her little brother.

Denae

As a target for dad's anger, Elaine seemed to be singled out most often – whether because she was the oldest or for some other reason, I could not say. My memory has been indelibly branded with the image of one unhappy morning in March at Greenacres. We kids were raking away last year's leaves, removing them from the emerging crocus and early-budding forsythia bushes in an effort to ready the yard for a brief visit with our cousins who would be arriving soon.

Dad had begun drinking at 7, and was in a fine rage by 11 am, looking for trouble. Elaine, had committed the unpardonable sin of overlooking one pile of leaves that was meant to be burned in a 55-gallon drum at the back of the garden. Hurling his spittoon can at her, he shoved her into the kitchen, kicking and belting her with, "Goddamn son of a bitch, can't you even complete a simple job without me getting involved, always having to oversee and check up on you?"

Pitched from one wall into the other, buttons popping off her blouse from his manhandling, Elaine was tossed back and forth like a rag doll until she lost her balance. Crashing to the floor, she covered her face for protection. The abuse was sickening, violent, despicable. She never said a word, as dad in his Heart of Darkness continued to kick and lash her with his belt, while his mouth roared out profanities.

My ears went numb. My very skin recoiled from the blows as though I was the one being assaulted. The blackness of his rage coated the kitchen ceiling, walls and floor. All of us in the room felt sticky, tarred with the density of his madness. I felt a wild craziness, like we were all inmates on a psych ward. Desperately, I wanted to scream out

144

at the top of my lungs: "Mayday! Mayday! Murder in the house! Stop the killing! Call the police! Call an ambulance! Madman on the loose! Give him the noose! MAYDAY! MAYDAY!!"

No one came, of course … no one but the relatives. We heard the crunch of their tires on the gravel as they pulled into the driveway. Dad stuffed Elaine into the broom closet with, "You damn well better be quiet in there!" Then turning, "The rest of you get in the living room," adding out of breath, "Act natural."

*Yes,* I thought, *you son of Satan. Hide the body. Wash your hands. Smile for the camera. Make us all feel guilty, guilty as you while our sister is half dead in the closet!*

So we passed the time, along with the tea and cookies, to Uncle Wes and Aunt Ethel, sitting on the couch in the living room. Chicken puppets, one and all. Wooden dummies afraid to cut our strings, still dancing to the mad puppeteer's tunes. Scraping, bowing, "yessir … no-sir." Sing along, then – sing, sing your little song, all the way to Sing Sing, right where you belong.

# REPORT CARD DIARIES
## Ode to A, Requiem for F

Denae, Karen, Elaine, Diane

<u>Elaine</u>

I remember third grade in Moose Bay, Minnesota, along with the below-zero, waist-deep snowy winters when my bare hands would stick to the icy metal of the outside pump when I tried to draw up water for boiling our morning cereal.

My school dresses were hand sewn by mom with matching hair bows tied to my braids, while the farm kids all wore milk-stained blue coveralls smelling of horse manure and cow barns. Much as I wanted to fit in and make friends, in reality I felt more like a kitten in a herd of mustangs. Those kids were built for hard work and accustomed to a harsh environment. Social niceties like welcoming the new girl with the hazel eyes and dark brown pigtails into their community were about as likely to happen as plowing the fields with a pig.

I dreaded going home from school every day because the bigger boys would call me names and chase me across alfalfa pastures, where I had to dodge cranky goats, bulls and barking dogs before reaching our house. "Scaredy-cat, scaredy-cat," they'd yell, "stupid, skinny and blind as a bat!"

I became the quietest, most invisible student in class until the day daddy was taken to the police station for stealing some bundles of old clothes. Even though he wasn't officially arrested, the story made the front page of the *Moose Bay Courier,* and next day at school I was the center of attention, with every kid in class laughing at me and retelling the ridiculous story.

*If he was going to commit a robbery, why couldn't he just rob a bank like any other self-respecting thief? No, my father has to steal a bunch of old rags, thinking it was a business opportunity.*

Fourth, fifth, sixth grade – we were now living in Washington State. Classes, teachers, subjects are all a blur because I changed schools so often. Mom would sign me up; I'd be there three or four months, then we'd move again. No time to find a best girlfriend, learn long division, or gossip about boys and movies. Our family was a band of gypsies, itinerant fruit pickers following the apple, peach, and pear crops from orchard to orchard, like migrating snow geese looking for seeds and grains on their way back from the Arctic plains.

Central Washington was the heart of the state's apple belt – parts of it bordered by the mighty Columbia River, while other areas were sandwiched in between the Yakima Indian Reservation and the Hanford Atomic Energy Site. We lived in pickers' shacks, collecting rainwater for cooking in wooden barrels which stood outside the front door. The terrain was a composite of glacially gouged scablands intermixed with sagebrush prairies, green irrigated fruit orchards, tumbleweeds and dusty roadsides littered with abandoned cars. Street signs in this odd landscape read: Pothole Reservoir, Trinidad, Dry Falls, Moses Lake, Moxee City, Batum and Schrag. Out-of-the-way bergs, I mused, where you might run into outlaws like Doc Holliday or Calamity Jane, had they lived long enough to settle into retirement.

Ours was a fairly spartan existence, short on amenities, most especially in the personal grooming department. Mom cut daddy's hair, while he cut ours. At recess one day in fifth grade, my teacher, Mr. Hauser, walked up to me and asked, "What happened to your hair? It looks like you got run over by a lawn mower!"

Thanks a lot, daddy, I mutely responded. I knew it was bad before I ever got to school and had dreaded hearing the kids' comments. It must be *really* bad if my teacher was ridiculing it. Apparently daddy had been trying to re-create Audrey Hepburn's "Sabrina" cut from the movie we had seen the previous week. About the only thing our hair had in common was the color, dark brown. Otherwise, I'd say my butchered hairstyle was more like Elvis Presley's on a really bad hair day – kinda like, well... like he'd been run over by a lawn mower.

Living as we did among other itinerant Anglo and Mexican families in the orchards as "apple knockers" – the prevailing slang for this occupation – I was perfectly aware of our poverty and the low status

148

of fruit pickers. I recall one September morning when the crows, orioles, woodpeckers and blue jays were chattering noisily in the fruit branches outside, gorging on breakfast, while inside I was hanging my head over the bedrail trying to *dis*gorge the Hong Kong flu into a red plastic bucket on the wood floor. Feverish, with a fierce headache, the slightest touch of the bed sheet was inflaming my already tender skin.

Mom and dad were walking out the door to begin their 10-hour day of apple picking while Karen, Diane, and Denae had already boarded the school bus. Turning slightly in my direction as she tucked dad's blue work shirt over her seven months pregnant belly, mom grumbled, "All right, Elaine, you can stay home from school today, but be sure to have some lunch ready for Frank and me at 12:30. You don't need to give me that look, either; you've got nothing to do all day except lay around in bed, so I don't think it's too much to ask."

No aspirin or juice left for me on the chair next to my bed. If I got thirsty, water would have to be collected from the communal pump, outside. So, after they left, I got up slowly to address the water problem. On most days I didn't mind standing in line with my pail, waiting my turn as I watched the other migrant pickers – all those dark-skinned strangers wearing bandanas in reds, blues, greens and citrus yellows – a Gauguin painting of tropical parrots. But today I dreaded the wait. Dizzy with weakness and fever, I nearly fainted a couple of times before I could start pumping my drinking water. Monday became Friday as I struggled through each day, putting soup and bologna sandwiches on the table for dad and mom's lunch, then crawling gratefully back into bed. I might just as well have been one of those anonymous, chattering birds flitting in and out of the tree branches, so little attention was directed toward my care.

In those days I'm sure mom suffered from Stockholm syndrome – identifying with dad, her abuser. She became victim to her circumstances, finding it easier to be indifferent, even abusive to us kids. How else could she cope, with six children crammed into a two-room shack and another on the way? Her days were spent climbing up and down 12-foot ladders carrying a heavy bag of apples on her back. And she was married to an alcoholic, who was also a sociopath and a paranoid-schizophrenic. I guess a twelve-year-old with the Hong Kong flu seemed pretty insignificant by comparison.

My teachers struggled to deal with the transitory families of the fruit pickers. In sixth grade I was the only student without a math book. Dad and mom could not afford one, so I tried keeping up with the assignments by borrowing a book once a week from the blond girl in front of me. However, with my grades dropping, I finally got up the nerve to ask my teacher if he had an extra math book. "Why?" he asked unsympathetically. "Do you know how to do the work?"

"Yes, I do," I said, eyes lowered.

"All right. I figured you for one of those migrant kids. Their families never stick around long enough to finish the school year. Just a waste of a good book in their hands.. and they never return them, either."

Ninth grade geometry was my nemesis. Despite my high IQ, all the moving around had completely disrupted the progression of my math studies. So at quarter's end, I received the lowest possible passing grade, a D-minus. As we lined up at home in front of daddy for the report card "revue," I headed for the back, mentally listing possible punishments for such an unheard-of grade. Cleaning out the spooky lower basement? Raking the front lawn with a fork? Anything was possible.

Next quarter, same grade. Hard as I studied, I still got a D-minus. So, hoping to avoid a repeat of daddy's temper, I went to an empty classroom and changed the minus to a plus. Once home, I headed for the back of the line again, ignoring the confident smiles of Karen, Gail and Denae standing nonchalantly at the front.

"Well, I'll be a dirty name; you actually *improved* in geometry," was daddy's hearty response (I didn't know about "snide" at the time), signing FJV with a flourish. Now if I could just convert the

D-plus back to a D-minus without raising my teacher's suspicions. Stealthily removing the blade from daddy's razor, I sat on the toilet seat in the bathroom and carefully scratched out the down bar on the plus sign. If only I had Diane's daring resourcefulness. Realizing the incomparable value of blank report cards, at the beginning of the year she had shrewdly signed up for office duty with the school secretary. Those few hours of volunteer filing guaranteed her access not only to blank report cards but also to absentee forms as well. Thus she could skip class or relax her homework schedule as she pleased, with no fear or retribution. As for me, I was just plain stuck with that D-minus.

## La Traviata, Dejeuner
Elaine

As the oldest at age 15, I was in charge of packing the school lunches: for myself, Denae and Diane, Karen, Keith, Gail and Gwen. Seven lunches for seven kids. It was the last thing I did after my schoolwork was finished before going to bed at night. A simple task, right?

To begin with, I had to use cheap paper bags, the brown ones mom bought once a month, 30 for 29 cents. Rustle, rustle. The paper was as thin as the tissue sheets you line gift boxes with. Not for us those shiny metal lunch boxes that snapped open and shut with that lovely, precise, middle-class clicking sound – lunch boxes that were colorfully decorated with images of Superwoman, Bullwinkle and Bugs Bunny.

Inside the brown sacks I placed the sandwiches wrapped in waxed paper. Since every disposable item in our household had to be rationed and recycled whenever possible, each day after school everyone was expected to return their bag *with* the waxed paper to the kitchen counter, to be reused on the following day. The trick was to keep both intact for the entire week until Monday rolled around, when mom would allow me to start fresh with seven new sacks and seven glossy sheets of waxed paper.

As the week progressed, the lunch bags would be increasingly oil-stained, pencil-marked, and black smudged by playground hands. Rain or snow further weakened their condition. After four days of folding and unfolding, they were as wrinkled as crushed poppy petals. Come Thursday night, I handled them with the delicacy of a surgeon lifting damaged lung tissue. Not to mention the waxed paper, which by then was so tattered that I had to resort to rubber bands to keep it in place around the sandwiches.

Obviously, on some days not all of the lunch bags made it home, resulting once in daddy recycling two old fishing tackle boxes for Keith and Gail. Much as I scoured and purexed them, they still carried the smell of shrimp bait and dead fish. By way of replacing the missing sacks, I would often salvage from our kitchen bin of large used grocery bags, cutting off the tops to make them more manageable, yet knowing perfectly well the consequences at school. Seated at the lunch table with that oversized shopping bag was like reaching into a suitcase to get at the pathetic sandwich inside.

Inventiveness was key in the event the waxed paper didn't make it home with the lunch sack. Sometimes I cut up our plastic bread wrappers. At the time we were buying Boge's Bread, its packaging vividly stamped with yellow polka-dots and red letters. When that wasn't available, I tried encasing the sandwiches in school notebook paper, carefully cutting off the left side margin with the line of little holes. Even by folding the corners with crisp tight edges in origami fashion, the paper was still too stiff to stay in place, so once again I had to resort to the rubber bands.

Karen and Diane got very upset over the notebook paper wrappings, so I decided to use it only for emergencies with the younger kids. However, as payback for their criticism, a couple of times I just dropped their sandwiches without any wrapper at all into the lunch bags when there was no waxed paper.

Equally problematic was what to put between the slices of bread, or, in its absence, between the halves of homemade biscuits. In those days our surplus commodity margarine came white, like Crisco, and was packed in little plastic tubs. Attached was a tiny packet containing yellow dye, which I mixed with the white oleo to achieve the store-bought effect.

Twenty-nine-cent a pound bologna from Horseman's Meat Market was the standard filler for our sandwiches. However, prelude to buying was the necessity to first earn the purchase money. This unhappy task entailed a lonely mile or two walk along Sprague Avenue or the railroad tracks with a sturdy plastic bag for collecting discarded beer bottles, to be turned in for the refund money. Occasionally I could talk Karen or Diane into assisting me. 30 bottles would buy one pound of bologna, while 60 (were we excessively energetic) would net us two pounds of the lumpy, irregular end pieces, which the butcher had packaged up from the rolls of uniformly sliced meat. Most people did not want these end chunks because they were often dried out or too bulgy to make a nice flat sandwich. So I did the best I could to level them by chopping them into tiny bits, but the meat still ended up falling from between the bread slices, looking suspiciously like dog food.

Horseman's Market was also the place where we bought fresh cow tongue and our school shoes. Every size imaginable, from triple A's to extra-wides, was jammed together in a huge wooden bin next to the door. At $1.49 each, they were a bargain. However, there were no color choices; every single one of them, year in and year out, was hush-puppy brown. Mr. Horseman, the owner, was a good businessman, I thought, but with a weak sense of aesthetics. Apparently, he didn't mind that the shoes matched the meat rather than our clothes.

As the month progressed and food supplies shrank, I would fry up potatoes or mash overripe bananas to fill the school sandwiches. A couple of times I put in dad's homemade sauerkraut, and in extreme cases I had to resort to just plain lard. We all dreaded the lunch hour at school; there was simply no way to camouflage our hideously wrinkled brown bags and their contents. Trying to hide things was just a way of life for us – hiding bruises, hiding our feelings, hiding the holes in our shoes and our clothing.

Absolutely worst were the 1950s, when the school nutrition programs were being re-evaluated. All across the country, school boards focused on educating teachers, parents and students about the value of the basic seven food groups. For at least two years in the Gestapo-like mania, students would have to line up during noon hour at the teacher's desk. One by one, we were to hand over our lunch for inspection. Then, our teacher, like a diver opening oysters for pearls, would examine the contents with intense scrutiny.

"Why, Elaine, weren't you listening yesterday when I told the class that each lunch should contain whole-grain bread, milk, a fruit item and a vegetable? I'm giving you a note for your mother. . . and tomorrow I expect to see a much more acceptable lunch."

Then she would mark a big red "U" for Unsatisfactory next to my name in her grade book. *One hundred ways to humiliate the poor kids.*

So mortifying. The entire class was both spectator and participant in this daily drama. Students would approve or condemn the exhibited lunches, right along with the teacher. In essence, your noon meal was on trial as a sign of your economic status. Its contents revealed the whole story. On those days when all I had was a biscuit swathed in four-day-old waxed paper, I prayed for a sinkhole to swallow me. At the same time, I couldn't help but reflect on Diane's technique for extracting a sandwich from her lunch bag when the waxed paper was so tattered it was almost spectral. Like a fox scooping a hare from its burrow, her fingers would plunge deftly into the sack, detaching the raggy shroud. And before you could blink, she was holding aloft the naked sandwich, nary a lump of bologna falling to her lap.

Lacking her dexterity, I longed for a blanket of invisibility so I could get through the day without all the demeaning roadblocks. And if I couldn't become invisible, I wished I could silence once and for all that damn noon bell, signaling the lunch hour. Ah, the sweet rapture of taking a sledgehammer and bludgeoning that red gong into smithereens, or, at the very least, flattening it into sheet metal – its final *cling, clang, clon-n-ng* – music to my ears. And then the blessed silence. A way to avoid the daily agony of watching rich, overweight Agnes haul

154

out the lavish smorgasbord from her large painted lunchbox (a pink poodle with black bows): salami, pickle and onion on rye – sometimes pumpernickel – with sliced celery sticks, chocolate milk, and ginger snaps. If I lived to be a hundred, my lunch bag would never hold such a banquet. More realistically, I dreamed of reaching down into my sack one day and pulling out a set of Hostess Twinkies; whether chocolate iced with the white squiggle, or coconut sprinkled on marshmallow pink, I didn't care. How I longed to poke my finger into its mooshy center and feast upon its rich creampuff filling.

Diane

Our house was a five-minute walk from school if it was cold outside, or it could be a 15-minute walk if I had to remove my mascara at the bus shelter across from the junior high before going home, so dad would not yell "Jezebel" at me and try to pull off the mascara, himself. He was home a lot because he was unemployed. And my mascara was on pretty thick because the smaller refill tube was easier to steal than the larger mascara tube *with the brush*, so I had to apply it to my lashes with a twig or a toothpick.

Returning home from school could take up to 20 minutes if I had to remove makeup *and* pull off stolen nylons, replacing them with my ankle socks. Eventually, I mastered this artful exchange by peeling off the forbidden hose while walking down Sprague Avenue and slipping on each white anklet while my bare foot was still in midair.

With only one bathroom the size of a closet in our house, five sisters and three brothers did not make it easy for me to get ready for school in the morning. I calculated that to be ready in time, each of us had three minutes of mirror-time in the 8-by-12-inch glass above the sink. Fortunately, Elaine left earlier because she was attending high school. Being two inches taller than Karen and Denae, I could gain several extra minutes by standing behind them to put the final touches on my hairdo.

At night, I used cotton rag strips to curl my hair, because when mom gave me a permanent she used the old waving solutions given to her by the ladies whose houses she cleaned, and they always burned my hair.

Once ready for school, there were three choices of doors to make my exit. One stood just behind the dining table, which had no chairs, just two long benches on either side. This doorway took you down rickety wooden steps to the first level of the basement where dad had cabbage fermenting in three-gallon crocks, weighted down with big rocks sitting on plates so we could skim away the gray scum once or twice a week. Other crocks contained cukes from our garden – soon to be pickles – fermenting in sweet brine. This particular exit route was an obstacle course of old car parts, beer bottles, rusted tools, fishing tackle boxes and a manual wringer washing machine standing at attention on the concrete floor, waiting for the call to duty on laundry day.

Below this level was another flight of broken concrete stairs that took you to the lower basement, a pitch-black room with a dirt floor where all our canned goods were stored on shelves, including our pet rabbits that got canned one day when we were at school.

I usually left by the first-level basement door when I didn't want to be seen by dad, on those days when I was wearing stolen clothing or clothes borrowed from a girl on Barker Road. It was not easy to push open this door because dad had once jammed it shut when he was trying to redirect a stream of sewage from our overflowing septic tank. Since there was no doorknob, just a fist-sized hole, you had to lean hard against the wood to force it open. Once outside, I could breathe in the sweet, fresh air. What a relief to be free of the basement smells: fermenting sauerkraut, the sour odor from stacks of empty beer bottles piled up so dad could get the refund money, and the indescribably foul fumes from the dirt in the lower basement that never really dried. That bottom level was the spookiest place on earth.

Most days, Karen, Denae and I walked to school together. They actually liked school. I, on the other hand, couldn't help lagging behind, not wanting to transition from the freedom of outdoors to the prison awaiting me within the red brick walls of the junior high. Once inside I felt trapped, like the rats I saw through the school's basement windows one night when Denae and I had snuck out of our house. A pack of 16 rats – brazen, tails twitching – were slowly making their way down the central hallway, straight toward our disbelieving eyes.

The combination of being poor and not finishing my homework made school a living hell. Not to mention our principal, Mr. Voege – tall, dark-suited and dark-eyed – stalking me in the corridors from the moment I entered the front doors, hoping to be paid the $5 for my registration fee, owing since the beginning of the year. Once, he even came into my home-room looking for me and told Mrs. Collier to send me out into the hall.

"You can work in the lunchroom at noon to pay it off," he said, staring critically at my bleached-blond hair.

"But I go home for lunch," I countered.

I think this is when I began to practice the art of being invisible. I didn't want to be gone altogether, I just wanted to see without being seen. I was very much interested in participating in life, but without the judgments and prejudices of others. So at those times when I was unprepared for class and terrified to be called on, or hiding behind lockers and doors to avoid the ever-watchful Mr. Voege, I would go into invisible mode – focusing on not being there, not being seen, as though I was located somewhere above the ceiling.

The first time I read about a near-death experience where the soul leaves the body and looks down from the edge of another dimension, I could totally relate. That is how I spent most of my time in school.

Not completing assignments was due in large part to my wardrobe, or lack of it. We got our clothing from St. Vincent de Paul, Goodwill and Salvation Army. In a poor community like Greenacres, clothes donated to these outlets were one step from rags. I did try to remodel my second and third-hand outfits, but I much preferred new clothes. In clothes-trading arrangements with classmates (forbidden by dad), it became obvious my own were just too shabby for barter.

The only outfit I had fit for trading was a blue sweater and skirt I had stolen from one of Karen's girlfriends. In a class-conscious society like ours, I realized our family was well below blue collar, we were "torn collar."

I believed that with stylish new clothes I might be accepted and even become friends with one of the popular girls. Consequently, I became obsessed with clothing and its acquisition. This preoccupation left little time for homework, though I did try to skim-read and cram while in class or between classes. One of the few courses I actually enjoyed in junior high was World History with Mr. McCleod. Since he spent most of the period reenacting the people and events, he didn't ask many questions, so I could just relax and enjoy his performance.

When assigned to give an oral book report in Mrs. Collier's eight grade English course, I memorized the synopsis on the book cover of Lewis Carroll's *Through the Looking Glass*. As I stood there trying to articulate, the words were strange and arranged quite unlike any I had ever spoken. Mrs. Collier knew I had plagiarized – I wondered how.

Finally, the bell would ring at 3:15 – total ecstasy. No more hiding at my desk, aligning myself behind someone's head, hiding the holes in my shoes, hiding from the principal, or trying to be invisible. The outside air was like sweet perfume as I rushed past the big double doors across Appleway to Sprague Avenue and freedom.

Denae

I started first grade with four eyes, even though when I left home that morning I was sure I had only two. But at recess the boys yelled at me from the teeter-totter, "Hey, Four-eyes, you sure do look ugly with those specs! We sure don't want *you* sitting next to *us* at the lunch table!"

There was nothing wrong with my vision – it was 20/20. The problem was, I was cross-eyed. So my doctor had put strips of white tape on the inside of both my lenses, hoping to make my eye muscles stretch out instead of in. To say I did not enjoy first grade would be an understatement. The only person I felt sorrier for than myself was little Josie Mattson. At recess when she turned upside down on the monkey bars, you could see the big holes in her underpants. The other kids all laughed at her. I didn't, because my underpants had holes in them too – but at least I had the good sense to stay off the monkey bars.

In high school we were assigned to read Homer's *The Odyssey*. Memories of first grade returned when I came to the chapter on "Cyclops." Bonding with him immediately, I understood perfectly why he would want to kill Ulysses and his men in the cave. Life can be very difficult if you do not have the correct number of eyes. One – however large – is too few, while four is too many. Without the anticipated two, you could be called names, or even be hated. Aesthetically speaking, like it or not, two just looks more pleasing. Better feng shui, I guess.

My second-grade teacher, Mrs. Hempstead, was so beautiful I could hardly wait to get to school so I could sit and stare at her. She smiled all the time and was so nice to Diane and me. Unlike home. I waited months for the apples to ripen on our tree in the front yard so I could place one on her desk. Unfortunately, mine was a yellow variety –the effect not quite the same as the big red one you see on greeting cards for teachers. But her kindly smile assured me she liked yellow apples just as much.

It was a good thing the rest of my teachers were not as beautiful as Mrs. Hempstead, because in the absence of that distraction I was finally able to concentrate on my lessons and begin my extensive collection of A's. The only C I ever received was in ninth grade Latin class, which I immediately changed to a B-plus without even trying to erase out the C. I explained to dad that my teacher had made the mistake, so he passed me through the report card line with not a hint of suspicion. I kept the accolades coming by maintaining my near straight-A average right through college, where I graduated summa cum laude with a degree in anthropology and women's studies.

I have never been math-oriented, rather my interest and expertise have been in art and literature. This said, an occasion once arose in ninth-grade math class which caused me, at least temporarily, to re-consider my lack of interest.

Sam Carroll was the Greenacres Junior High math genius. Ev-eryone knew it, even the mindless seventh-graders. Had we all been students at *Harvard* Junior High, I am certain that Sam would still have retained his status of math prodigy extraordinaire. His father was a math instructor, as was his grandfather and great-grandfather before him. A genetic coup, a virtual monopoly of trigonometric genes was guaranteed Sam – all he had to do was survive birth – which he did.

So my story begins one inauspicious day in math class when our teacher, Mr. Kallas, decided to supplement the usual daily assignment with an impromptu contest. Randomly calling up two students at a time, each was to position himself to the right or left of the blackboard and solve as quickly as possible the long division, square root, or story problem that was given. The loser would be replaced by another con-testant, while the winner would remain standing as long as he or she continued to be the fastest.

Not surprisingly, each time Sam was called, invariably he pre-vailed. Irregardless, an abundance of adolescent testosterone fueled spirited matches. Much as it seemed that he was a serious rival, still Sam's diminutive stature and Walter Mitty-like personality mitigated the obvious. Confidently, football and basketball jocks towered over him as they stood in turn to oppose him at the blackboard. It did not seem a daunting matter to defeat little Sam Carroll.

Day after day passed, yet no one could solve the math problems faster than he. The bell would ring signaling the end of class, and there would be Sam, still standing, grinning triumphantly, a worn stump of chalk between his fingers. It appeared that he really could not be beat-en. Much as the notion rankled, his mastery began to unnerve us all, and he seemed destined to join the ranks of legendary invincibles like Heisenberg, Einstein and Marconi.

This burden of defeat, after weeks of futile confrontations, began to undermine the morale of the entire class. Combatants no longer

160

strode to the blackboard with swagger and impudence, eager for revenge. Rather, apathy and resignation hung thick in the air like chalk dust. Even the simplest story problem now became an insurmountable intellectual challenge: "How many minutes does it take Joe and his date to reach the movie theater 50 miles away, if they are traveling by bike at 20 mph, and make four, 10-minute stops?"

By contrast, Sam seemed to have grown eight inches. Little Sam was now Big Bad Sam, exuding vitality and confidence. He owned the blackboard; he owned the classroom. Why did our teacher continue the competition? Morale was so low I decided that an intervention was necessary. No longer a benign competition, this had become a philosophical concern of the highest magnitude. Those classmates destined to become physicists, engineers and math professors had lost focus and certitude. They had become straw men and women of war, walking wounded across the battlefield without ever raising their weapons.

Sam's character was even more seriously jeopardized. Moral corruption seemed inevitable, as he saw himself soar prematurely into the dizzying heights of genius. It had been all too easy, unearned. Sam had crossed the line from hero to anti-hero. The incandescent light of his success was blinding us all. He thought, he *knew* he was invincible. And for that, he had to be stopped. A David must be found to subdue the overweening pride of his Goliath. We were on the verge of math massacre and clearly there were to be no survivors. Only Sam, unbloodied and victorious, would walk off the field, strewn with the fallen. And what was left? What would remain for the rest of us, but to whisper into his footprints, long after they had passed: "*I coulda been a contender.*"

Big Bad Sam became an object of extreme interest to me. Like a bloodhound stalking the spore trail of its prey, I became relentless, single-minded in my focus. I was Inspector Javert pursuing Jean Valjean; Sherlock Holmes on the trail of Professor Moriarty. When Sam stood at the chalkboard raptly multiplying, dividing, square-rooting his columns of numbers, I analyzed his method, measured the tilt of his head, the alignment of his spine, evaluated how he held his chalk. No aspect of his movements escaped my attention as I probed deeper and deeper, past bone and muscle, beyond capillaries and corpuscles into the very essence of his soul.

And then it came to me – suddenly I knew how to beat Sam at the blackboard! All I had to do now was wait for Mr. Kallas to call my name.

It was a short wait. At last I found myself gazing across the length of blackboard at him – the kingpin of computation – chalk in hand, poised for action as the math problem was given. Before the teacher had finished, it was easy to discern what comprised the rest of the story problem, so I began writing the numbers and equations on the board – while Sam, not noticing, was still standing there waiting for the instruction to end. And that was precisely what I had learned during my intense observations. Sam never put chalk to board until the teacher stopped talking, nor had anyone else. No rules had been established forbidding this; it had simply not occurred to anyone to do so.

My few critical seconds of lead-time were Sam's undoing. Close to a photo finish, but not quite. I dropped the chalk a half second before he did. And the contest was mine.

Sam nearly fainted. The class went wild. There were a few cries of "Foul play! Unfair! She started too soon," from his best friends. But Mr. Kallas upheld my victory.

Sam, of course, did not thank me for saving his immortal soul that day.

Looking back on all those years of books and homework assignments, not easily forgotten was the morning in Mrs. Dean's ninth-grade English class when she called students one by one to give their prepared speeches on "How to do" something. Nadine Olson, my archrival, once again had outdistanced everyone with her artfully devised concept of "First-aid in an eggshell." Wizard-like, she extracted antiseptic, gauze, band aids, needle and thread from a hollowed-out egg, so large it must have been from an emu or a pelican. No one wanted to follow that act.

Football jock and school heartthrob Lonnie Barron stood at the front desk holding the microphone for each speaker as Mrs. Dean pointed to me with, "Next." Even Diane, my twin, sitting impassively two rows away did not know my topic, since I had purposely avoided rehearsing near her at home the night before. Now, nervous as a three-legged rabbit on the Serengeti, I walked to the front of the class to begin: "Mama Mia! This trainsa leavin' the tracksa. . . and I'm nota even ona boarda yet," I intoned with an *Italian* accent, continuing to narrate the adventure of "Luigi" as he traveled alone from Rome to Brindisi, his first solo trip on a train.

"Thatsa my bambina there. . . Squeeza the banana, nota the baby! So clumsy you city boysa." (An elderly woman with a child criticizes Luigi as he jostles other passengers in moving from one crowded compartment into another).

Since the cultural diversity of Greenacres and Spokane at that time was fairly lopsided – about 95 percent Anglo-Saxon – the only "people of color" likely to be seen were red-skinned casualties from too many hours on the beach under the hot summer sun, I doubt that anyone in our class had ever heard a foreign accent, except on television.

Looking up just once during my oration, such was my anxiety, I caught a brief glimpse of Diane, head on her desk, shoulders convulsing – whether from embarrassment or from mirth, I couldn't tell. An awkward moment of heavy silence ensued when I finished, followed by a storm of applause and laughter. My unexpected, broken Italian accent had so decomposed the normally unflappable Mrs. Dean that I could barely decipher, between the coughs and sputters, her intent to give me an A-plus on the spot. "In twenty years of teaching," she claimed, "that is the most unusual oral presentation I have ever heard."

But the best compliment came from my twin (albeit years later) when I asked her if she remembered my speech. "Are you kidding?" Diane laughed, "I'll never forget that day as long as I live. I could not believe you had the nerve to talk in front of the class with an Italian accent!"

Mr. McLeod, at Greenacres Junior High, was Jimmy Stewart with Buddy Holly glasses and a Jerry Lee Lewis grin. Who could resist such a combination? Not me, nor half the student body. During school assemblies, students would jump to their feet, rocking the wooden bleachers with their stamping and yelling, "McLeod! McLeod! McLeod!" when he walked in, as though he had just made the winning touchdown.

It was in his seventh-grade history class that I savored my first time ever experience of being the focus of attention and admiration – a situation which normally would have terrified me since I was so extremely shy. At the time, we were studying Eastern European countries and he knew our family was Czech. What he didn't know was that dad quizzed us weekly on the spellings of world continents, as well as state and country capital cities. On that particular day, Mr. McLeod stood at the blackboard, natty in a blue serge suit and starched white shirt, his long wooden pointer tapping the colored wall map. "Does anyone know how to spell *Czechoslovakia*?" He might as well have asked the class to speak in Apache. One lone hand was raised. Mine.

"Yes, Miss Veselits," he beamed in my direction, as though he had just placed a bet on the winning race horse.

"C-z-e-c-h-o ..." I spelled the blessed word, enunciating each of the 14 letters with the aplomb of a Shakespearean actor. A star was born. And my regard for him swelled to near idolatry as he continued to shepherd my academic confidence and success throughout the next three years.

Not only was Mr. McLeod outstanding in the classroom, he used every available opportunity outside his classes, as well, to mentor and inspire his adoring students. In study halls, school corridors, even in after-school detention rooms, he would hold court – I can still see that roguish grin, a merry twinkle in his Gaelic blue eyes, advising us: "Don't be afraid to be different. If everyone else in the grocery store is buying tuna, try the sardines. Forge your own trail. Believe in yourself. If you like the harmonica, don't pick up a guitar just because everyone else is playing one."

Mr. McLeod, top right; Gail, bottom right

Gail

Mr. McLeod had a huge impact on my life. I always felt so different – because of dad, our poverty, our crazy home environment. We were used to hiding our feelings about so many things, trying to pretend that we were just like the other kids. Mr. McLeod had a way of validating being different. Not only did he think it was okay, he thought it was *better* than being status quo – something to be admired and *encouraged*!!

Denae

Coincidentally, these credos were the same ones espoused by our father. Why did they sound so substantive and visionary coming from

Mr. McLeod and so disingenuous coming from dad? We see-sawed between the experience and perceptions of our father and those of our teacher, trying to heed the philosophies of both.

To our great good fortune, this remarkable man was also an actor in private life. Never to be forgotten was the day he reenacted the spread of the bubonic plague. Crawling up the back of a classroom chair, he began the lesson by impersonating a ship's rat, chewing through the mainsail ropes on a transient freighter adrift in the Atlantic. From rodent, he transformed himself into infected deckhand, first-mate, then captain – as the deadly pestilence traveled person to person, from ocean going ships to the soils and populations of medieval Europe. The "curtain" of his performance came down on his twisted figure, writhing in agony on the floor as he suffered through the final stages of the Black Death, his last gasp exhaled just before the bell rang.

He championed me right up to the last day of junior high, when at the graduation and awards ceremony, I was *not* named among the Top Ten achievement recipients. Devastated, I refused to look up at a triumphantly smiling Nadine, standing next to Sam Carroll and the rest of the "exalted ten." Blinking away tears, I threaded my way out of the noisy, packed auditorium to find a quiet hallway. A moment later I felt a warm hand on my shoulder and Mr. McLeod's voice behind me. "For what it's worth, Miss Veselits," as if he could read my mind, "I thought you should have received one of the Top Ten awards."

The moment had been transformed; if Mr. McLeod thought I deserved to win, that was good enough for me.

# DUST MARKS ON the BLACKBOARD

Keith and Gail

<u>Karen</u>

My first day of school, fifth grade, was filled with giggles and shrieks as Diane, Denae, Keith and I pelted each other with potatoes from the newly harvested fields we were crossing, on our way to Foothills Elementary, a two-room structure, housing grades 1-6, and presided over by the intrepid Mrs. Johnston. We were living in the foothills below Mt. Spokane, a rural area of milking goats, alfalfa pastures, beekeepers and orchards. Our home, a sagging two-story farm house sat on a bluff overlooking the school, a half mile away.

Today, however, was a different matter entirely. Rain had fallen all night, dripping from the bedroom ceilings onto our faces and bedcovers. Now in the foggy gloom of morning, it was streaking brownish trails down the drafty windows as I peered unhappily across the puddly stretch of dirt road. There, well ahead of me, having taken the short-cut across the potato field were Denae and Diane, trudging along in high rubber wellies, one pair of which I had hoped to be wearing, myself. With no thought for me or my smaller stature, they had left the house early, and were now completing their sloppy trek to school, without incident.

I, on the other hand, got only about 100 feet in mom's too-large overshoes. Descending the hill, my heavily booted feet were soon sucked knee deep by the treacherous sludge. Unable to move and with no prospect of rescue, I struggled out of mom's galoshes, and slogged my way barefoot back to the kitchen door – a scourge and lamentation to all – soaking wet and utterly defeated.

The following morning mom penned a note for Mrs. Johnston. It read: "*Please excuse Karen from school yesterday. She got stuck in the mud.*" *Rose Veselits*

Mr. McLeod and Mrs. Harrington were my two favorite junior high teachers, who, coincidentally, taught my two favorite subjects, history and English. Diane, Denae and I would spend hours after school discussing Mr. McLeod's classroom antics. One year we made a Christmas card for him, a tree and stars sprinkled over with glue and lots of silvery glitter. I wanted to sign it "Your loving daughters," but Denae said we couldn't. That didn't stop us, however, from continuing to pretend he was our father and fantasizing about taking the school bus to his home in Coeur d'Alene – hoping he would invite us to stay.

I remember always being very concerned about grades. Even though I was an A student, I must have been afraid that eventually I'd slip up and get a B, so I became obsessive about accumulating extra credit. In eighth grade, I began copying words off book jackets, which I gave Mrs. Harrington as my book reviews. Diplomatically, she told me I didn't need more points. "Just read the books, Karen; you've already got an A."

So I took her advice, oftentimes choosing books that were too advanced. While my friends were reading *Girl of the Limberlost* and *The Nancy Drew Mysteries*, I was devouring *Lady Chatterley's Lover*, *The Collected Letters of D.H. Lawrence* and Tolstoy's *War and Peace* – until I discovered the magic of cinema. From then on my passion for movies equaled my passion for academics. In fact, I loved school so much that I went all the way through a Ph.D. program and became a teacher, myself.

75 cents, the price of a movie ticket, provided me entry into someone else's life, a welcome escape. And if not a movie ticket, a movie fan magazine – the first was on Liberace – which I impudently read in Mr. Filbert's ninth-grade science class, in part because he was such a bad teacher (It was rumored he had been a used car salesman).

My first screen love, Spencer Tracy, was the subject of my numerous scrapbooks, along with George Maharis ("Route 66") and Richard Chamberlain ("Doctor Kildare"). However, my Jackie Kennedy albums totally eclipsed the others in thoroughness and sheer volume. Such was my idolatry that I spent hours perfecting the "K" of Karen to identically match the "K" in Kennedy.

As a ninth grader, I heard that *Judgment at Nuremberg* had opened at the Fox Theater in downtown Spokane. Although I had no idea what the movie was about, I dreamed of going by bus with my girlfriends, Pam Jewitt and Anna Allison, because Spencer Tracy was the star. After lying to all three sets of parents and getting into serious trouble with mom, Mrs. Allison and her husband rescued the situation by agreeing to drive us to the movie and act as chaperones. I now realize they sat through the show only because I had made such a grown-up choice. However, Pam and Anna hated it. They thought we were going to something like *Beach Blanket Bingo* with Annette Funicello and Bobby Darin.

The second most memorable film I saw was *West Side Story*. Now there was a film just like home – but set to music. Natalie Wood was so beautiful as Maria, I dreamed of being just like her. Of course, I had no idea what Puerto Rican gangs or rumbles were, and most certainly knew nothing of New York City or Leonard Bernstein. But with this movie, somehow I felt I had "arrived."

Denae

Karen was so obsessed with *West Side Story*: I will never forget the afternoon I came home from school and there she was in a torn T-shirt and jeans, holding court by the kitchen sink, singing, 'Gee, Officer Krupke, krup you!' to all the little kids. She continued to reenact every song and scene, alternately playing Tony, Anita, Maria and half the gang members from the *Sharks* and the *Jets*. After a few weeks of these impromptu performances, we finally begged her to stop, because by then we knew every line by heart and could hardly bear to hear one more chorus of 'I just met a girl named Maria…'"

Karen

Our taste in films and music was considerably influenced by dad, who often brought home scratched 78 and 33 vinyl recordings of classics like the "Hungarian Rhapsody" and "The Gypsy Love Song," along with the greatest hits by Caruso and Mario Lanza. While our friends might be listening to Pat Boone and Chubby Checker on

170

American Bandstand, we would be humming "Ah, Sweet Mystery of Life" from the operetta "Naughty Marietta."

With all those bus trips to the Fox and State movie theaters in downtown Spokane, I developed a taste for big city life and decided to abandon Greenacres altogether – the deciding factor being the hostile environment at Central Valley High School during my freshman year. Like most of the girls in my class, I was terrorized by the hulking senior boys in their blue letterman jackets, who lined the hallways as members of the "Paddle Squad." No female felt safe from their leering eyes and lewd comments. They were supposedly there to maintain order between classes. Instead, they acted more like stalkers, trolling the school corridors like they were ghetto alleyways, looking for girls to fondle or bully.

So when my friend Liz O'Reilly said, "Why don't you come to Marycliff?" I did, without ever asking mom. And what a sight it was! The school was two huge mansions on Spokane's prestigious South Hill that had been donated – along with their expansive green lawns and towering shade trees – for the purpose of creating a Catholic girls' music academy. Every room had a baby grand piano, and nearly all the students (except me) had a hefty musical background. We wore uniforms, grey and blue pleated skirts with white blouses, which I loved because I had no nice clothes. On dress-up day, which came once a month, I relied on Diane for my outfits. I also borrowed her semi-formal, as well as her boyfriend, for my first prom (I provided the tiara).

In addition to my movie addiction, I was also incurably hooked on politics. While still at Marycliff, both Gail and I became "Foleyettes," campaigning for U.S. Rep. Tom Foley before he was elected Speaker of the House. We were so thrilled to be given special passes the day Bobby Kennedy arrived at Spokane Airport to support JFK's bid for presidency. Standing together at the front of the crowd, we were close enough to touch his shirt sleeves. Everyone was screaming!

Busy as I was, I had also been accepted as a House page for then

Speaker Bill Day in the State House of Representatives. I loved taking the train for the 300 mile trip between Spokane and Olympia, so much so that I stole small sums of money from time to time to pay my fare. By then, mom had no idea *what* I was doing. So I widened my options by competing in a United Nations writing competition, and won first place. The award was ten dollars, with which I bought my first bikini (and which mother promptly returned).

By then it was obvious to me that my future was to be on the East Coast, not the West. So after high school I signed up as a VISTA volunteer, working in Pittsburgh. From there it was just a puddle jump to Washington, D.C., where I participated in the Poor People's Peace March and finally found my political soul.

Keith

I learned a lot in third grade – a lot of things that usually don't show up in the average 9-year-old's curriculum, like love and kindness. I had been playing outside at recess; it was winter and very cold. The lines on my knuckles were cracked and bleeding, so when I came back into the classroom my teacher noticed and asked, "Don't you have any hand lotion?" Mystified, I responded, "What's that?" She looked at me incredulously, then opened her purse and offered me a tube. Not knowing what to do with it, I just stood there. So she squirted some into her palm and began rubbing the cream against my palms and knuckles. The experience of feeling her soft warm hands massaging my chapped red ones was so unprecedented that I felt like crying. No one had ever given me that kind of attention before.

I also learned about love letters in the third grade. While standing in line at the water fountain one day I noticed a note being passed forward from farther back in the line. Eventually it reached my hands, and to my surprise it had my name penciled in on the front: K-e-i-t-h. Yep, that was me. Hurrying to gulp my drink, I rushed back to my desk and discovered the letter was from none other than Linda Paine – the prettiest girl in class. As a young boy, I had never had a very high opinion of myself. But that day, I was near the top of the

172

world. She had written "I love you," and I can't remember much else. The point was, someone had actually taken an interest in me; a novel experience.

School has always been a challenge, partly because as a kid growing up in an abusive, dysfunctional home, I struggled to find my identity. Consequently, class assignments weren't always a high priority. Who am I? Who can I be? Why am I here? were the more compelling issues, so I used school as a safe haven to experiment with various personas that I could inhabit or discard, as suited me –athlete, scholar… or parking lot smoker and ne'er do well. Many years were to pass with much soul-searching and self-improvement before I felt my ego and psyche were in a healthier place.

However, periodically fate would step in and throw me a curveball to rouse me from my academic lethargy. For example: Sophomore civics class was an exercise in staying awake. One afternoon in the middle of stifling a long yawn, I vaguely recalled hearing our instructor mention a documentary we'd be watching on public service buildings in Spokane and outlying areas. Included would be the Veterans Hospital and Eastern State Mental Hospital – which nominally raised my interest, since dad was currently a patient there.

This building was about ten miles from town near West Medical Lake, one of the better trout fishing spots in the area. Adjacent to the hospital grounds was a dock with chairs and benches that patients could use. When visiting dad, invariably we would end up fishing there –one of his favorite activities. Needless to say, while waiting for a strike, I met some very strange characters. It seemed to me, by comparison, that dad was out of place and certainly did not fit the profile of the typical resident.

With the class half over, my eyes were nodding in disinterest when I noticed the camera panning some vaguely familiar landmarks, eventually halting at a long wooden pier. With the lens slowly zooming in, you could make out images of a few people fishing. As the shot became tighter, facial features became more distinguishable. Finally the camera came to rest on one angler, intently studying the tip of his bamboo pole, cheek bulging with chewing tobacco as he anticipated the jerk on his line. To my horror – eyes bulging in disbelief – I realized, THAT'S MY DAD!!!

I'm not sure whether I went into cardiac arrest or, simply stopped breathing – maybe it was the rush of adrenaline you get when you are in danger. All I could think of was escaping that larger-than-life image before me, the super-magnified features of my father fishing off the dock of the mental hospital for all my classmates to see.

Clamping my eyes shut, I tried to block out dad's face, but the familiar contours were imbedded in my brain in blazing Technicolor, still larger than life, still testing his line, waiting for the "big one."

Sitting there in the darkened classroom, with the only sound the steady whirling of the 16mm movie projector, I waited for the inevitable words that would shatter my anonymity, revealing the secrecy of my father's whereabouts: "Hey, Veselits, isn't that your old man?"

*Steve Pettibones, the traitor. Thanks a lot, buddy!* I grimaced. The bell rang, lights came on, and I had to open my eyes while Steve's words were still bouncing off the walls in echo. I staggered from the room like someone who had just been shot. Thankfully, the rest of my classmates were considerate enough to remain quiet on the subject for the rest of the day.

Gail

The one thing you could always count on in our family was that you could never count on anything. As a painfully withdrawn grade school student, I joined the Library Aides, not just for my love of reading but because it was a way to escape the terrors of recess and the noon lunch hour. When I learned this group met in the library during these times, I jumped at the chance to join.

As a member, you got to wear a special badge. For each significant accomplishment, a jewel would be added. The jewels on my badge matched the jewels in my glasses. Finally, I felt I belonged. As a member of this group and with the library for refuge, I began to feel less lonely and vulnerable.

In third grade, a local TV program called "Bar 6 Roundup" randomly selected school kids to participate in the show. The format was similar to "Captain Kangaroo," but with a western twist. Inexplicably, I was among the elite few chosen for the coming week's production. See-sawing between fear and anticipation, I waited for the big event, feeling like a celebrity of sorts, since no one in our family had ever been on TV before. Despite my shyness, I was nonetheless anxious to have everyone in the family, especially daddy, see me perform – my one and only chance for glory in an otherwise nondescript existence.

The day finally arrived, and I was in a hurry to get to school, where we would be chauffeured to the Channel 6 studio. Daddy had assured me that he would have the TV on sharply at 3 p.m. to watch the show.

Thankfully, I was not required to do anything other than sit on a hay bale, but still my stage fright was off the Richter scale. I forced a smile, slowly warming to a glow inside, as I imagined daddy watching the program, wanting him to be proud of me.

With the hour over, all had gone well. I couldn't wait to get home and hear daddy rave about my divine performance. In a large family where individual recognition was rare, I felt my 15 minutes of fame had finally arrived.

The front door opened into the kitchen, and as I bounded in, I knew immediately that something was terribly wrong. The first thing I noticed was the quiet, which was odd, what with homework and meal preparation usually in progress. Then I noticed the darkness; not a single light was burning. With extreme trepidation, I slipped through the black, silent kitchen into the living room.

"Daddy, are you in here?" I whispered timidly. No response. As my eyes adjusted to the gloom, I could make out daddy's form, sitting with a beer bottle between his legs, staring absently at a lifeless television. Moving closer, I felt my shoes crunching on glass and realized with alarm that something had been thrown at the TV; its screen was broken, shards of it scattered everywhere. Fearfully, I asked, "Daddy, what happened? Did you get to see me on TV?"

"The goddamned set went dead right before the show started, and I missed the whole bloody thing. Go on upstairs with the rest of them so I can drink my beer in peace."

Even in triumph, there was failure. Those jagged bits of glass littering the floor, mirrored for me all the promises made, then broken over the many years of childhood. No matter how great our pain or disappointment, we were always expected to ignore our feelings, never to question why – just dust ourselves off and carry on as if nothing had happened.

I crept upstairs to join my siblings. They explained that when daddy couldn't get the TV to work (a common occurrence, since nothing, including our parents, was ever in very good working order), he hurled his his beer bottle at it and then banished everyone to their bedrooms. So now we waited for daddy to either leave the house or pass out so we could return downstairs to finish our homework and eat dinner. So much for my 15 minutes of fame.

Food was a preoccupation, something we thought about constantly, whether we were in school, at home, weekend camping or swimming in the river. Contrary to the indigestible, government-issued powdered milk we drank at home, I found utterly irresistible the milk at school, which came in small, red and white cartons. Every day at noon, little Johnny Allen would wheel the milk cart around, offering the half-pint containers for 3 cents apiece. It was my introduction to credit. If you didn't have the money at the time, your teacher would mark it on your account, to be paid in full at the end of the week. For most students this was not a problem, since their parents provided them with milk money in addition to their regular allowance. For me, however, it was a catastrophe.

The watered-down milk at home became even less appetizing after I had tasted the authentic stuff at school. My calcium-deprived bones and I were instantly addicted – I simply could not abstain from ordering that milk. Day after day I charged it, agonizing over my accumulating debt, but unable to produce a satisfactory solution. I was six years old and unemployed; asking mom and daddy for the money was out of the question. They would punish me severely for ordering the milk and for racking up a bill we could not pay.

Weeks went by, and my debt continued to mount. Finally out of patience, my teacher spoke firmly to me after class, "Gail, you are going to *have* to pay me by tomorrow." With no recourse except debtor's prison, I burst into tears and confessed my sins to her. Sympathizing with my misery, she volunteered to settle my account, which was by this time a whopping two dollars. It might just as well have been $200, because either way I did not have the money. Furthermore, she offered to treat me a carton of milk each week. I cannot express how much I looked forward to that one glorious day when I could consume without guilt my 100% Grade A, homogenized, fully paid for carton of whole milk.

Now that I had a milk patron, I began strategizing how to finagle my classmates out of portions of their lunches. Peering into my own nearly empty sack was so depressing, when all around me was such mouth-watering bounty, displayed on other kids' desks. So in third grade I befriended the fattest, ugliest girl in class. Her name was Susan, and she was constantly ridiculed by the other students. Consequently, she had the personality of a porcupine. However, her lunches were par excellence, and I drooled daily, watching her consume such sumptuous delicacies as ham and roast beef sandwiches, potato chips, vegetable sticks (with dip!), cookies and grapes. But the piece de resistance was her Hostess Cupcake and/or Snowball. Some days she even had *one of each* in her lunch! I coveted her food to such a degree that in desperation I concocted a scheme I hoped would be foolproof.

It seemed reasonable to assume that if I became her friend and sat with her at lunchtime, in return she would surely reward me. So after a month of shared conversation, she was in the palm of my hand. However, lest I appear too greedy, at first I accepted only small offerings – a half-sandwich here, a few carrot sticks there – until she spoke the words I had waited weeks to hear: "Gail, you've been so nice to me; why don't you take my lunch today?" and pushed a veritable banquet onto my desk (not to worry about Susan starving, her mother always packed extra snacks in case she got hungry later in the day). In my defense, I rationalized that Susan had been losing weight since meeting me, and my scrawny frame could certainly use the extra calories, so it was a win/win situation.

This charade continued for months until the day my teacher, Mrs. Larson (whom I was devoted to) asked me to stay after class. Smiling in approval, she said, "Gail, I just wanted to tell you how pleased I am that you have become Susan's friend. I know because of her weight, the other kids are always laughing at her. But you have been able to see beyond that. I am proud of you for being so compassionate."

Well, you can imagine how that made me feel – lower than a snake. Looking down at the floor, I accepted her misguided compliments. By next morning I devised a plan to make amends and to restore myself into her good graces.

Subsequently, for penance, I abstained from eating any part of Susan's lunch, quid pro quo. I had consumed my last Hostess cupcake. For the rest of the term, I continued to sit with her at noon and, painful as it was, became a real friend to her. Susan got fatter, while I got thinner, but I had learned a valuable lesson.

As a fourth-grader, I struggled terribly with cursive writing because I was left-handed. No amount of tears or practice would make those letters come out right. Even so, I was horrified at the end of the term when my teacher, Mrs. Kaiserman, gave me a D in penmanship. With trembling hands, I waited my turn in the report card line behind the older girls. Daddy was furious at the grade – even though I had A's in all my other subjects – and yelled, "How could anyone be so stupid as to get a D in penmanship? That's the *easiest* class there is!" I stood there like a statue.

To make matters worse, I had brought home other school assignments which required a parent's signature, to be returned to Mrs. Kaiserman the next day. Well, of course, a simple signature was not enough for daddy. In his rage, he scrawled every profanity he could think of in heavy black ink all over my schoolwork, words I had never heard before. I figured they must be really bad and certainly didn't belong on a fourth-grader's classwork. Shoving them back at me, he sneered, "Now give these to your *precious* teacher and see what she thinks of you now!"

I gathered up the soiled papers, thinking how dirty they looked, and dreaded the next day. For us, teachers were nothing short of saints. Our main objective was to always please them, and in so doing, we hoped they would reciprocate with praise and attention. Conversely, to be humiliated so completely in their presence was unbearable.

Surprisingly, I noticed a significant shift in our relationship after returning my paperwork. Where before, Mrs. Kaiserman had always been considerate and pleasant, she now *lavished* me with her time and attention. You would have thought I was an accomplished calligrapher by the way she praised my handwriting. And, no, I had not miraculously conquered the discipline of cursive writing; my writing was as abysmal as ever.

Even more preposterous, she gave me an *A* the next term! It wasn't deserved – we both knew it. However, as a caring and sympathetic teacher, she weighed giving an accurate grade against a little left-handed girl's inability to satisfy the impossible expectations of a perfectionist father. Compassionately, she tipped the scale in my favor. To this day, I refuse to write in cursive; instead I print anything that needs to be hand written. Best to not press my luck, I decided.

In fifth grade, my fruit cravings began. Since we were rarely given anything except apples or canned peaches at home, I began to lust after oranges. A homely boy named Mike sat in front of me. I think he had a bit of a crush on me. He tried to make inroads, somehow guessing the way to my heart was through my stomach. One afternoon he gave me the orange from his lunch, and from that day on I was hooked. I became a citrus junkie. Coyly, I let him borrow my pencil, loaned him comic books – in short, did anything I could think of to separate him from his orange. And each noon hour he succumbed to my flirtations, happily turning over the coveted fruit. Heaven only knows what might have become of our relationship had his mother one day put a grapefruit instead of an orange into his lunch box.

# A WATER TRILOGY

Dad on the river

Denae

Langston Hughes famously wrote "The Negro Speaks of Rivers," wherein he reminisced wistfully and eloquently about the muddy Mississippi, pyramids along the banks of the Nile, and bathing in the Euphrates "when dawns were young."

His poem evokes an entirely different set of memories for Elaine and myself as we too travel back in unrhymed recollections to rivers and streams and other water images, both real and metaphoric, from our own past. We wish we had known those same "ancient, dusky rivers" that Hughes wrote of. Instead, we must journey back to images more like Ophelia floating atop an indifferent current, or the Lady of Shallot adrift on her barge, disappearing into doom, far from the protective shores of Camelot. Let us speak, then, of the rivers and waters we have known.

It is Saturday night, wash night. Not our clothes. Us. All the kids. Mom drags the metal wash tub into the middle of the living room. Daddy has water boiling on the wood stove in the kitchen in two big pots. He pours the water into the tub until it's half full, then adds some cold water. Mom is putting old rags around the tub so the floor won't warp when the water sloshes out. Elaine is 12, Diane and I are 9, and Karen is 8. The younger kids, Keith, Gail and Gwen, are sitting on the couch naked. They always get to wash first. I guess mom thinks they are cleaner than us big girls and won't get the water so dirty.

One by one daddy drops them into the tub, scrubs on the soap and rinses them. When he lifts them out, mom towels them dry. Elaine's turn. We all watch as she pulls off her clothes. My turn. I really don't like Saturday night. I don't like being naked in front of everyone, especially not in front of daddy. But I have to do it. Everyone does. No one questions what he says; we are not allowed to. So I lift my leg over the washtub edge to step in. Grey scum floats on top like pond algae.

The water is barely warm. *Lucky little kids – they always get the clean, hot water. Be quick,* I tell myself. The quicker I wash and get out, the quicker I can get into my pajamas. Karen is next. Glad *that's* over.

The dilemma of the bath at home became the dilemma of the shower at school. That same wolf who had so terrorized Little Red Riding Hood and her grandmother was now residing not between the pages of that fairy tale but in the hallways and locker rooms of Greenacres Junior High. How can I be so sure? Well, he showed up in the eighth grade girls' P.E. room right after baseball practice one day when we were undressing and showering in preparation for our next class.

The old Greenacres Junior High School in 1962 was an outdated, two-story red brick structure, overburdened with its student population. Classrooms were low-ceilinged, square and tight, corridors narrow and jammed with book-toting students who often bruised themselves against the heavy combination locks jutting out from vertical metal lockers lining the hallways.

Even more outdated was the girls' locker room. Ten or twelve concrete cubicles, which served as shower stalls crowded the center of the space, while alongside were wooden benches and wire mesh baskets for storing clothes and shoes. The stall partitions were about six feet high and open at the top. Once inside, if you looked up you could see the dozen shower heads streaming with hot water, their heavy mist darkening the room, obscuring forms and edges – an effect similar to being trapped in the back streets of London on a dense, foggy evening – Jack the Ripper weather. Within this claustrophobic milieu, each of us hurried in and out of our clothes, trying to shower and towel dry as speedily as possible to accommodate the impatient, noisy line of girls still waiting for their turn.

Yes, the wolf had learned a thing or two about disguise and deception since those early days when he so provoked me by the transparency of his masquerade. He was no longer impersonating grandmothers. But clearly he was still gobbling up little girls, this time disguised as a P.E teacher. I was fooled for a while, even though "she" looked more like a "he" with her dark, short-cropped hair, stocky muscular build and raspy unfeminine voice. Not for her the starchy-collared, floral printed dresses that the other teachers wore. She fooled us all as we took her instruction, practicing gymnastics, baseball and basketball.

My guard was down because this was school and not home, where I never felt safe. Here adults observed the rules, praised you with A's and wrote nice things about you on your report cards. So, yes, I had relaxed my guard and had forgotten Rule Number One: Vigilant, be ever vigilant.

I was standing naked in the close, steamy shower stall – all around me the sounds of giggling girls and running water pelting concrete floors – when I heard the wolf. His voice was low, insinuating, authoritative: "Sally, don't you know how to wash properly? Your underwear always looks dirty, like the rest of your clothing. I guess I'll just have to get in there with you to show you how to use soap and water."

My body went rigid as I strained to hear Sally's reply, her outraged refusal. But there was none, only the continuing sound of splashing water from the twelve stalls. Somewhere in that maze of cubicles beneath the thickening smog was Mrs. Turk, our gym teacher, washing down Sally. The wolf had gotten into the showers! Poor Sally with her prematurely large breasts, stringy blonde hair and timid demeanor. She was not my friend but still I knew her like one knows any student who is in class day after day, answering questions, receiving test scores, or gossiping at recess. She came from a large family, not unlike ours – abusive, poor and hungry. She could not speak up to defend herself, nor could she run from that tight, dark cubicle – because she did not know how. No parent had taught her what to do or to say. She was trapped in that shower stall as surely as if she were in a prison cell.

I could have been Sally, so keenly did I feel her shame, her fear, her ignorance, her inability to protest or to run in escape. And so the water – guileless, guiltless – kept gushing from above her head over her stringy blonde hair and down her too-large breasts, as we both kept our silence.

In a panic, I rushed from my partition to yank blouse and skirt over my dripping skin, my thoughts a desperate jumble. *Would I be*

*next? Who else had attracted the wolf? Was Sally to be his only victim?*
The other girls – naked beneath the rushing waters, trapped by their undress and their innocence – surely they too had heard the wolf's words. Did they think they were at risk? Did they hear the words with the same fear I had experienced? Did they know about wolves that pretended to be teachers?

I had to get out of the locker room. In the days that followed, I stopped taking showers after I heard the wolf go a second time into Sally's bath. I waited to see if the other girls would sound the alarm and tell their parents or the principal. Eavesdropping on them I had hoped to hear some plan for reprisal, some action to stop this outrage. The subject was never mentioned.

Even though I did not know how to help Sally, I did know enough to stay clear of those rooms where the wolf could watch you undress, could watch you step naked into the shower, and then join you in that act of cleansing – making you dirtier than you had ever been before with all that fresh soap and water. Then try and make yourself clean again. See how hard you have to scrub scrub scrub to get rid of the dirt.

Oh, that wolf was a crafty one; he had mastered the art of deception. This was not to be the last time I would encounter him either. He would cross my path several more times as the years went by – once as a therapist who was treating both me and Gwen. Another time he would disguise himself as a boyfriend. But thinking back, what pains me most deeply is the number of times he masqueraded as my own father.

A few more details are necessary to complete this story. Sally did not go on to complete ninth grade at Greenacres Junior High; she stopped attending classes mid-term. Soon after, word got around that she was pregnant. After that I never saw or heard of her again. But I did not forget her. I cannot because she is lodged permanently in a chamber of my mind. We visit there, she and I, from time to time. Our conversation varies little, with me doing most of the talking. "How are you today, Sally? I am so sorry; can you forgive me for not reporting

Mrs. Turk to the principal? Did your life get any better? You did not deserve what happened to you."

Many years later I read these words in a book's preface:

> *Let us remember, what hurts the victim most is not*
> *the cruelty of the oppressor, but the silence of the*
> *bystander.*        *Elie Wiesel*

My chest tightens with anxiety each time I ponder these memories. No, I could not protect Sally – but even worse, so much worse, were all those times at home when I stood by, stiff with fear, unable to protect my own sister in the bath with my father. Neither sister, brother, nor mother – I could not protect any of them.


Elaine

We were crossing the River Styx, all four of us, with Charon the Boatman guiding the oars like a gondolier in Venice – the water falling from his paddles quiet, almost musical, with the cadence of his rowing. We had no shirts on; our bodies were bare from the waist up. "Take off your shirts," Charon had said, his voice sounding just like our father's. "It's a good way to get a tan."

The sun was hot – I was 13, Denae and Diane 10, and Karen 8. We didn't want to take off our clothes. Why did we need to be tanned? We were only crossing the river. Who would care when we reached the other side whether our skin was white or brown? Hands stretched across our chests, cowering and ashamed, we passed other boats bearing curious faces and lingering stares, while blue herons waded in the shallows through yellow marsh iris.

Such a long, wide river. How far away the green banks of the shore seemed. We bunched together to hide our nudity, like a lotus unwilling to open its petals. Where were we going? Charon was so slow, deliberately so. Why did he look so much like our father?

"Give me an oar," I said, reaching for the long handle. Two can row faster than one."

"No, no – that's my job. Not for you. Besides, we're in no hurry."

Hardly glancing at the water lilies we were passing in the sluggish current, I thought only of my shirt and how much I wanted to put it back on. Usually I enjoyed pulling up their long slippery stems, those sinewy roots that surely must stretch all the way to China. But not today.

Pensively, I thought of the Lady of Shallot, drifting peacefully in her barge along the river current, her loosened hair and flowing garments coloring the water like a floating flower garden. She had no need of a boatman in her gentle passage down the riverway. Would she mind, I wondered, if we four sisters were to join her – five damsels then, trusting a kindly current to see us safely to shore.

# TWO BITS, FOUR BITS

Elaine, Mom, Diane, Karen

It was clear to me at an early age that employment was a very desirable activity, a necessity in fact toward acquiring bubble gum, movie fare, roller skates, comic books – all those luxury items lacking in our household. And, although not employed himself, daddy was an eager and innovative mentor in familiarizing us with the nuances and complexities of the workaday world. Indeed, such was his influence that by the age of ten, holding down a job and earning my own money seemed perfectly normal.

My inaugural experience was in grade school when I sold Camp Fire cookies outside the tavern door at the Greenacres Shopping Center. Daddy came up with the brilliant idea of posting me there while he went in for a few beers.

"You've got to smarten up, Gail," he had said. "Why go to the trouble of knocking on all the neighbors' doors when no one really wants the cookies anyway? Hell, those bums at the tavern will buy 'anything' once they're liquored up with a few drinks!"

So there I found myself the next Saturday afternoon standing below the "Lucky Lager" sign in my red and blue Camp Fire outfit, praying that the exiting drunks would just buy my cookies and leave me alone. Even though daddy's theory proved profitable, and I did sell a lot of cookies, I always felt afraid standing outside that door. My mind was filled with thoughts of Candy Rogers, the young Camp Fire Girl from Spokane who had disappeared the previous year. Her picture had been posted all over town, and the newspapers had run front-page stories about the round-the-clock searches for her. But she was never found.

Someone, I thought, could just as easily nab me… and I would never be heard from again, either.

In fifth grade that same shopping center provided other opportunities for making pocket money. Each Saturday, Keith at 12 and I, would arrive at 5am with brooms and a dustpan to sweep the sidewalks, huge parking lot and all eight business storefronts. Once the customers began arriving at 9am, each shopkeeper would pay us 50¢. My cut, as assistant, for the four hours of filthy grueling work was about two dollars.

At 12, I began babysitting, preferring it to strawberry picking, which was the primary summer employment for Elaine, Diane, Denae and Karen. I was paid fifty cents an hour (sometimes more after midnight, which never made sense to me, since by then the kids were in bed, so there was little else to do).

Our family was a popular source for babysitters in Greenacres because there were so many of us—all reliable and the right age: 12-18 – and because our neighborhood had dozens of children whose parents loved to go out drinking and partying on weekends.

The homes we entered, although often dangerous due to alcoholism, domestic violence and varying infidelities, nonetheless attracted our labors – partly due to the money and partly due to the many temptations not available at our house. Such amenities included: diet pills, gin, whiskey (which Diane and Karen mixed with Kool-Aid before drinking), potato chips, nylons, soda, ice cream – and the magazines! "True Detective," "Crime Magazine," "Adults Only." All graphic and gritty, exposing us to unimagined appetites and behaviors. All of which we duly confessed to Father Brunner at St. Mary's.

One hot summer night while fast asleep at home, we were awakened by shouts and an explosion of breaking glass. Peering out our 2nd-story bedroom window, we saw a naked teenage boy burst from the doorway of the house across the street. More breaking glass, then gunshots, followed by ear-shattering threats helped us piece together a story of love-gone-wrong. Apparently, the homeowner, a 35-year-old schoolteacher and mother of four, had not counted on her husband returning that evening.

Despite another hour of slamming doors and yelling voices, no one called the police. In our blue-collar neighborhood where tempers often flared, it was not considered a neighborly thing to do.

<u>Denae</u>

My own babysitting experiences can be summed up in one word. Normie. Actually that word represents the low point in an otherwise exemplary career.

As I think back, perhaps it all began with the chocolate chip cookies. Mrs. Porter had given me permission to make a batch of them, just before patting Normie's little sandy-haired head good-bye, on her way to the podiatrist. And there lined up on the counter before me, like a banquet table in Bangladesh, were a full package of Hershey's chocolate chips, a half pound of shelled walnuts, *real* butter, *real* eggs, and a two ounce vial of *real* vanilla extract.

Mr. and Mrs. Porter lived across the street from us in a small white clapboard house with black shutters. Since Lee (Mr. Porter) was tall and thin, while Geraldine was short and fat, I always associated them with the nursery rhyme, "Jack Sprat could eat no fat, his wife could eat no lean, and so between them both, you see, they licked the platter clean."

Little Normie was at present living with them as a foster child. At age six, he was regarded as a slow learner. In those days his mental condition would have been described as retarded. Which made him, no doubt, harder to place. But nonetheless he was a sweet quiet boy with fair skin and cornflower blue eyes.

My babysitting duties that day were relatively simple: "Keep Normie out of the dirt. And be sure he has lunch and an afternoon nap." Then as an afterthought, as Mrs. Porter was attempting to squeeze her ample proportions, corseted by a too-tight sunflower printed dress through the door frame, she remarked, "And if you'd like to bake some cookies, the ingredients are sitting there on the counter."

I smiled the smile of lottery winners everywhere. Bliss beyond measure. Had I heard her correctly? Alone, entirely alone with all those delectable items, and no adult to monitor how much cookie batter I ate or how many additional chips and walnuts I might stuff into my mouth. Uncounted and unsupervised. What more could a babysitter ask for?

In my euphoria I actually forgot about Normie that first half hour as I tore open the bag of chocolate drops, inhaled the vanilla extract and checked out cookie recipes. Bustling happily about the kitchen, a lone treacherous thought began inching its way into my awareness. *What if this baking invitation is really a test of my honesty? A ruse by Mrs. Porter to determine how reliable I am?* Possibly, she, like dad, had spy cameras concealed around the house to monitor and record subversive activities – like babysitters gorging on her food. I made a quick room to room search, looking for tell-tale signs of surveillance equipment: inside broom closets, around light bulbs, atop door frames. However, since we kids had exhaustively searched our own rooms at home without success, I was not entirely certain what these devices looked like, or if I would recognize them were I to find one.

Returning then to the kitchen, my initial elation was dampened by the necessity to now exercise restraint in my consumption. With all the ingredients at hand, the only item lacking was a mixing bowl, so I reached into the lower cupboards towards a thick-walled green bowl just visible inside the dark space. Clumsily, in my haste I knocked it against the wood siding and Calamity! It broke into three pieces – fell apart as cleanly as a coconut cleaved through by a machete blade.

I was horrified. What would Mrs. Porter say? At home, such a misdeed would earn me a night without supper – at the very least. Now, two punishments were inevitable: one from Geraldine, who would surely withhold my babysitting pay and another from dad when she told him what I had done.

I was sick. Desperate. And then I remembered Normie. Yes, Normie, indeed. Where was my little charge? In that instant his person – not his whereabouts – became the sole object of my attentions. A solution to my dilemma illumined the moment as though a religious epiphany. Mentally, I began to fine-tune its choreography.

In my defense, I am not proud of my actions, but after all I was only 14 and facing two punishments for an honest accident. At the time it seemed the only reasonable course to follow.

Among the criminal classes there must exist a certain pride in successfully executing a crime. Now finding myself within this membership, I will admit my deed was premeditated (although with no malice of forethought) and that yes, I did feel a certain vanity over how artfully I discharged the fait d'accompli.

But first things first. Returning to the scene of the crime, I thrust my hand below the counter into the jumble of cooking vessels. Collecting the green shards, I carefully reassembled them, pushing other pots into place around them for support so that once again the bowl was whole.

Now to locate Normie. "Normie! Normie!" I called out the front door, hoping he wasn't chasing cats or squirrels down Sprague Avenue. He would never find his way back. "It's lunch time. Aren't you hungry?" So quietly did he enter the house that at first I didn't realize he was in the room with me.

"Oh, Normie, there you are. Say, will you do me a favor? I'm baking cookies and need a bowl. Would you be a good boy and hand me that green one inside the cabinet?" Holding my breath, I watched as his awkward pale fingers closed around the container, struggling to lift it. Which, of course, made it fall apart all over again.

"Oh I broke it. I broke it!" he began wailing. "Mama'll spank me…"

"Now don't worry sweetie," I reassured him, patting his quaking shoulder. "It wasn't your fault, I saw the whole thing. I'll explain to mama that it was just an accident," adding "and I promise you won't get in trouble."

My blackened soul filled with relief since now the guilty party was no longer me. And even if there was a hidden camera in the kitchen, since I had never actually pulled the bowl out from the cabinet, I reasoned that the lens could not possibly have recorded me causing the breakage. Safe. On all counts.

After calming Normie sufficiently into falling asleep for his nap, I proceeded to finally make the cookies – eating only a few chocolate chips, and no batter at all, because I was beginning to feel guilty over my deception, and was a tad bit worried that Normie might be punished after all – in spite of my lengthy, prepared list of excuses for him.

So when Mrs. Porter returned a few hours later, the words came tumbling from my lips – how poor little Normie tried to be "so helpful in handing me the bowl…that it was definitely *not* his fault…."

Amazingly, she seemed genuinely unconcerned, dismissing the matter airily with "Oh, that's all right. It was an old bowl – probably had a crack in it that I didn't notice." Giving Normie a big hug, she headed out the door with him to pick some string beans from the garden.

Unbelieveable. My eyes trailed their retreating figures in disbelief. *She didn't even care. She wasn't the least bit mad.* I was more shocked by her complacency than by the actual bowl breaking. No fireworks at all. Was this really how other families reacted when you did something wrong?

Then a bleak thought occurred to me: I had just sold my immortal soul for a handful of chocolate chip cookies – in order to avoid a punishment that would never have transpired. A sobering reflection. Clearly, six year old, mentally retarded Normie was my moral superior, in every respect. I was humbled by the realization.

Gail

By age 14, I was working part-time as a housekeeper for an upper middle class woman, who was recovering from a hysterectomy. I'll never forget how dumbfounded I was the day she asked: "Gail, would you make up my bed with these linens?" and handed me two sheets. As I stood there eyeing her king-sized mattress, I could not, for the life of me figure out why rich people slept on top of *two* sheets. However, reluctant to show my ignorance, I waited until returning home to question mom.

"They don't sleep on *top* of the sheets," she replied. "They sleep *between* them." What an epiphany. In our house where you were lucky to have "a" sheet on your bed, the idea of two seemed a monumental extravagance. Quickly, I calculated how much longer it would take me to do our family laundry with two sheets per bed. It was a daunting thought.

Further mystifying to me was why you would *iron* pillowcases – such an unbelievable waste of time and energy. Yet my employer insisted all pillowcases, including her children's, be starched and ironed. Rich people certainly had some peculiar ways.

My ignorance of domestic technology was further challenged the day I was asked to use her vacuum and carpet cleaner. I had never before seen such devices. We didn't even own a clothes dryer until I was in junior high – its long awaited arrival celebrated by displaying it prominently in the kitchen next to the stove (the dryer also served as a repository for dirty dishes at those times when Diane's boyfriends showed up unexpectedly). How could I explain to my employer that our house contained no cleaning equipment that you plugged in? Rather, we swept our carpet with a broom (raising clouds of choking dirt, like a Texas dust storm). When the carpet was too stained for sweeping, we scrubbed it on our hands and knees with a steel-wired brush and a bucket of Tide water.

One of my more memorable jobs as a teen was working at the greenhouse of Imogene and Atticus Preach – hardworking, god-fearing Baptists from the Oklahoma Bible Belt, who expected an honest day's labor from their children and employees.

By way of keeping our thoughts focused and spiritually inclined, Atticus kept the sound system tuned to local radio station KCFA (Keep Christ First Always). Consequently, I watered, thinned and transplanted thousands of seedlings to the beat of "Rock of Ages" and "What a Friend We Have in Jesus."

Wednesday was my favorite workday because the Preach's would be away for hours at Prayer Meeting. As soon as their car left the parking lot, my best friend Shelly and I would switch the radio knob to a rock 'n roll station, smoke cigarettes and chase each other through the greenhouse while belting out, "I Can't Get No Satisfaction," "Ruby Tuesday" – anything by the Stones. Imogene and Atticus would have been horrified by our blasphemy, but it was the only way Shelly and I could tolerate the monotony.

Unquestionably, the most lucrative of my early jobs was waitressing. Even though the hourly wage in 1970 was only 90¢ an hour, I could usually earn $30 in tips per shift, which was a fortune to me.

That first summer, Diane and I both worked at the same restaurant, a Denny's in downtown Spokane. We were saving for a Club Med vacation. The hours were long, the dining area cavernous, and the manager, Mr. Hay – the reincarnation of an S.S. officer from the Third Reich – insisted that Diane and I waitress the busy 40-table room by ourselves. The only thing that made it bearable was that Diane and I worked together in this madness. I lost ten lbs that summer, and my feet have never fully healed.

Instead of helping us when the restaurant was packed, Mr. Hay would stand at the register, imperiously calling out: 99! 85! 68! Each number a secret code for such things as: your order is up; customer at the door; a table needs to be bussed.

At summer's end, for our vacation we ended up at the Oregon coast rather than the Mediterranean, but I still felt like a millionaire. The balance of my earnings was banked for a trip to Europe the following year when I turned 19.

When the time came to depart, I did not have the bus fare from Spokane to Seattle, where my plane was scheduled to leave from, so I asked mom if she would drive me to the I-90 freeway entrance. From there I hoped to hitch a ride to Sea-Tac Airport.

Her actions in response have bothered me ever since.

"Sure. We can leave right after breakfast," she had agreed, then drove us the 5 miles to the freeway. As I stepped away from the car, she rolled her window down and called out, "Have fun!" leaving me standing there with my backpack and 300 miles to go.

Years later, still upset and still hoping for some maternal concern, I questioned her as to that long ago day and her total disregard for my safety. "Mom, didn't it occur to you that it would be dangerous for me to hitchhike 300 miles by myself?"

With a look of bewilderment, she responded, "But Gail, you have always been so mature and responsible that I didn't feel I had the right to interfere."

Funny, that's what I thought mothers were supposed to do. Oh well, on the bright side – at least I didn't end up like Candy Rogers.

# STRAWBERRY FIELDS FOREVER

How aptly this Beatles tune reflects for us older girls the single most defining activity of our childhood. However, just as you cannot comprehend a pig by looking at a pork sausage, likewise "Strawberry Fields Forever" does not tell the whole story. Although the *forever* part does characterize the seemingly endless, mile-long rows picking berries beneath the merciless summer sun. Time lost all meaning, melting as it did into forever. Surely at least one lifetime passed before we could graduate from high school and begin passage into our next existence.

Diane and I were seventh-graders, Elaine a ninth grader, when in 1961 we were hired by soft-spoken, church-going Phil Hurry – considerably fattening the home coffers, especially when younger sister Karen joined us a year later. Working full time in the summer, collectively, we brought home about $350 a month, which paid the $60 mortgage payment, utilities, and half the food bill. With dad unemployed and mom busy at home with the five younger kids, we four teens were at this time the family's sole financial support.

Granted, such domestic stability was immensely gratifying, but the real motivator for us was even more primal. Escape from dad! Sanctuary among the strawberries. With his explosive temper and obsession with keeping us isolated, we were ecstatic at the thought of 8-10 hours a day, UNSUPERVISED! We might even get to practice some flirting skills with the better-looking teenage boys. Possibilities of the forbidden loomed infinite.

Denae

Typically, our day began about 7 a.m. (Buenas dias! Cisco) as we began the mile trek from the Greenacres house, straight as the crow flies, along Sprague Avenue to Mr. Hurry's. Not a daunting hike, even on the 90-degree July mornings, since we were all in superb health.

No, it was not the mile walk that undid us each morning; it was the homes we had to pass to reach our destination – most specifically *Bev Southern's* home.

Cheerleader, Lilac princess, Homecoming queen – she was in all our classes. Every morning, six days a week, we had to walk by in our rag-tag clothes – cotton babushkas tied on our heads, dirty sneakers on our feet. Slogging along as we did through mud and dirt over crushed red strawberries, it was pointless to try and keep them "tennis-white" for appearances. Rather, they looked more like paint-spattered scraps from a Jackson Pollock canvas.

We could have been migrant workers up from the Southern California fields. In fact, one day while reading a magazine article on Cesar Chavez, I was disturbed to learn that strawberry picking is regarded as the most grueling of all manual harvests, requiring as it does a chronic stooping or kneeling position.

But it was on blonde, beautiful Beverly that our thoughts centered as we four neared her brick house with the oversize picture window in front. I can hear Diane voicing our feelings: "She's probably at the breakfast table right now, pouring milk over her cornflakes, watching us parade by. I can *feel* her eyeballs on me. Or else she's still asleep in her bed, dreaming about sunbathing at Sandy Beach in her blue string bikini, with all the boys ogling her." Continuing, her voice deepening with resentment, "I just bet she's already told JoAnn Walker, Rondy Wallace and all the other girls at school that we work in the fields across the road from her. They can all have a good laugh. They think we're just a bunch of nothing-burgers."

"Yeah," Elaine had agreed. "It wouldn't be so bad if this was a babysitting job. No, we have to be day laborers…working like men… always something to make us look different – one more thing to humiliate us."

By the time we reached the strawberry patch, Mr. Hurry would have already assembled the flimsy wooden flat-carriers and crates. "Hey," he'd quip, "it's my elite crew! First to arrive, as always! Excel will be out in a couple of minutes. She has a few instructions about topping off your flats the way she likes it done."

Naturally, it was flattering to be heralded as the "elite" pickers, but considering the rest of his crew – scrappy teenage boys looking to earn weekend, drive-in-movie money and random transients hoping to pay for last night's motel bill – we kept the compliments in perspective. It was a continuing source of exasperation for Mr. Hurry that his work force was so unreliable. Only the four Veselits girls exhibited the constancy and superior work ethic that he so prized.

At his side, through 25 years of farming and marriage, was his much-esteemed wife, Hazel, whom he called Excel, so excellent were her standards. Not as enamored of her virtues, we called her "Witch Hazel" – behind her back, of course. Dour as a spinster school marm in expression and manner, she would march Gestapo-like through the fields – a veritable field marshal, with her sombrero-brimmed straw hat – surveying our progress, timing our breaks and checking for over-looked ripe berries.

Mr. Hurry, too, was like-minded, if not single-minded in his efforts to make us ever more efficient. Even his name presaged his obsession with speed. Complimentary he might be, but we were not blind to his ambitions to prod, flatter, and develop us into the highest order of berry pickers – the "summa cum laudes of the field."

Only one other came close to equaling our amazing performances – one of the three Rapp brothers who worked alongside us. I cannot recall his first name, so indistinguishable was he from his kin – all Abe Lincoln-tall, and quiet as moss grass. But this one brother was so fast in filling his flats that in admiration we dubbed him "Vacuum Hands."

Ever competitive and wishing to retain our high status with Mr. Hurry, we kept a keen eye to his progress through adjacent rows, watching as his fingers seemingly suctioned the berries from the plants. A shame that his dazzling technique so indiscriminately gathered the hard white ones as well, along with the occasional green leaf or caterpillar – a fault that inevitably barred him from membership in our elite summa group. A grievous fault indeed, which drew heavy criticism from the ever-vigilant Hazel. Grim faced, several times a day, she would confront him and his overflowing flats, flinging the offending debris at his feet.

However, all things considered, I do believe Elaine ("Speedball," as we called her) was consistently the fastest picker. Adding to her fame was the fact that she had never left behind an unpicked red berry – not once! As mistress-in-charge of quality control, Witch Hazel simply could not concede such perfection. She became as a blood hound in Elaine's wake, probing a thousand, ten-thousand plants for that orphaned object. To no avail. In Elaine, she had met her match.

Yet, much as we all admired her abilities, we knew that dad was partly responsible, since he constantly pressured her to be the best: "As the oldest, I expect you to pick faster than your sisters. It's up to you to set the pace. If not, I'll damn well know who the lazy one is!" So the satisfaction that should have been Elaine's reward was all too often subverted by this immutable mandate – a dark cloud following her even on the sunniest day.

"That's it! Nada. Nyet." Even the crème de la crème have a breaking point. And Elaine had just reached hers. It was time for revolt. "For my next flat, I am going to do the worst job possible. Goodbye, Queen of the Berry Pickers!" She was on her way to becoming, in H.G. Wells' words, "a fine flower of insurrection."

Ah, the bliss of sabotage, the sweet revenge of deception. A puckish smile settled upon Elaine's lips. Turning slightly to scan the fields for Hazel and Mr. Hurry, she then reached into the foliage for the hardest, whitest strawberries she could find, filling the bottoms of all 12 hallocks with them. Next, a fistful of leaves. Humming purposefully, she gaily wadded them into the boxes. Then, scooping up some loose pebbles, she gently tucked them into greenery for all the world like a mother robin arranging her newly laid eggs.

Yes indeed, the joys of mutiny. Her humming became louder, more pronounced – a full orchestra of sound. Was it the "Hallelujah

Chorus?" With building crescendo, her flat was nearly full. Gingerly raising it, she tested its weight. And now – Elaine beamed to herself – the coup de grace. Meticulously, she gathered the biggest ripest strawberries, layering them thickly and uniformly, as though drawing a rich red tablecloth across the surface.

Voila! The deed was done. She carried her flat to the storage shed where dozens of others were already stacked and set it down.

Adieu and adieu, the infidel departs. Elaine returned in the most exalted of spirits to her abandoned row, resuming her picking and the monotony of field protocols. But today it did not really matter, so buoyant were her thoughts, brimming with freedom and the intoxicating exhilaration of insurrection.

Whether viewing Mr. Hurry's property as a customer or as one of the field crew, the seven-acre vista in summer was pretty as a picture postcard. Wide, pleated ribbons of green rows alternated with the rosy pink swathes of soil, seeming to replicate the tulip fields of Holland before the blooming season. Shoulder-high hedges of raspberries, like boxwood thickets bordering an English cottage garden, were fragrant with the soft rouged fruits, as ruby-throated hummingbirds and frisky sparrows nipped in and out of the foliage. With scarlet-stained hands, sun-browned skin, and colorful bandanna-wrapped heads – immersed as we were in our labors – we could have been tropical birds gathering seeds on some Jamaican plantation.

In early summer, each morning upon arrival, surprisingly enough, the first order of the day was of poetic consideration:

*I come to the garden alone*
*While the dew is still on the roses...*

Not only did the dew need to be off the roses, more importantly, it needed to be off the *strawberries* or we could not begin picking for the day. To fill our flats with wet berries was to invite disaster – that fuzzy white fellow, mold – which could form within hours under the hot sun, spoiling the entire crate. Glumly, impatiently, we would sit in a semicircle next to the plants, Mr. Hurry leaning against his hoe. "Nope, not yet. Still too wet; it'll be another half-hour, at least." Mother Nature was not to be rushed, no matter how fixedly we stared at those uncooperative bushes. Our thoughts soon teetered less on the poetic and more on the dogmatic – Dew be damned. Let's get on with the show!

Tedious as the picking was, it could not compare to the boredom of weeding and hoeing in the early spring. There we would find ourselves after school and on weekends. In the fruit paddies. Chop, chop… clunk, clunk. Our metal-edged hoes clanked noisily against rocks and pebbles as we tilled the hard soil around the plants, occasionally pausing to look ahead at the endlessly long rows bristling with thistles and dandelions – while behind us was the ubiquitous Hazel.

To occupy our thoughts, Diane and Karen invented a mythical kingdom, co-existing in parallel time beneath the fields we worked in – a reverse Hades. It was here that we longed to dwell, munching on Sumatran oranges and pecan biscotti, instead of clearing dusty brown acres of rocks and weeds.

As in any good fairy tale, transformation was key. On rainy or sultry days when our bosses were missing from the fields, we imagined them to be in the glades below us – their everyday forms replaced by more resplendent guises. Magically, Witch Hazel would step out from her dry, wrinkled hag-skin to become a beautiful young princess. Coyly leaning against the arm of her now rakishly handsome consort, Prince Philip, she would guide them to wandering merrymakers, laughing and eating.

Like them, we too sipped pomegranate nectar and lunched on broiled quails' eggs, caviar and chocolate truffles as our Scheherazades of the Field spun ever more complicated narrations. To be sure we would not miss a single diverting detail, Elaine and I on adjacent rows would weed at exactly the same pace as our storytellers, causing the rising and falling of our four hoes to achieve a rhythmic timpani in the otherwise silent terrain.

Between them, Karen and Diane invented a troupe of characters with diverse names and distinct personalities. Occasionally, when the sun rose to a blistering 103 degrees, while the clock was stuck at three in the afternoon, the cast's adventures and misadventures would degenerate into bizarre Fellini-esque scenarios . With ghosts, shamans and skeletons rising from the heat waves and our DNA strands dissolving into refracting puddles, you can imagine the resulting schizophrenic liaisons and psychotic breakdowns. Such that, some evenings returning home for dinner, we could not be sure if we were waking up from a deranged nightmare or if we were still in the middle of a heat-induced delirium.

One exceptionally searing August afternoon, we noticed Karen lagging far behind. Motionless, she was bent over a strawberry plant as though studying a rare Egyptian scarab. Peering back several more times, increasingly perplexed, we realized she was not so much bent over her row as she was *slumped* over it – not having moved for a half-hour. Fearing Mr. Hurry would notice her napping and fire her on the spot, Elaine stood up with, "I'd better check on her and see what's going on." Shaking Karen's shoulder determinedly, she whispered, "Wake up! Wake up! Get up, for heaven's sake!" Not a ripple of movement. Finally realizing she was unconscious, Elaine raced over to Mr. Hurry so he could summon help.

Poor Karen was carried from the field like an extra-heavy crate of strawberries and returned home to be diagnosed by mom as suffering from heatstroke. She registered an impressive 105 degrees on the oral thermometer.

That was the end of Karen's career in the berry patch, because she was fired. An unjust action, we felt, coming as it did from our usually compassionate boss. Perhaps, we theorized, he feared reprisal for violations of child labor laws. After all, Karen was only 13, working eight to ten-hour days in the summer months. More perversely, we further speculated that his response might have been redress for her self-appointed position as bookkeeper. Shortly after being hired, she had brought to work a stack of 3-by-5 index cards to record our weeding hours and flat totals, ensuring a check and balance on the company records.

Understandably, Mr. Hurry was offended and not at all amused that a seventh-grader would dare question the accuracy of his accounts. Undeterred, Karen was polite, if not adamant, in reviewing the tallies at the end of each week with him before he wrote out our check.

This predilection for justice and fairness, as an adult saw Karen through two lawsuits, both of which she won. One was a sexual harassment case against a College of William and Mary professor, the other a class action regarding unfair firing practices at a New Jersey college where she had been teaching. The latter case resulted in a court judgment authorizing new case law.

Still upset over Karen's termination, we continued to seek explanations. Perhaps Mr. Hurry was recalling her first day of work – that long-ago morning when she arrived with the rest of us at 7:30 wearing sandals, pink shorts, a halter top, dark sunglasses and a matching ribbon tied to her ponytail.

"Karen, you absolutely cannot leave the house in that skimpy outfit," Diane had protested. "Hazel will have conniptions, and we'll all be in trouble. Do you see what *we're* wearing? This is *not* a fashion show. You've got to be practical; there *is* a protocol to be observed, even as a strawberry picker."

Unconvinced, Karen headed for the door. By noon, she was a conspicuous lobster red with tiny white blisters blossoming on her neck, back and shoulders.

"Get thee to a shade tree and take an ice pack with you!" is a loose translation of Hazel's decree expelling Karen from the fields. Once home, mom and dad took turns applying Lipton tea bags and vinegar compresses to reduce the frightening swelling of her skin.

Diane, too, was a casualty of the fields during raspberry season one year. On a hot afternoon while trying to stay cool in the shade of a row of sunflowers, and with tiger-tail butterflies dotting the bushes like pats of butter, Diane reached into the dense foliage for a handful of berries. Instead, she disturbed a well-concealed hornets' nest.

We all heard the angry storm of buzzing as the thick cloud swarmed over her like piranhas in a feeding frenzy. Screaming, leaping, dodging, Diane fought her way down the row, flailing her hands and arms to ward off the attack. Mr. Hurry rushed her to a hospital emergency room, where she was treated for dozens of stings, her face, arms and legs grotesquely swollen.

So for good reason we did not rush to judgment, in consideration of our employer's customary protectiveness. He was in effect a surrogate father, much the same as Mr. McLeod was in the classroom.

Diane

Mr. Hurry was a stable, old-fashioned farmer, representing good solid values, the salt of the earth. I liked working in the fields with him; it gave me a structure, an organization to my life. He ran a tight ship, but you always knew what was expected. At the end of the day, I always felt good.

When I first saw his strawberry patch, it was at peak picking when the plants were thick and bushy – hundreds of heavy red berries hanging from the stems, some spilling into the dirt like rubies from a broken necklace. Who would have guessed as I stood there half a year later on the first day of planting that this is how it all began? Looking around me at those vast empty furrowed fields – like the first day of creation in the Book of Genesis – I marveled at the straightness of those dark-etched rows. He took such pride in their straightness.

"Be careful with the roots," Mr. Hurry would caution as he knelt in the soil beside me. Nestling one in his leathery pouch of a hand, he would continue, "Set them straight down in the hole, then pat the dirt around them." Lovingly he would arrange the soil around the plant – a father wrapping his newborn in its baby blanket.

I felt honored to be helping him, humbled that he would trust me with the lives of these young seedlings. And when the orange-pink shadows of sundown approached, I would stand and pause, looking toward the darkening horizon and at all those little green shoots. I knew they would survive to become strong and healthy. How could they not? Hadn't Mr. Hurry shown us the right way to plant them – and hadn't we completed each step *exactly* as he had taught us?

Denae

Mr. Hurry surely did leave us an invaluable legacy from those long-ago days in his fields. Oftentimes on a midsummer afternoon with crows and red wings swooping down to carry off juicy squashed berries, he would reach up to wipe away the sweat from his brow, tilting back the faded brim of his grey fedora. At that moment, the milky whiteness of his high forehead would be revealed, all the more distinct because his lower face was so sunburned.

"I liked looking at his blue eyes, beneath that full veranda of shade," muses Diane. "There were little flecks of green in them, as though the berry plants that he so loved were always reflected in his eyes."

That stark line of demarcation – the brown against the white – reminded us of our own skin when we took off our berry-stained shorts in the evening after work. The tops of our legs and stomachs were chalky as his forehead. Below that we were gypsy-brown, the same as our faces, necks and arms. We were *two-toned*, just like Mr. Hurry. But during the day no one could tell, with his hat down and our shorts covering our pale flesh – almost like we were members of a secret society.

In an entirely different way, our two-toned skin was the scourge of the summer months. Down at the Spokane River's Sandy Beach in our two-piece swim suits, we were like walking billboards advertising our employment.

LOOKING BACK *Swimming in Spokane River in 1962*

"Here they come, the two-tones, the Veselits girls with their farmer tans," jeers Karen, mock-miming the comments of fellow swimmers.

"Yes," continues Diane, "a big part of my self-image were those ghastly two-toned legs – like I was a genetic mutation, a freak. As soon as we'd get out of the car, I'd race for the river, diving in as fast as possible to hide my legs. Then I felt like I was equal, the same as everyone else. My defects were now buried beneath the river's surface."

For an alternate perspective, we might have benefited from listening to our sister-in-distress, Black singer Alberta Hunter, who sang her version of our fate in the 1930s:

> *Look what the sun has done to me…*
> *Tell me, tell me, am I out of style*
> *Just because I'm slightly shady?*
> *…You can't tell the difference after dark.*

After long hot hours of picking, the perfect ending for the day would be when Mr. Hurry had a last-minute errand to run. "Say, do you girls want a ride home tonight? Hop in the back!" And he'd pull down the tailgate from his old farm truck where we would seat ourselves in a row – all four of us fit perfectly.

"With our legs dangling over the edge, the wind blowing tangles in our hair, I loved it!" enthuses Diane. "It was like riding in an open convertible! The best part was speeding past Bev Southern's house (*Faster, Mr. Hurry, faster*). I imagined we were just an unidentifiable blur, streaking past her picture window."

Inevitably, however, the day must come when we had outgrown the lessons and labors of the strawberry fields. Elaine was departing for Vietnam as a Red Cross worker; Diane and myself had been accepted as volunteers in President Kennedy's VISTA program. We older girls were passing the torch on to Keith, Gail and Gwen, the next generation of field summa cum laudes. Looking back, we gazed a final time upon those seven acres that had so profoundly imprinted us – Milton on our minds:

> *Farewell happy Fields*
> *Where Joy forever dwells: Hail horrours, hail*
> *Infernal world, and thou profoundest Hell*
> *Receive thy new possessor...*
> *The mind is its own place, and in itself*
> *Can make a Heaven of Hell, a Hell of Heaven.*
> *Paradise Lost*

# IN SICKNESS & in HEALTH

Elaine, Karen, Diane, Keith, Denae, Gail, Mom, Dad

Karen

To some of us, it seemed like daddy was nicer to sick kids than to healthy ones, so we learned how to get sick as a way of getting attention. I was a case in point. When the mood struck me, I rechewed old wads of bubble gum – from off the sidewalk or under a school desk. Sometimes I would lick pennies picked up from the street, or, suck on gravel from our driveway. Once I even drank the water from a mud puddle.

That escapade with Denae, when I was nine, resulted in a severe case of trench mouth with a 106-degree temperature and fever blisters all over the inside of my red-hot face. I didn't mean to get quite *that* sick, but it was great nonetheless. To help cool me off, daddy brought me a cherry popsicle, which I rubbed over my burning cheeks and open sores, and licked with my white-coated tongue. Everyone in the family visited my bedside, sympathizing with me. In return for their concern, I let each one of them lick my popsicle.

This habit of inducing illness continued on into high school. One wintry week, rather than face my English class at Marycliff with an un-prepared speech, I sold tickets to the neighborhood kids so they could watch me take a midnight plunge into a tub of snow. My goal was to get pneumonia, or at the very least laryngitis, so I could stay home from school. For the 25 cents admission price, my audience would be treated to watching me take a snow bath in our front yard, clad only in a bikini. The midnight viewing time was top secret. A lot of tickets were sold, but only Denae and the two Kokot brothers showed up for my barefoot performance.

Diane had her own techniques for getting sick. Her most mem-orable attempt, although not a success, was still remarkable for its ingenuity. She had convinced dad before school one morning that she was in desperate need of medical attention. He actually drove her to Dr. Nowak's office– quite a feat since normally we had to be hemorrhaging blood or exposing broken bone to warrant a trip to the doctor. Even then, dad might postpone the inevitable by declaring, "Nahh, that's not so bad. Wait a day or two. The body has amazing healing abilities: Rose, tear a couple of strips from that diaper and we'll make a tourniquet. That should stop the bleeding."

As a seven year old, Denae once fractured her skinny leg in two places by jumping off a ladder (on a dare) onto a patch of snow-covered ice. She had to wait three agonizing days before dad was sufficiently convinced that it merited a doctor's visit. The high point of her exam was when the doctor put a plaster cast over her entire leg, and then sent her home with crutches. For the next month, whenever possible, she would hobble slowly and pathetically in front of dad – a gratifying means of pointing out his grievous neglect.

Meanwhile, back in Dr. Nowak's office, Diane had been left alone in the examining room with a thermometer in her mouth while dad sat impatiently in the waiting room. Those were the pre-digital days when thermometers took four minutes to accurately register a reading, which Diane had counted on. Unfortunately, the nurse returned with still one minute to go. Opening the door, she was startled to find Diane standing up on the white, paper-draped exam table, holding the thermometer against the light bulb in the ceiling. Not without humor, she first relieved Diane of the thermometer, then glancing down at the mercury, commented wryly, "Doctor would never have believed you, anyway – the reading is 107.3. With those numbers, you'd be either unconscious or dead."

Denae

Late-night television in the 60s was a great combination of science fiction, horror and suspense – all of which we watched raptly and indiscriminately, grateful for the weekend nights when dad would go off to the tavern, leaving us to stay up as late as we wanted. Mom was just glad to go to bed early with a calm and quiet house. So, as we bundled together on the couches with our popcorn, wrapped up in old quilts, she would call out: "Remember, the last one awake has to turn off the TV set!"

Not infrequently, our viewing repertoire featured lurid images and hallucinations, as in "The Lost Weekend," with a boozing Ray Milland. I was spellbound by these eerie, fanciful visions, but thought they were made up or overly exaggerated to heighten the impact of the film – certainly not anything that real-life people experienced. Nightmares I understood, because I had them. But hallucinations were beyond my mental reach. However skeptical as I might be, still I thought about them a lot, the same as fainting or sleepwalking (which Curt did) – and wondered if I would ever have the good fortune to experience any of these extraordinary states.

One dull and cloudy afternoon, I found myself lying on the sofa in the living room, listlessly watching dad in the chair opposite me as he peeled off the wrapper to his Copenhagen. The rest of the kids were outside in the yard playing a game of tetherball. I hadn't been feeling well, so it was pleasant to just burrow into the worn fabric, with no noise except for the faint rustling of paper as dad's thumbnail worked its way around the waist of his can.

Then suddenly I started laughing. "What's so funny?" asked dad, glancing up. Pointing to the wall behind him and still giggling, I responded, "those newspapers behind you – three of them, folded up, walking along the back of your chair, and they're all wearing big pink sunglasses!"

Astonished, dad flipped around, scanning the furniture, apparently seeing nothing. I continued laughing as I watched the little parade of newspapers circle the room. Walking over to me, dad laid his hand on my forehead, exclaiming, "Holy moly, mother of Christ!" then rushed toward the bathroom to fetch the thermometer – our household god, divining rod for all disease.

After my temperature had dropped to a more acceptable level from the cold cloths and ice packs, it dawned on me that I had actually *hallucinated*! Now, 45 years later, I have no recollection of my high fever or what caused it, but I can still recall in photographic detail those three folded newspapers with their oversize pink sunglasses, parading along the sofa and chair backs of our living room.

Gail

I was about 8 when daddy dropped me off for my first appointment at the dentist. No one had coached me beforehand in office protocol – like checking in at the front desk. To be so presumptuous as to address an adult before being acknowledged seemed to be overstepping my training of being seen and not heard. (We had learned long ago how to speak without making any noise). So I crept in, unnoticed by the receptionist, and sat in the corner of the room, invisible, as was the pattern of my life, thinking that someone was going to call my name – but never did.

After a couple hours waiting, which seemed like two lifetimes, the receptionist started to pack her things, preparing to leave. I was dumbfounded, not knowing what to do. *Would I be locked in the office.. all night?* Even worse, daddy was going to be really mad about my missed appointment, since welfare patients had to wait the longest to be rescheduled.

The lights had been turned off and the receptionist was locking the door when she finally saw me. "How long have you been sitting there? Why didn't you say something?" Realizing she was partly to blame and would probably be reprimanded, she continued angrily, "Am I supposed to be a mind reader? How could anyone be so stupid as to not check in at the front desk?!" Had I the courage, I would have told her that she seemed like such an important person sitting there – maybe even a doctor – that I didn't feel I had the right to address her.

Setting her purse and keys down, grimly she penciled my name in the appointment book. So there I was several days later, sitting in the dentist's chair, looking up at Dr. Riley. Terrified. With a scowl on his face, he tapped each tooth needing to be filled, pointing out that I had a mouth full of decay due to poor (actually, nonexistent) dental care at home.

"You've got a lot of cavities, young lady" he criticized. As he adjusted the light, and the gigantic needle appeared, he was quick to add, "And since you're a welfare patient, the state only reimburses me for one shot of Novocain per visit; so this should keep you numb until I finish."

Of course I proved to be the exception to his misguided expectation. Two-thirds of the way through the procedure, I could definitely feel the drilling at the root of my tooth. I was in dire need of another shot of anesthetic. Wincing in pain, I gripped the arms of my chair as he continued to drill. Young as I was, somehow I knew he was getting some perverse satisfaction out of controlling the Novocain supply. What was I to him, anyway? Just another welfare patient that he was losing money on because he had to discount his fee.

When the interminable drilling and filing ended, he handed me a mirror. I was horrified to see two black lines etched across the bottom of my lower front teeth. Smugly, he explained that as a welfare patient, my allotment was only for *black* fillings and not for the more expensive white porcelain that would have blended with the tooth enamel. It looked like I had two pieces of rotting spinach in my teeth. As for smiling – on those rare occasions when I did have reason to laugh or smile – I did so self-consciously, terribly ashamed of the way I now looked.

Years later, when I could afford it, I had the two hideous black fillings removed, replaced with white porcelain. My dentist was appalled when I told him the story, exclaiming, "I can't believe any medical professional would actually put black fillings on a child's front teeth, no matter *what* the price differential!!"

Going to the eye doctor at around the same age was another humiliating experience. At first, I thought there might be some status in wearing glasses, since I had seen fashion magazines with models and movie stars wearing them and found the effect quite glamorous. I imagined myself sitting in a comfy chair—a blue-eyed Sandra Dee—looking through row after row of frames to select a perfectly alluring pair for myself.

After the exam (when I was told I had significantly-impaired vision and a cataract in my left eye), I couldn't wait to visit the optical shop to make my selection. Sitting across from the lab technician, I carefully tucked my short blonde hair behind my ears so as not to obstruct the full glory of my brand new glasses. I watched as he set down a small box containing four pairs of frames. *Four*?! All the same style, with a pronounced wing at either end. Each had a strip of white paired with a border of either pink, blue, brown, or grey, with black speckles scattered through the line of color. To make matters worse they were heavily glittered, making them even more unseemly. Sensing my dissatisfaction, the technician explained my choices: "These are the frames we carry for welfare people – it's all your allotment will allow."

I did not want to pick from his paltry selection and could not imagine myself wearing any of them. All I wanted to do was cry, but I desperately needed corrective lenses because I was starting to have migraines. I may have been poor, but I did possess some aesthetics. Even with limited fashion sense, I knew these glasses were an aberration of some demented designer and that my schoolmates would have a field day when they saw me.

Realizing I had no other options, I made my selection. That first year I picked blue, pink the next, followed by brown the year after. By sixth grade, I was wearing the gray. Even though I felt like a freak in my sparkly, bejeweled glasses, at least the headaches had subsided.

# PART TWO
# ARREST & LAMENTATIONS

*He looked with his very soul, it's hidden chamber saw,*
*Inscribed with records dark and deep, of many a broken*
*law.*

-Elizabeth Oakes Smith

It was on Valentine's Day, 1965 that the police pulled up in our driveway in an unmarked car and took dad away in handcuffs. Quietly, with no drama. We kids watched dumbstruck through the panes of our kitchen window, unable to process what we were seeing. *What was he being arrested for? Who turned him in? Would he be sent to prison?* Our minds became question factories, desperate for clues to what had just happened. We looked to mom for some clarity – but she wasn't saying a word, not one word.

Denae

Elaine took the little kids upstairs, everyone crying, while the rested of us drifted around the house in an uncertain limbo, wondering and waiting. Truth be told, with the heavy silence and all the ominous possibilities, we weren't so sure we wanted to know anyway.

A week passed with the domestic atmosphere still funereal. But school attendance being mandatory, I found myself sitting in high school English class writing a paper on "The Troubadours of the Middle Ages" when my teacher tapped me on the shoulder, motioning me to follow. We walked without speaking to an empty classroom where I was received by two burly policemen in uniform and Miss Browiak, the Girls' Advisor, all seated in chairs.

Uh oh. I had a sinking feeling the Big Secret at home had something to do with this officious looking group sequestered with me. No preamble or semblance of social niceties, either. The big boys in blue were on business, meant business and weren't going to engage in any monkey business, like polite platitudes, in order to make my interview more comfortable.

Nope, straight to the jugular. "Where are the bedrooms located in your house? Who sleeps in which rooms?" Followed by questions on road trips, bathing habits – whether washing alone or with *others*: "Does your father bathe with you?" (Domestic routines and parental schedules were examined in exhaustive detail). Then, back to the bedrooms. Certain words from the interrogation stood out like roadside flares at the scene of an accident – words like *pedophile, molesting, mentally ill, felonies*. Scary sounding words that might tell a story if you fit them together properly. A dark and ugly story, from the look of things… that no respectable person would want associated with their father, or with their sisters and brothers.

I was not sorry that dad had been taken away. It was a relief, actually – like having a bullet finally removed from a festering wound. I hoped he would never return home. But beyond that, I did not want to contemplate the details and innuendo that these men were trying to force upon me. Mom was walking around the house like a zombie; she surely knew what was going on. So if "knowing" made you act like mom, I wanted *nothing* to do with it.

One of the policemen drummed his thick, stubby fingers impatiently on the desktop as he waited for my answers. Miss Browiak, succorer of young women, sat farthest from me, her hands piously folded, her eyes cold – offended perhaps that she must sit witness to such undignified, licentious inquiries.

I thought of Spencer Tracy, the kindly, white-haired magistrate in "Judgment at Nuremburg." For indeed, this gathering did seem like a trial to me, an inquisition with no jury, with me as the defendant, trying to protect the reputation of my family. I didn't even have a defense team, no erudite barrister to plead my case, support my claims or protect my innocence. If only Spencer Tracy could be here with me now, sitting alongside my interrogators, forcing them to comply with the laws of decency, forcing them to more considerately question a naive high school student.

Suddenly the thought occurred to me, *Did mom know about this questioning? Had she given her permission without warning me first? Had Diane, too, been pulled from class to suffer this ordeal?* Leveling my eyes at the two officers, I thought, *You brutes. How dare you do this to me?* I was furious at my vulnerability, my inability to stand up to them and refuse to answer their sordid questions.

To this day, when I think back to those humiliating hours and the total lack of sympathy extended, I am enraged all over again. Absolutely no counseling follow-up was provided by Miss Browiak in the ensuing weeks. It is my one regret of adulthood that I did not write her a detailed letter of censure before she died of old age. It would have assuaged a good deal of my anger to itemize her breaches of responsibility, both as a paid professional and as a member of the human race.

As it turned out, all three of us older girls were called from our classrooms for interrogation – Elaine from college, and Diane and myself from high school. (Karen was a ninth-grader, thus spared). When the boys in blue were finished with us, guess what? They sent us back to our classrooms, unable to extend the simple courtesy of letting us go home. Diane told me later she cried so uncontrollably during the questioning that they finally just excused her from the room. And no, mom had *not* given her permission for the questioning. She was furious with the police department when we told her they had subjected us to such an ordeal.

Elaine

After dad was taken away, I had nightmares – we all had them. I was afraid to open a door or look out a window for fear I would find him standing there like the bogeyman come to get me .. come to get mom, Diane and Denae .. and do awful things to us for turning him in and for not lying to save him from jail.

Denae

The court ordered dad committed to Eastern State Mental Hospital for observation and rehabilitation, while mom proceeded to have a nervous breakdown from the stress of the whole mess. Three weeks after dad was in residence there, she joined him at the nut house. A fine kettle of fish for the nine of us left at home. Although it came as no surprise when mom was taken away; we all saw it coming. It began with the scraps of paper – torn envelope flaps, coffee-stained fragments of stationery, used notebook paper and discarded doctors' prescriptions. Mom would scribble down odd number sequences, birth dates, grocery items, neighbors' names and partial phone numbers in random criss-cross arrangements on these paper bits; then she would read them to us as though they were important Bible passages.

Sinking ever lower into the nether realms of passivity and despair, she had even begun following 5-year-old Curt around the house, writing down everything he said, with an expression of intense determination, as though she were a courtroom stenographer – visibly upset if he talked too fast for her to keep up. Unaware of his mommy's fragile mind, Curt would chatter away about fishing worms, his tricycle, a broken kite, or who would be reading him his bedtime story.

Randomly at meals or in the middle of our homework, mom, in agitation, would interrupt us to read from her messianic transcripts. "Shhhh! I want you all to hear this ..." Following these recitations she would drift into illogical interpretations, attempting to predict future events or catastrophes. In effect, our little brother – the one she hoped would become a priest – had became her Cassandra, her oracle or crystal ball by which to discern an uncertain and frightening future.

The Department of Social Services intervened by taking mom away and replacing her with a state homemaker, who apparently was primarily in our home to oversee Curt while the rest of us were away at school. Kelly was her name, and we all equally detested her. Slovenly, fat, coarse of manner and speech, she did not have a maternal bone in her body. Within a week of inhabiting our living space, she had set up Karen, Diane and me with her teenage son and two delinquent buddies to triple date to a drive-in movie.

None of us had ever been out with a boy; Diane and I were 16, Karen 15. Dating had been strictly forbidden by dad. Besides which, we had no desire to spend even five minutes in the company of her short, pimply, greasy-haired son Johnny. His friends, we had not yet viewed. However, having been raised to submit unquestioningly to adult authority and on the verge of nervous collapse ourselves, we grimly agreed to the movie date.

I will spare the reader a detailed description of the trio of misfits we were forced to share company with – their lewd conversation and odious gropings inside the darkness of their bald-tired, hot rod. Having no experience whatsoever in managing six-handed teenage boys, Diane, Karen and I uniformly pretended to fall asleep.

How very long ago was that dreadful night, when the three of us were trapped in the car like canaries in a cage with hawks. I did not want to see what would happen to me, did not want to feel the rough touch of those grasping fingers or the boy's hot, smelly breath against my bare flesh. So I closed my eyes, closed my mind, turned off all my senses to protect myself. Had I done this before? Somehow, it seemed familiar, a means of escape I had used in the past.

At one point, weary of my cramped position on the back seat, I slitted my eyes open toward the movie screen to see if the credits were running, signaling the end of the film. No! No! It could not be! For there, staring down at me, his face filling the entire screen, was daddy. Huge. Furious. His eyes were big as dinner plates, glaring at me through the darkness, glaring at all of us. A purple tyrant in a purple rage.

It was not allowed, he had told us. Boys were bad. They did bad things to you. Bad girls with bad boys. Sluts. He had told us over and over and over.

Nowhere to hide. He knew. Even though he was 30 miles away in Medical Lake at the mental hospital, still he knew. Oh yes, he knew exactly where we were, exactly what we were doing, that we had defied his rules. He always knew. Everything.

I wanted to scream, to flee from that awful image of his face on the screen. But I couldn't. Caged birds don't scream. They shut their

222

eyes, shut their ears and their thoughts. So that when "it" happens – whatever "it" is – they won't have to feel it or know about it.

Seeing dad's face at the drive-in movie was only the beginning in a long series of unpredictable sightings of him – a parental omniscience and presence it seemed I could not avoid. In my 20s: I am standing next to my boyfriend's car as he changes a flat tire. "Hand me that bolt," he says. His voice sounds just like my father's! Snapping my head in his direction, I peer down to see who is really fixing the tire. That person looks exactly like daddy.

Another time, at 32, I am making out on the couch with my date, while a nearby lamp illuminates his sandy hair and fair skin. Reaching up to touch his face, I am horrified to see my father's image instead. *But my father's hair is black, his complexion olive. How can he look like my blond boyfriend?!*

In restaurants, on road trips, dancing at nightclubs, sunbathing at the beach – with every man I ever dated, the moment I fear inevitably arrives when it is my father's voice I hear, my father's face I see, and at the most inappropriate, most intimate of times. I feel revolted, defiled; my skin crawls with invisible worms. I want to vomit and run away as fast as I can from this changeling that can so quickly become my father.

This chapter title reads "Arrest and Lamentations." The lamentations I can tell you plenty about. But the arrest – what is the crime? What, goddamn it, was he arrested for? What did he do?

You want the truth? The whole truth and nothing but the truth? Well, it's not that easy. We can't tell you the whole truth because none of us really knows what it is. Who was molested? How many times? Who with a finger? Who with a penis? Which of the daughters? One of them? Three? All of them?

As many crimes as we can remember, an equal number have been forgotten. Treacherous, violent parental actions create dangerous and painful memories. Memories that can destabilize you, paralyze you, make you crazy and sometimes even kill you. So the human body developed a natural defense against trauma to protect us from memories of such searing magnitude. Call it amnesia, repression, suppression, fugue state – call it anything you like, but its effect is universally similar: to restore peace and achieve homeostasis so life can go on.

Following dad's arrest, the official, court-generated document describing his crime reads: "one count of carnal knowledge of a minor." A prosy adjustment (a *GROSS* maladjustment, if you will) of details and events, deliberately minimized to expedite passage of a civil crime through a 1960's legal system anxious to save on expenses incurred by a jury trial.

However, lest the dirty deed come back to haunt the professional record of the presiding magistrate, he cunningly covers his tracks – the infamous paper trail. Calling mom into his chambers, he invites her to sit on the simple wooden chair reposing before the towering oaken desk which is his domain.

Yes, our barely functioning, gaunt-faced mother in her drab housedress seats herself meekly, head bowed, as His Honor points out to her that the publicity of a jury trial "could be very embarrassing and painful to an already damaged family," and did she really want her children's father "to be a convicted felon, sitting for years in a federal penitentiary when, as an alternative, the court could commit him to one or two years in the state mental hospital for rehabilitation? In no time at all, Frank could rejoin society and once again contribute to the family's financial support. After all, you are on welfare, aren't you?"

"So, Rose, which is it to be?" inquires Solomon as he delicately rearranges the folds of his great dark robes. "Prison or the mental hospital? I leave it to you to decide your husband's fate."

Do not ask me to name names. It is enough that the offender has been identified. We were all violated, in one way or another – all of us, along with our mother. Some of us remember a lot, some a little. Some do not remember anything at all. But the signs are there, the disturbing signs that lay beneath our unwilling memories. Hymens that were broken long before puberty. Phobias about big black, hairy spiders and rat tails and mice. Difficulties with intimacy and sexual relationships. Chronic sleep disturbances. Nightmares of being trapped and held against our will by faceless demons. Memories of naptimes with daddy that didn't seem quite right. Memories of lining up at the couch at bedtime, where daddy was reclining – and being forced to kiss him goodnight, mouth to mouth, while lying against his chest.

So, who was molested? Who was not? Who was beaten? Who was spared? We remember selectively and we forget selectively; the mind makes its own arrangements. Do not ask me to name names. Each of us suffered through personal assaults as well as the assaults committed against others. Much of the violence we were forced to watch, while at other times when it happened in our absence, we could only imagine at what had caused the bruised arms, the tears or the deafening silence.

When reporting cases of sexual abuse, the media subscribes to an ethos requiring them to withhold the names of victims under the age of 18. Shall we then be less decent, less considerate by publicly naming the victims in our own family?

"But don't you want to know? Don't you want to know if you were molested?" ask well-meaning friends. "Why don't you undergo hypnosis?"

ARE YOU KIDDING? Why in God's name would I want to remember my father forcing himself on me? What a *ghastly* image, were it true, to forever hold in my mind. Elaine's theory of "reverse hypnosis" makes more sense. She once asked her therapist, "Is it possible to use hypnosis to help you *forget* instead of remember?"

Pontius Pilate rinsed his hands symbolically, not realizing that no amount of scrubbing would ever rid him of his sin. Nor could Lady Macbeth ever cleanse entirely from her royal hands the stain of that "damned spot." Do you think it would be any easier for me or any of my sisters to obliterate the terrible picture of dad's crimes against us once we had willfully called them back into our minds?

Memory loss protects us. And we are grateful for that protection. We do not wish to lift the veil of remembrance. Much as there are inconveniences to memory loss, inconveniences such as entire years lost to our recall, for many of us – like Gwen, Keith and Diane, who have the poorest memories – we accept what cannot be recalled of the violence, the rejections, the daily terrors of living in our household. The loss of memory is a gift, a kindly protection to keep us safe from the fearsome specter of our past.

### Denae

The six weeks that mom spent at Eastern State Mental Hospital were difficult for all. To have had both parents removed from the home within the same month was emotionally devastating. We were left adrift in a sea of uncertainty, afraid to look into the future, equally afraid to confront the reality of our present.

I was seventeen. In one photo album was an enlarged black and white image of mom at the same age. I would sit on my bed holding her picture, pretending she was still at home. Today that same photo hangs framed on my living room wall. It is my favorite picture of mom. Standing at the road's edge, a beautiful, full-lipped blonde, she smiles easily and provocatively into the camera as she raises her pant leg above her knee in a faux hitchhiking pose.

I never got to know this self-possessed, happy-go-lucky young woman. By the time I was old enough to distinguish emotions and personality, she had withdrawn into a silent, submissive, bony-limbed woman who smiled rarely – partly due to the grimness of her environment, partly because her teeth were loose and discolored, badly in need of dental attention.

"The world is too much with us, late and soon" – and so it was with mom. Too much responsibility, too much isolation, too much work; too much criticism and abuse from her husband. She had become a woman of silence. Silent because it was expected of her. Silent because it takes less energy to be quiet, an important consideration when you haven't had enough to eat. Her silence was society's silence – a reflection of the larger social milieu of the 1940s, '50s, and '60s, which all too often looked the other way when fathers drank too much, shouted too much and abused their families.

This was an era when police departments interrogated rape victims for hours, with no female officers present. A time when domestic abuse calls were received with patronization. With little more than a glance in the direction of the sobbing, black-eyed mother, a policeman would step outside with the man of the house, sharing some old boys' counsel: "Gotta slap 'em around a little to keep them in their place to show them who's boss." Wink, wink. "They *like* a man who lets 'em know he's a man. Sorry we had to come out and interrupt your evening."

Court systems were filled with men in charge – judges, prosecutors and defense attorneys – many who didn't think domestic abuse qualified as a criminal act. Occasionally, newspapers or television specials would rally to the cause by featuring an isolated incident, guaranteed to boost ratings and increase circulation, yet rarely investigating sufficiently to reveal just how pervasive and damaging the problem really was.

First-person memoirs of domestic violence garnered responses of "Dreadful! Shameful!" because authors had dared reveal family secrets.

Indeed, when *The Color Purple* book and movie came out, mass media's male-dominated voice seemed more outraged by the author's seeming black male bashing than by the victimizing of defenseless women and girls.

As Christina Crawford points out so compellingly in her book *No Safe Place, the Legacy of Family Violence* (following *Mommie Dearest*), the silence which is so highly prized by diehard family loyalists, only protects the perpetrators, not the victims. Why must we abstain from naming the abuser, naming the crime? She rightly asks. How else will the innocent be protected; how else will society become aware how profoundly domestic violence impacts lives and how widespread it has become? Why should the victim be made to feel guilty for turning in his or her parent?

Who's to say that cheeky "What happens in Vegas stays in Vegas" did not have its origins in "What happens in the home stays in the home" – a dangerous philosophy for wives and young children.

So, while dad was doing time in the city jail, the court ordered a series of evaluations. Some of the results were passed on to mom. Paranoid-Schizophrenia, Narcissistic Personality Disorder and Antisocial Personality Disorder were among the maladjustments red-flagged for consideration. Elaine looked up the latter in the *Diagnostic and*

*Statistical Manual of Mental Disorders* to see if it would clarify dad's behaviors. All of us were looking for answers to explain the craziness and unpredictability of our home life. (Not surprisingly both Elaine and Gwen chose careers in the field of psychology, one earning her master's degree in social work, the other her master's degree in counseling).

The diagnostic manual's text on Antisocial Personality Disorder was particularly edifying – a word-perfect description of dad:

1.  Fails to conform to the social norms in respect to lawful behavior
2.  A reckless disregard for the safety of self and others
3.  Tends to be irritable and aggressive, prone to committing acts of physical assault
4.  Often irresponsible and exploitive in sexual relationships
5.  Irresponsible and neglectful as a parent
6.  Shows little empathy, or little remorse for the consequences of their acts
7.  Indifferent to the feelings and rights of others
8.  Deceit and manipulation, central features
9.  Inability to tolerate boredom or depressed moods
10. Exhibits an inflated and arrogant sense of self
11. Tends to have a "dishonorable discharge" from military service
12. Fails to be self-supporting in financial matters
13. Consistently and extremely irresponsible

*Thirteen Ways of Looking at a Blackbird.*

Gail

Following mom's month and a half absence from home, we were all looking forward to her return. Even though we had not put up balloons and crepe paper, mom's first day back was marked by cheer and relief. Yet, inexplicably, her first decree was that Keith and I participate in a local square dancing event—leaving us to conclude that mom had been released a tad prematurely, and was still off her rocker.

Our neighbors, the Sherrodds, had a 14- and 15-year-old girl and boy, Aileen and Alden –the same age as Keith and me – who were involved in square dancing. Following a phone conversation, both mothers agreed that Keith and I should attend a few performances, presumably to improve our social deficiencies. For two teens who had never danced publicly, the idea was appalling. However, dutifully we agreed, fearing a refusal would precipitate mom's going over the edge again.

With the jamboree days away, we had little time to practice, so Alden and Aileen formulated a workable crash course. I think they felt sorry for us, knowing some psychodrama was always taking place at our house, and that no doubt this sudden interest in western dancing was based on something deeper than mere whimsy. They flipped "Jingle Bell Rock" on to their record player – full volume – then proceeded to demonstrate our choreography.

As we tried to emulate them, Keith and I were overwhelmed by the complexity of the steps. Not only could we not distinguish a *do-si-do* from a *tour jete*, but it was also becoming evident that we shared four left feet and had no sense of western rhythm. Then there was the problem of where to put our hands. It was all so confusing. Was my hand to go around his waist or on his shoulder? If so, which shoulder? Which hand was I to use, the right or the left? When did I turn clockwise and when did I turn counterclockwise?

Not wishing to prolong our distress, having failed in teaching us any steps, Alden and Aileen wisely moved on to wardrobe selection. Generously, they opened their closets, explaining that costumes were a large part of the dancers' success. Since my musical tastes at the time were the Beatles and Rolling Stones, the only clothes I wore were bell-bottom jeans or mini skirts. So when Aileen presented me with a long, fire engine red skirt with layers of ruffled petticoats, I was mortified. To make matters worse, a stiff wire had been sewn into the hem, hugely extending the skirt's circumference. *How in the world did you go to the bathroom in this getup?* A short-sleeved, polka-dot blouse completed the ensemble, accessorized with a red kerchief for my neck.

Keith's costume was equally unseemly. Since he didn't own any dress slacks, Alden loaned him a pair. Unfortunately, Keith was two inches taller, so the borrowed pants gave new meaning to the term high-waters. A blue plaid shirt with mother-of-pearl buttons completed Keith's outfit. (He did draw the line at donning a matching Stetson). Finally outfitted in these togs, we laughed despairingly into the mirror, knowing we looked like adolescent versions of Roy Rogers and Dale Evans. Now we truly were participants in the Theater of the Absurd. Mom owed us big time for this!

Rehearsal over, we walked home still in western drag, praying mom would sense our embarrassment and end the masquerade. Conversely, she beamed with joy and declared that we looked stunning – totally confident our square dancing debut would be a huge success. Hee haw!!

The big day had arrived; it was show time whether we liked it or not. With trepidation we donned our ridiculous outfits and went to the ridiculous dance. The noisy auditorium was packed with girls in colorful, flashy costumes. At least from that standpoint, I felt like I blended in. But when the music began, Keith and I moved discreetly to the refreshment area, waiting for the moment when we could sashay our way out the back door.

It was not to be. From the stage the Caller shouted out, "Oh Johnny Oh!" because it was the easiest of the square dances. Beckoning to Keith, me, and a huddle of other reluctant newcomers, he continued with, "Now you all join hands and you circle the ring; stop where you are, give your honey a swing." With firm resolve, my sweaty hands joined my brother's and we commenced circling the ring. We were briefly in sync, at least until Keith proceeded to give his "honey" a swing with such momentum that I lost my balance and torpedoed into the next couple, leveling them like bowling pins.

"*Allemande* left with the girl on your left," the Caller continued. More confusion. What in the world did *allemande* mean? Uncertain, we came to a dead stop, mercifully obscured by the tide of swishing skirts and petticoats.

When "*Do-si-do* your own" was called, Keith, in a final attempt to salvage the situation, folded his arms across his chest, bent his knees, and performed a maneuver around me resembling that of a Russian Cossack dancer. My face went scarlet, with no idea what to do next. Keith in turn, realizing he had mixed up his nationalities, not to mention his dances, gave up as well, and joined me in my stupor. Once again we were two inert dummies stranded in the chaos.

Meanwhile, the Caller was getting more and more aggravated by our disruptions. He issued a stern warning, "Take your corner; go walking with your maid." As we pondered *which* corner, his face darkened in wrath and he pointed us to the door. Ecstatic, Keith and I promenaded our way across the room, and then bolted.

Mom has no idea the sacrifices we made that disastrous evening. When she expressed surprise that we were home early, we assured her we'd had a wonderful time. As for the bumps and bruises to our pride, it seemed a small price to pay to keep her mentally stable.


Denae

Mom has been gone since December 1998. Two images of her stand out in memory. The first is of her peeling potatoes at the kitchen sink. I see her only from the back, but still I am aware that her eyes and thoughts do not inhabit this quiet form leaning with such resignation against the counter – they have already taken flight. Only her hands mindlessly paring away brown potato skin suggest at a life force still present in this otherwise silent landscape of stove, refrigerator and cupboards.

"The soul selects her own society, then shuts the door … Safe in her alabaster chamber," writes Emily Dickinson. In like fashion, mom's mind has transported her beyond the wooden-paned window to our half-acre vegetable garden – the second image I hold of her – where she stoops contentedly for hours, weeding and planting. Or perhaps her thoughts have winged their way a further distance yet, all the way back to her father's tobacco farm in Minnesota, where as a child she felt loved and indulged.

Two poems by Langston Hughes speak to these images. Her form and demeanor are mirrored in his description of "The Weary Blues," while I, her daughter, can only yearn that she might one day escape the harshness of her plight. "Magnolia Flowers" captures this longing for change: "… I went lookin' for magnolia flowers… there was only this corner full of ugliness… There ought to be magnolias somewhere in this dusk."

It is third, possibly fourth grade – one of the school holidays where the students' mothers alternate in providing the refreshments. It is mom's turn. Earlier that morning, I plead with her to let me stay home. "I've got a fever and a stomachache. I'm way too sick to go to school." The medicine cabinet thermometer treacherously registers 98.8, when I firmly believe my anxiety alone should have raised the mercury to at least 101.

"Nope. A perfectly normal reading," disputes mom. "Now go get ready for school.

All day at my desk I squirm restlessly, watching the round-faced clock above the green blackboard tick-tock its way closer to 2 p.m. – party time. An almost inaudible knock at the back classroom door announces the arrival of my mother. I can't bear to turn around, knowing what I will see. The pain of my anxiety is exquisite – like a hummingbird's beak slicing through the center of my heart.

Mom stands there, a character from Steinbeck's *Grapes of Wrath*, one arm balancing an oil-stained cardboard box containing flat sugar cookies I watched her bake last night. Her other arm wobbles a little from the weight of the two-quart plastic pitcher of watered down Kool-Aid, which only suggests by its pale red color that it is slightly more than tap water with a little food coloring. The merest trace of a smile sits uncertainly upon her lips, as uncertain as the wan smear of pink lipstick, which seems almost brazen by contrast with her plain blouse and brown skirt, her bare legs and flat, worn walking shoes.

Pausing a moment from his absorption with wadding up paper for spitballs, the boy next to me pokes me in the arm, whispering loudly, "Hey, is that your mother?" When I mutely nod yes, he finishes with,

"Well, she sure is ugly."

Time stops and the whole room goes blank. I wish I could die, or fly up to heaven – go somewhere, anywhere that is not filled with so much pain. The echo of his words rebounds against my ears. *Was that boy whispering…or was he talking out loud, loud enough for the whole class to hear, including my poor mother? No, no, it must have been a whisper. It's better to remember it as a whisper.*

It wasn't that I was ashamed of mom. Rather, I felt sorry for her, as sorry as a young girl could possibly be for a mother who certainly knew the difference between a flat cookie with no raisins or chocolate chips and a real dessert cookie with marshmallow creme, walnuts and pink frosting. She hadn't been raised poor. She knew what kids were looking for in a party cookie – and that fruit juice, punch or soda were certainly preferred over Kool-Aid.

But she wanted to be a good mom, who went to school events, parent-teacher conferences and mother-daughter teas. It was her way of showing she loved us, that she cared about us. She could have said no like a lot of the other poor mothers and spared herself the shame and humiliation of bringing the worst treats for school parties, knowing no one was going to thank her for the tasteless cookies. But she came anyway because she was the mother, and that's what good mothers are supposed to do.

# THE CHANGING
# Of the GUARD

Diane, Denae, Elaine, Grandma

*...it was as though they were a pair of birds of passage,*
*caught and forced to live in different cages.*

– Anton Chekhov

<u>Karen</u>
<u>Denae</u>

Life at the Greenacres house changed dramatically after daddy was taken away in 1964 to be rehabilitated at the Medical Lake mental hospital. Grandma Hartmann, now in her late 70s, had moved from Everett, Washington, to live near us. And mom divorced dad within a year after sufficiently recovering from her nervous breakdown. With these changes, a whole new order was established at 17907 E. Sprague.

The Confucian straightjacket of daddy's restrictive rule-oriented "I want to know *everything*" regime was replaced by mom's lax "I don't want to know *anything*" policies. Both systems netted equally chaotic results, the one from too many rules, the other from too few. Worn down by 18 years of violence and abuse, mom was just barely capable of fulfilling her social worker duties. Thank goodness grandma decided to park her trailer permanently in our backyard. In the midst of such uncertainty and tumult, she provided both levity and ballast.

A no-nonsense, hard-working Irish woman who had married into the Norwegian farming community of St. Cloud, Minnesota, grandma certainly knew a black Angus stud from a Rhode Island Red. Human nature, by comparison, she opined was not so dissimilar; she could live as easily with one group as with the other.

Such hardy equanimity was a tonic to us all, so we viewed with alarm those first few weeks of disorientation when her unflappable

236

pluck was seismically disrupted by the mayhem of our household. For a time, a pernicious vertigo kept her atilt and in collapse until finally her resilient Irish stock rallied, dispatching her unaccustomed malaise. In admiration we watched as she, like the fabled Phoenix, rose in triumph from the ashes of her not inconsiderable adjustment.

Nearsighted and considerably less fat since Dr. Nowak had slipped amphetamines into her pillbox, grandma frequently supervised our house while mom was working. In an effort to bring order she would air out the blankets, wash the clutter of breakfast dishes and hide the boys' ashtrays, while at the same time baking chocolate chip and oatmeal raisin cookies. She had a habit of writing the baking times on the stove and countertops rather than on scratch paper, such that on busy days she would forget to wipe away the numbers, giving the effect of some Russian espionage ring that had set up in our kitchen – leaving cryptic equations and uncracked spy codes – when we returned from school.

Granny and her wooden canes were legends among our Greenacres friends. Well into her 80s, she wielded them with an authority and accuracy of aim that would make any marksman proud. Of especial interest to her were our blouse necklines and skirt lengths. "Shameful!" she would remark. "In my day we'd never get away with this," her cane sweeping up a too short hem, revealing bare legs. "And no slip, either. Anyone a'tall could see your bloomers if a good wind came up! How do you expect to get a decent husband with such floozy ways? I'm going to have to speak to Rose about you girls. . ." and off she would stomp to find Keith or Charles to inform them they were ruining their lungs from smoking, their shirts were wrinkled, and they had missed three cans of cutworms the last time they weeded the tomato plants.

Truly, grandma was mom's eyes and ears, and attempted to be our consciences as well. Our brothers' friends – Jeff Belknap, Dave and Alan Kokot, Lonnie Miller, and Steve and Paul Skeen (the Greenacres gang) – would hide in closets and behind doors when they heard the thump thump of her cane (too late to fan out the telltale odor of marijuana or cigarette smoke). Grandma acted as house bouncer and was perfectly capable of shutting the door on a mouthy teenager or any juvenile who got too obnoxious. "Rose doesn't need any monkeyshines like that in her house!" However, they all loved her home-baked cookies and thought her morality lectures and clothing reviews to us older girls madly funny.

No one in Greenacres responded to visitors as she did. In response to a knock at our door: "WALK IN! WALK IN!" she would command, rather than invite, in that extra loud voice so common to the hard-of-hearing.

None of us can forget the Saturday morning grandma came marching in to the kitchen from her trailer to announce to mom, "Rose, I've got so much money now, I'm starting to burn it!" Chuckling, she continued, "Baking brownies this morning, I smelled burning, and it wasn't my batter, either. Nope, it was the money I hid in the oven last week – afraid the neighbor boys would steal it. I forgot all about it, and now it's burnt to a crisp!" Adding as an afterthought, "but the brownies turned out fine."

Many an afternoon, following TV's *Oral Roberts* and *General Hospital,* grandma would bribe us girls with cookies or ice cream to entice us into washing and waxing her tiny kitchen linoleum, or setting her thinning white hair with bobby pins for Sunday morning services. Her judgment and sense of propriety were always impeccable until the morning she asked nine-months-pregnant Karen to scrub her kitchen floor.

Partly due to her inch-thick bifocals and partly because Karen had been careful to conceal her ballooning figure with extra-large sweatshirts, grandma had no idea that her 19-year old granddaughter, recently returned as a house guest, was hours away from becoming an unwed mother. Days later when the baby girl (her first great granddaughter), Rachael Elizabeth was presented to her, she wept with joy and shame – recalling with remorse the many mornings she had ascended the narrow stairwell to the second floor bedroom to roust Karen from her bed. Prodding her with the end of her wooden cane, she would protest, "Wake up, wake up for heaven's sake; are you going to sleep all day?!!" Which of course was exactly Karen's intention, immured as she was in the uncertainty of her pending future as a young mother.

When Rachael's birthfather Joel met grandma Hartmann for the first time, she was a sight he would never forget, dubbing her "Trailer Face" on the spot. She was being filmed in 16mm by Denae, using a rented movie camera – a tape intended as a Mother's Day tribute to the out of state relatives.

With a wooden cane in each hand, wire-rimmed bifocals propped on her nose, and wearing a gingham housedress sitting atop her brown, rolled-up support hose, she stepped out into the May sunshine, pausing for a moment on the cinderblock doorstep. A rose corsage was pinned upon her ample chest and a huge smile lifted her pink Irish cheeks. Behind her, miming every wobbly step was five-year old Curt, leaning on two broken tree branches. Denae, intent on capturing grandma in all her considerable glory, failed to notice him hamming it up from the rear.

The following evening's movie preview revealed his mischief, so the relatives never saw the video. We, however, consider it a family treasure. When we want to remember grandma in all those hilarious years she lived in our backyard, ruling Greenacres with her pluck and wit, we just pull out that movie and enjoy her all over again.

# THINGS FALL APART

Mom, at Greenacres

*Turning and turning in the widening gyre, the falcon*
*cannot hear the falconer;*
*Things fall apart; the centre cannot hold; mere anarchy*
*is loosed upon the world;*

— W.B Yeats, *The Second Coming*

Gwen

*It's my weekend to visit daddy. He is living across the street*
*from Lucille Ball, the woman who gave me my first real job – cleaning*
*her house. I had to get a Social Security card and have my taxes taken*
*out. I am ten-years old and have a Social Security card so I can work.*

*I go to bed and pray the mice won't come out. Why do they always*
*show up when it's dark? Everything is scarier then. I try not to listen.*
*I don't want to hear their scratching and their gnawing. Oh no, I hear*
*it. I know there's plenty of garbage for them, so they will be here a long*
*time, probably all night. What if they come into my bedroom? I know*
*they could crawl up the covers. I tuck the blankets in tight around me.*
*The gnawing sounds so close now; I can't protect myself. Where's dad-*
*dy? Daddy, is that you…?*

Gail

Once daddy was discharged from Medical Lake and living on his
own, he was anxious to resume communication with us. However,
the court's restraining order barred him from coming closer than 100
yards to our house, which made synchronizing our visits rather tricky.

Directly behind our house was the vegetable garden, and beyond
that a long expanse of open field in the shadow of the two-story-high
signboards. Our property ended at a deep ditch below the railroad
tracks. These three elements – the signboards, the railroad tracks and
the ditch – were not only geographic landmarks, but also emotional
markers that represented unforgettable events from our childhood.

Since the signboards were far enough from our house to satisfy the
restraining order, they became our meeting place with daddy. (It didn't

take him long, however, to inch his way back into the driveway). At the time, both Keith and I attended Greenacres Junior High and daily walked the four blocks to home. As we approached the signboards, we could see daddy's parked car waiting for us. Climbing inside, we would join Gwen, Charles and Curt, and visit with him for an hour or so.

On a long list of humiliating experiences, these visits were near the top. Since many of our schoolmates took the same route home – either walking or by bus –they would pass us like the paparazzi, craning their necks to catch a glimpse of the Veselits kids, all packed like sardines into their father's car. His old red Chevy became a roadside distraction, and I would imagine their comments: "Why in the world are the Veselits visiting their father on the side of the road? Why doesn't he just meet them at their house? It's only 100 yards away!"

When Saturday rolled around, we would stand waiting with a brown shopping bag filled with our clothing changes, concealed in the shadows beneath the signboards. Our destination? A succession of ragtag addresses in cheap hotel rooms, motels, or rented houses— wherever he was currently living.

But at least we had a real home to return to. We were reminded of this blessing one summer when a neighboring teen ran away from his violent, mentally ill mother, and camped up in the rafters of our signboards with an old sleeping bag. We kept his secret for two months (along with the other Greenacres kids), and kept him supplied with sandwiches, water, and other necessities until the weather got too cold and he went back home.

I always felt our visits with daddy had more to do with him wanting to control our lives than with missing us. He couldn't stand the thought of being cut off; he wanted to keep his finger on the pulse of whatever was going on. We were the conduit that provided him this information. During these visits, he constantly criticized Keith with such taunts as, "What kind of a weakling are you that you can't even bench press the same weight as your old man?" Easily lifting two-20lb bar bells above his own head, he would continue, "If you wanted to be a *real* man, you'd keep practicing until you can beat me."

Charles, he ignored altogether, as though he didn't exist. Eventually, so hurt by the rejection, Charles simply stopped seeing dad.

Curt was the only one he seemed to care about, whether because of his sweet nature or because he was the youngest. But the fact remained, Curt lived more with daddy than he did with mom. I never understood her allowing this, and always worried about him when he was alone with dad.

Years later when these visits came up for discussion with Elaine, she was outraged: "What do you mean '*overnight*, weekend visit?' What could mom have been thinking? Sleepovers with any of the kids were strictly forbidden by the court!"

Smiley, Charles, Keith, Curt

Daddy's residences were always scary, usually mouse-infested, with strange, unidentifiable noises at night. His bathroom facilities were dubious, with most flushing done by pouring water from a plastic bucket. While he continued to preach "Cleanliness is next to godliness," apparently that did not apply to him, since his sinks, bathtub and floors were rarely ever clean.

One night when I was staying alone with him in the spare bed-room of his rented house, I heard horrible scratching noises coming from the walls – even, it seemed, from beneath my bed. Terrified, I considered the possibility of going into daddy's bedroom for comfort. What would be worse, I wondered, staying alone in my bed trying to shut out all the awful sounds, or, asking daddy if I could sleep with him? Both options seemed equally dangerous, but in desperation I de-cided if I tip-toed into his room and crept into his bed, he'd never notice I was there. Which I did. The next morning, he was startled to find me on the other side of the mattress, lying motionless, straight as a board. I hadn't slept all night.

The mouse infestation at daddy's could have been manageable, but he refused to put his garbage in a closed container, preferring to use a paper bag on the kitchen floor. With plentiful food, the mice happily procreated and flourished.

Knowing we girls were terrified of them, his response bordered on the macabre, if not outright malicious. Curt and I had been spend-ing the afternoon when daddy decided to play a "joke" on me. Earlier, he had trapped a particularly fat rodent and placed its dead body, still in the trap, on the top shelf of the fridge between a can of soda and a jar of sauerkraut. His plan was to ask for a coke, at which point upon opening the door, I would have fainted from fright – while he had a good laugh. Fortunately, little Curt knew about the scheme, so he tipped me off. Motioning me to be quiet, he whispered anxiously, "Gail, whatever you do, *don't* open the refrigerator when he asks you for a soda. There's a big fat dead mouse in there, and I don't want you to get scared."

"Thank you, Curt!" I whispered back, hugging him with all my might. "I love you – you're such a good brother." With that, I dashed out the door, hopped on my bike, and pedaled away as fast as I could. To this day I cannot erase that image, of opening the refrigerator and seeing the dead rat staring me full in the face.

Normally you would not think of a ditch as a place of refuge. But the deep gully behind our property was for many years a haven of immeasurable worth. During the first half of childhood – before daddy was taken away – we were all terrified when he would punch holes in the walls, overturn furniture and lash us with his belt. Whenever possible, we would run to the ditch, leaving mom alone in the house to cope with dad. There, with our backs pressed against the dirt banks, we sometimes waited for hours... second-guessing what new atrocities dad might be committing, sharing secrets, or just drying our tears.

Periodically, the monotony of hiding would be interrupted by the shrill whistle of an oncoming train. Both Keith and I *loved* that sound, fantasizing about hopping onboard and being carried far away from our dreary life in Greenacres. I would watch wide-eyed as Keith would swing himself up onto the slower moving freight cars, preparing for the day when we would both jump aboard and ride the tracks to the end of the rainbow to claim our share of a pot of gold.

Denae

Changes indeed had taken place in the Greenacres household since mom had replaced dad as parent-in-charge. No room in the house had undergone such a radical transformation as the big girls' bedroom on the second floor, once we had vacated. It was still a bedroom, Charles' bedroom – but now everyone, including mom, called it the Gestapo Room.

The prim, almost Quaker-like neatness of our room, with its three quilt-covered beds and modest wood bureau, topped by white doilies and a few stray hair curlers, had become a cyclone-rearranged nightmare. Dangling chains hung from the ceiling while Jimi Hendrix and The Doors posters were taped onto graffiti-sprayed walls in Day-Glo greens, reds and mind-altering yellows. Glass bongs, empty beer bottles and overflowing ashtrays littered the floor beneath the boarded up main window, which was scrawled over with black swastikas and *Make Love Not War* slogans. Stringy wads of chewing gum and phlegm lugies hung erratically from the ceiling like stalactites in a dim cave.

To enter the room (usually posted with a menacing *NO*

*TRESPASSING* sign) was to leave behind sanity and order, as you crossed into a horrorscape of Dead Man Walking. Janis Joplin's whisky-edged voice reverberated, trembling and stuporous from too much acid, peyote, and hashish: "… put off, put down, strung out and stoned." A leering Jim Morrison poster mouthed, "It seems that you got lost somewhere in the wild …" while the Full-Tilt, Kozmic Blues Boogie Band was strumming Charles' guitar, singing off-key and drunk, "Cry Baby … Bye bye baby, bye bye … too bad you had to drift away."

You couldn't really think in the middle of this Dead Zone – it wasn't meant for thinking. It was meant for hiding, escaping, obliterating reality. The Den of Iniquity was its other name, or simply, the Den. Charley's world. Not a pretty place.

It was here at age nineteen, he tried to kill himself by swallowing a bottle of aspirins, washed down with a half liter of wine. Not an alarming discovery for mom when she was alerted. No, not really alarming, because by now she was past feeling panic when calamities occurred. Sure, she'd take you to the hospital, and then, when you returned home after your stomach had been pumped, she'd leave you in your bedroom to finish recovering with a glass of water on your nightstand and a couple of aspirin next to it.

No irony intended. Denial was just part of her coping arsenal. And not wanting to know things. Because if she knew, she'd have to do something about it – make a decision, take some action. Mom just wasn't up to it. She was perfectly straightforward and honest with us about her deficiencies. "I don't *want* to know every little thing that goes on in this household. If you can't take care of your problems, don't bring them to me. I've got enough of my own."

Gail

On occasion, mom could be fairly dramatic – slamming metal pot covers together when she was really upset. Like a deranged circus performer, she would bang away on her make-believe cymbals, tromping up and down the stairs, in and out of our bedrooms. Usually when she exhibited this behavior, we would escape to the upper rooms where

246

the noise wasn't quite so deafening. Irrespective of time – it could be three in the morning or three in the afternoon – she could keep up this racket for an hour or more until she finally wore herself out.

On one such night, both Karen and I were hiding upstairs, intermittently laughing hysterically and crying at the absurdity of mom's behavior. Even though we were seasoned veterans to these crazy outbursts, all semblance of sanity disappeared on this particular evening when mom, who had now given herself a splitting headache, began searching the house for an aspirin. With pot covers still clanging, she shouted above the din, **"You can't even keep a goddamn aspirin in this house when you need one, because if you do, someone will try to commit suicide!!"**

<u>Denae</u>

Much as the Gestapo Room reflected Charles' dark, wounded side, it certainly did not represent the sensitive, artistic, intelligent aspects of his nature, nor his keen sense of humor. He was an intrepid practical jokester, just like Curt. His best friend Dave Kokot recalls one especially inventive Gotcha! Charley at his prankiest. All the Greenacres boys knew that Dave was finicky about his food. A stray hair lodged in a tuna sandwich or a spider leg dangling from a lettuce leaf in a Caesar salad would send him gagging from the room. No one razzed Dave for his queasy stomach because they had their own idiosyncrasies. So one Friday afternoon, Charley left for a haircut, sharpening up for a Saturday night movie date, and promising to pick up a hamburger for Dave. He was waiting, hungry and impatient in his backyard, when Charley finally showed up.

"Here you go! I even remembered the mayo and onions," he called out with a big grin. Dave whipped off the flimsy wrapper, lifting it up toward his salivating tongue. "A-a-gggh-h-h!!" His double cheeseburger was piled high with two meat patties, catsup and all of Charles' sandy brown hair, cut off by the barber. He had scooped it up from the floor and carefully padded it into place between the whole-wheat buns of Dave's Double-Deluxe, extra onions, hold the mustard, burger.

During their teen years, the two of them were virtually inseparable. Like Batman and Robin, Jagger and Richards, or Cheech and Chong, they did everything together – dating the same girls, cramming for school tests, shooting pool, or doing drugs.

At that time in Spokane, you could get LSD for a few dollars a hit in some of the downtown clubs. Pot was just as accessible. So one hot, lazy Saturday night, instead of hallucinating as usual in the Gestapo Room, the two of them decided to stretch out on our front lawn beneath Orion's Belt and the Big Dipper, curious to see if the change of setting would affect their acid trips.

With four dilated pupils gazing heavenward, the midnight sky was pulsating with psychedelic colors and intergalactic explosions. After an hour of watching these pyrotechnics, Charles turned to Dave. "Hey, let's walk up to the junior high and see what happens on the way." Then, with still a fragment of his brain intact, knowing how paranoid and delusional their trips could be, Charles paused for a moment, pointing toward our house.

"Wait a minute," he said, and disappeared into the kitchen, returning with an orange. "We may never find our way back, so we can use this orange to mark the road." Laughing easily, he peeled off a thumbnail patch of orange skin and dropped it behind him, repeating this action every few yards as they shuffled along the dimly lit pavement.

A few yards from the school, Charles stopped again. "Hey man, I've run out of orange. We gotta go back." And like a stoned Hansel and Gretel, the two of them laughed and lurched their way back to the yard by following the Clockwork Orange trail of fiery, gyrating fruit peelings.

Gail

While Charles sequestered himself in the Gestapo Room with his buddies – referred to as his "bum friends" or "the juvenile delinquents" by dad (they in turn referred to him as "Bat Face"), Gwen would be at cheerleading practice, leaving me at home to serve as mom's sewing assistant.

Sewing with her was almost as nerve-racking as cooking with her, the difference being that she actually enjoyed sewing, while cooking was a drudgery. Much as I had no interest in this craft, my home ec classes required making skirts and blouses, so I had no alternative but to enlist mom's help.

During the early '60s, when two-piece swimsuits were just coming into fashion, mom was one of the few neighborhood mothers who was not scandalized by seeing her daughters wearing bikinis at the public beach. Conversely, she was thrilled by how little fabric was required in their construction, so for years she made string bikinis for us girls.

It seemed to me all the homemade clothes just accentuated our poverty. Invariably, each new sewing project began at the remnants table in the Two Swabbies, where we rummaged for the rock-bottom, cheapest materials. Mom would pick up a handful of fabric, exclaiming to me with shining eyes, "Gail, look what I found! Isn't it beautiful?!!"

What she was really excited about was the price tag, 29 cents a yard. Every blouse or skirt I ever made always came from these stacks of materials, spilling off the shelves and sold by the pound at huge discounts – similar to our surplus commodities – food and fabric that no one else wanted. The first time you washed it, most of the dye came out and it usually shrank.

I think sewing provided a creative outlet for mom, a way to restore some of her equilibrium after her stint at Medical Lake. Unfortunately, this sewing period was also her shaky period, and we all know that shaking hands, scissors and sewing needles make for risky bedfellows. No matter how well-intentioned, her nerves usually got the better of her.

The vision I have of mom on sewing day is of her holding a Kent cigarette in one hand and a chipped, brown plastic coffee cup in the other. Thus fortified with enough caffeine and nicotine to make even a dead man shake, mom would proceed to the sunroom, where her antique treadle machine was located, with me following in her wake.

My primary function was to re-light her cigarettes, refill her coffee cup, pick up fallen straight pins and thread the needle when the thread snapped from her forgetting to adjust the tension release. Additionally, I was expected to act as house marshal, monitoring all phone calls. "Be sure and answer them by the *second* ring; otherwise it breaks my concentration" were her explicit instructions. No one was allowed through the front or back doors either; she demanded complete quiet – an impossible expectation considering the usual pandemonium created by five kids, grandma, pets, friends and neighbors.

At long last, the moment would come when the house was quiet – a fresh cigarette had been lit, her coffee cup was full and the phone was not ringing – when I thought I could relax. The moment would disappear in the time it takes a pin to drop, and mom would announce: "Gail, it's time for the first fitting."

The dreaded first fitting. Reluctantly, I would try the garment on, knowing from past experience that it wasn't going to fit. I never could figure out whether mom hadn't cut the pattern right or if her shaking hands prevented her from sewing straight seams, because invariably there was a malfunction in the fit. Either one armhole was smaller than the other, the zipper stuck, or a neckline was too tight.

Despite the inevitable problems, I always assured her that it *fit perfectly*, because god forbid she should have to rip out a seam and start over. I knew then that I'd be sentenced to another afternoon of sheer agony. All I wanted was for *her* to be finished so that *I* could be finished!

Elaine

Yes, the dreaded first fitting.

"Stand up straight, so I can see you. Suck in your stomach. Turn to the left... Slowly. You turned too much! That's not your left. Don't you know your left from your right?"

Grabbing me by both shoulders, oblivious to the tears spilling down my cheeks, mom would twist me into position like a well-digger shoveling around boulders. "Now, stand there. And don't move!"

From the age of nine, all us girls were expected to hem our garage sale/hand-me-down skirts and dresses. And of course, in those years there were yards of pleating around the waistlines. Nevertheless, our stitching was expected to be tiny, like our tiny awkward fingers.

"I don't want to see any 'elephant tracks'" would be mom's response as the stitches became larger and more disorderly. No wonder I hated sewing.

Denae

Much as mom could be a capable seamstress, the pressures of her life couldn't help but affect her, causing various wardrobe malfunctions. I can't tell you the number of times I sat on the hot sand at Liberty Lake watching Diane's bikini top or bottom sail off as she dived from the dock. Likewise, my own top or bottom could often be found floating like a discarded candy bar wrapper if I swam around too long without checking to see if it was still tied on. Invariably, mom forgot to reinforce the crucial seams, or else the fabric was so cheap it just shredded after a few trips to the beach.

My most memorable clothing disaster occurred on a trip to Ethiopia in my twenties (paid for by working three months as an au pair). I was boarding a crowded city bus with my Peace Corps boyfriend on my first day in Addis Ababa, when suddenly my miniskirt dropped to the floor (Mom had not finished stitching the elastic waistband to the fabric). All the modestly garmented Ethiopians – covered from neck to ankle – stared incredulously as I stood there in my pink underpants, clinging to my suitcase. My embarrassed boyfriend, standing behind me in the aisle, hissed, "For god's sake, SIT DOWN!!" But I couldn't, because every seat was taken.

Gail

One evening mom was helping me with a blouse, which I needed the next day for the Greenacres Junior High Mother's Day Fashion Show. We were running behind as usual, and I was frantic that it wouldn't be done. "Don't worry," mom reassured me, "I'll finish it up tomorrow morning and drop it off at school on my way to work."

The next day first and second periods came and went, but still no sign of mom or the blouse. By third period I was in despair with the show only half an hour away. Losing hope, I watched the clock tick-tock its way toward twelve, when I heard a knock at the door.

Wouldn't you know I would be in history class with hunky Mr. Lincoln. My initial apprehension was replaced with total embarrassment. Apparently, mom had dropped off my blouse at the principal's office with instructions to have it delivered ASAP. Upon receiving it, Mr. Lincoln couldn't resist exploiting the situation. Holding up the insipid paisley fabric between his thumb and forefinger, he announced, "Who would like to claim this lovely garment? Maybe its owner would like to model it for the class?"

Desperate to avoid sharing the limelight with that pink and lime shirt, I hurried to the front and grabbed it from him. Ignoring the snickers, all I could think of was hurling the hideous thing out the window. However, the fashion show was about to start, and I knew I had to participate. So off I went to the Girls' bathroom to change. As I pulled the material over my head and around my chest, I grabbed for a button to fasten it. Immediately I discovered that mom had forgotten to sew the buttonholes. What could be more obvious? It was like salt without pepper, a river without water. Buttons and buttonholes just naturally go together. How could mom have failed to notice?

Needless to say, I did not model my blouse along with the other girls. What did I care anyway? My mom wasn't even there. Instead, I sat in the audience next to Mrs. White, my best friend's mother, pretending that I was her daughter. We both watched as Shelly, her real daughter, sauntered down the runway in a picture-perfect blouse, complete with buttonholes.

Elaine

It's hard to entirely fault mom for the mayhem and malfunctions of her sewing efforts. For as long as I can remember, these ventures were dogged by adversity and sabotage. In 1959 when I was 14, dad bought her a brand new Singer sewing machine – she was ecstatic! Then, for months afterward, he would pawn it at a downtown hock shop for ten dollars every time he needed beer money. When the welfare check would arrive on the first of the month, he'd buy it back and bring it home. After months of this craziness, the day came when it was not returned.

"I was actually relieved," mom told me. "I could finally stop dreading that machine's disappearance. This time I knew it was gone for good."

For just such reasons, I don't blame her for the disaster of my college graduation dress. To her credit, she had volunteered to make the outfit, knowing the few clothes I did have were too worn and out of style for such a grand occasion.

The parcel arrived in the middle of finals week. Exhausted from all the late night cramming and with more tests ahead, opening mom's package was the one bright spot in my schedule. My hands tore away the brown wrapping to find inside the most beautiful soft green material. Sliding from the box, it fell to the floor. In pieces. Two sleeves, the front yoke, a skirt and the waist-band. *What the …?*

A note was pinned to the collar:

*Elaine, I didn't know your size, so I left all the seams open.*
*Ask one of your friends to sew it together. Love, Mom.*

My great shining moment. Four years of grueling study, paid for by berry picking, babysitting and cleaning houses so I could be the first in our family to graduate from college. And what was my final challenge in this rite of passage? Finding someone to finish sewing my commencement outfit. Frantically, I asked the girls in my dorm; lots of home ec majors, but all in cooking. Eventually, someone gave me the phone number of a student who sewed. I didn't even have the money to pay her. So a complete stranger finished mom's graduation gift to me.

Thinking back, I have no recollection whatsoever of the ceremony, but I sure remember the dress. I ended up wearing it to every job interview for the next ten years.

# THE SADDEST DAY

Curt and Charles

*Just as we take the train to reach Tarascon or Rouen,
we must take death to reach a star.*

–Vincent Van Gogh

Denae

Charles and Curt were due in to Spokane International Airport at 8 pm. So Diane, Karen, Gail, Gwen and myself were in the car driving through the December darkness, the windshield wipers pushing away the heavy fog and pounding rain as we strained to read the road signs marking our approach to the airport. But we didn't go to the regular terminal where dozens of passengers would soon be disembarking, anxious to be reunited and fussed over by waiting family or friends. No, instead we went to the freight annex. We had left home an hour early, to be sure we would arrive there before the hearse.

The week before, the boys, at 21 and 23, had been en route to a job site at Heideburg, Alaska, when their plane crashed. None of the eight passengers on board survived. So we had gone to the freight terminal to find them, to greet them, and say a few prayers before seeing them into the hearse.

What manner of purgatory was this space we were so reluctant to enter? Cartons and boxes, hundreds of them, filled the huge storage room – a virtual cemetery of stacked and toppled tombstones. How large a box should we be looking for? Or – our minds hardly dared go there – how small? Would they be together.. or separate? How would the containers be labeled?

We found Curt first… in a long cardboard box with "Curt Veselits" written in black ink on top. Fifteen minutes later, we found the box bearing Charles' name. Choking back tears, we placed a red rose on each carton.

That was in 1982. It is now 2017. The eulogy we wrote for them best expresses who they were as young men.

*...We will always carry with us the innocence and the beauty of their natures. There was a special quality in Charley and Curt that caused others to be drawn to them. Even when very young, their openness and brightness attracted the admiration and loyalties of the neighborhood children and their other friends. These loyalties became even more binding as the years strengthened and matured them all. If there was one thing known for certain among Charley and Curt's friends, it was that Charley and Curt would never let them down. Their friends were as special to them as their family; the line was never drawn to separate the two. In their profession as construction workers, they were regarded by their boss and co-workers as the two finest achievers.*

*But the love that Charley and Curt felt for each other was the most special bond of all and a testimony to each of us, of the profound power of human caring and devotion. We are comforted immeasurably that because they left us together, one will never have to mourn the other. 'Love bears with all things and believes all things and endures all things.'*

*Charley and Curt were like two young eagles who left the nest and dared to soar higher than us all, so high that they will never have to touch this earth again. They will return to us, but not as they left us, for in death life is merely changed, not ended. In their living as in their leaving, they helped us to know the joy and fulfillment of flying high. And by their example, we shall let our own spirits soar to reach the heights that they aspired to in life.*

*Our memories give them eternal life, and we will always know them as two proud men, ever young, ever strong, ever free.*

Gwen

To describe this day requires a vocabulary I don't possess. It was the day that changed each of our lives forever. Thirty-five years later, I still cannot think about it without crying, without still missing them. I look at their last photograph together – Charles' arm draped around Curt's shoulder, behind them an overcast Alaskan sky. Theirs were the first faces of love that I saw as a child.

As teenagers, and then as young men, they always maintained how much they loved and admired their sisters, and that they wanted to marry young women who were just like us. What more loving statement could two brothers make? Knowing this was the only solace I had to counter all my self-destructive beliefs regarding men. In spite of the many bad choices I made in dating and my poor self esteem, in the back of my mind was always that lingering belief that there must be something good about me, something redeeming, because my brothers could see it and had valued it.

My memory is probably the poorest in the family – maybe from drug use in my teens, or maybe as a defense against the filter of sadness through which I viewed life in general. But that day, December 9, 1982 – the day they died – is the saddest of all days. It is crystal clear in its detail and frozen in time, like their two names etched together on the copper memorial urn they share.

Since Charles was a year younger than me, we shared many friends and experiences. In reality, he seemed more like my twin. When others could not understand his moods or actions, I served as his interpreter. I understood his pain at being rejected by dad, while at the same time trying to comprehend why Curt was always so favored and loved. I was too young to protect him, but what I could do was always be there for him. We were two children trying to bear up beneath the weight of a father's mental illness, alcoholism and ignorance – a father's own lifetime of pain. It was a weight that would crush both our spirits for many long years.

After his death, I worried and prayed for a sign that Charles *really was* in a better place. I needed some affirmation that he was truly at peace. The long awaited sign came one Sunday morning in Portland, Oregon, where mom and I were attending a mass at Charles' church. Sensing the presence of someone to my left, I glanced over only to discover an empty chair. No one was there, yet I felt an energy that seemed very much like Charles. This essence began spreading, soon filling the entire sanctuary – a presence so compelling that it felt like a palpable force pushing in on me from all sides. I sat breathless, imbued with a fullness saturated with peace and goodness, light and grace. It could only have been Charles, his generous spirit filling the church. Then came a quiet and loving voice saying, "It's okay, Gwen. I'm okay now. All the pain and sorrow is gone." *All* the pain? *All* the sorrow? Somehow, I believed it was true. Charles was now all that he had been created to be, finally at peace, like Curt, both in the arms of their loving Father.

# I'LL FLY AWAY

Front: Keith, Karen, Denae, Diane
Back: Gail, Mom, Elaine

*Some bright morning when this life is over – I'll fly away*
*To that home on God's celestial shore – I'll fly away*
*When the shadows of this life have gone – I'll fly away*
*Like a bird from these prison walls – I'll fly away*
*I'll fly away oh glory – I'll fly away*
*When I die hallelujah by and by – I'll fly away*

Nine years after mom's death, Gwen penned the following entry in her journal. Not only does it speak to her own sense of loss and regret – a plaintive lament to recover a mother now gone – it also captures for all of us our bereavement for a mother so damaged by circumstance.

Gwen *(Journal Entry, April 16, 2007)*

*Mom, where were you? Where are you? I'm looking for you, but I can't find you. I'm trying to remember you. Did you love me? Were you glad I was born? Did I make you laugh? I don't remember ever sitting on your lap. I don't remember you hugging me or kissing me as a child.*

*Was I one too many? Were you disappointed that I was a girl and not a boy since you already had five daughters and only one son? Did we ever have a tea party together? Play dress-up? Did you feel anything – anything at all for me? What would it have been like to feel loved by you? How would my life be different today if I had grown up knowing that you loved me?*

*I have struggled so, mom. I have tried to be the mom I wanted you to be. It was easier to villainize dad than to think about what I missed out on with you. I always just accepted that you had too many kids, too much responsibility, that you were emotionally dead because of dad.*

*I miss my mom. I just want to walk with you, hold your hand, feeling like I'm the most special little girl in the world. Mrs. Langness made me feel special. That wasn't enough. I've been so sad for so long. I thought Charles and Curt were enough – thank God for them – but they couldn't take the place of a mother's love.*

*I forgive you, mom. I'm not mad at you. I know now that you must have loved me. How did I miss it as a child? Is there any way that you could still be my mom? I feel like I grew up without parents. In many respects, I'm still that little girl walking alone in the dark, the mile between the Two Swabbies and the Dishman Theatre (when you and dad accidentally left me behind) – trying to figure out what I should do, trying not to be afraid. I was just a little girl who needed love and protection...where were you?*

## Denae

Memories of personal time spent with mom are hazy at best. In actuality, she seemed more like the head matron of a boarding school. That said, there is nothing remarkable about this particular mother/daughter outing, except that it was one of the few times I can recall being alone with her – well, almost alone, as Gail was with me.

Gloomy is the best way to describe that Saturday afternoon. With so much rain falling, mom invited us to accompany her to Mrs. Dwinnell's home in downtown Spokane to pick up her paycheck, since mom worked there part-time doing laundry and other housework.

Never having been to a rich person's house before, Gail at 9, and I at 13, were eager to see the crystal chandeliers, Persian carpets, indoor palm trees (Imagine!) and flowering orchid plants that mom had described.

"Don't even think of wandering around on your own once we're there," she had cautioned. "Stay with me in the entryway until Mrs. Dwinnell invites us into another room."

Thus rehearsed, we followed mom up the stairs to the grand, three-story home with the grace and deportment of two young Audrey Hepburns, fresh from a French boarding school. The butler (if there was one) need not concern himself with following us around for any breaches of protocol. No, indeed. In fact, standing there before the gleaming mahogany door, I wondered if we were expected to curtsy to Mrs. Dwinnell. Was being rich the same as being royalty? Too late to ask mom; her finger was already pressing the doorbell.

Suddenly, there she was! a carefully coiffed, middle-aged woman dressed in a remarkably plain two-piece brown suit – her apparel nowhere near as fashionable as the clothes Diane borrowed from Oleta Maye. *This <u>was</u> a Saturday,* I reflected; *perhaps wealthy people dress down for the weekends?* My eyes traveled to her ears, neck and hands to see how many diamonds and pearls she might be wearing. I was delighted to see the enormous glittering stone on her ring finger – and poked Gail to be sure she noticed as well. *Now for the palm tree…* completely forgetting about the curtsy.

"Oh, Rose, you've brought your two daughters. How lovely. Come in, girls, to the sitting room. I'll have Myra make some tea. Follow me." We could have squealed with pleasure as we minced along behind her, discreetly checking our images in the large gilt-edged mirrors we were passing.

Finally settled in to matching maroon chairs, Mrs. Dwinnell pulled forward an inlaid mother-of-pearl table and began arranging saucers, teaspoons and creamer in preparation for Myra's arrival. So many different cultures drink tea, I mused – China, Japan, England, India. Doctor and Mrs. Dwinnell were well traveled and had probably drunk tea in every one of those places. No doubt the tea ceremony differed from country to country; so what kind of tea service were we going to have this afternoon? What manner of protocol was expected of us?

Niggling doubts were beginning to surface. Our anticipated time as accidental tourists in the Big House was losing its allure, and fast. We had only come to see the chandeliers and palm tree; how had we so quickly become entangled in high culture complexities like tea-drinking decorum? Uh oh. I began to squirm uncomfortably in my chair. Gail clearly had not yet perceived the enormity of our pending dilemma, perched as we were at the threshold of disgrace – the full catastrophe. Perhaps the butler *would* be ushering us out prematurely after all: "Stupid, poor kids. Riff-raff. Shouldn't be allowed in polite society."

Frantically, then – before Myra could make her appearance – I searched my mind for any scraps of information on tea etiquette. At home we had some Lipton tea bags in a tin canister, but they were rarely used for drinking. Rather, they were applied as compresses for sunburns or stove burns. Mom and dad drank Sanka and Maxwell House Instant Coffee – using water drawn from the hot water tap or water that had been heated in a pot normally used for boiling potatoes.

I tried recalling what details I could from *Breakfast at Tiffany's* or *The Prime of Miss Jean Brodie* – surely tea had been sipped in one of those dining scenes. Mentally, I rewound the Brodie film, carefully examining each frame. Karen had once informed me, "*Everything you need to know about life can be found in this film.*" Having seen it twice, I thought I was well prepared, but now I was beginning to doubt her judgment.

What exactly were the fine points? Do you pick up the cup *with* the saucer, or without? Was it permissible to blow on the hot water to cool it, or did you just wait? *Oh no, here comes Myra!* My panic increased. Was it acceptable to ask for an ice cube to plop in if the water was still too hot?

Palms now oozing with sweat, I glanced over to Gail. Not a worry crease on her face; she was staring into the next room at a pale yellow cockatoo, eating its birdseed while hanging upside down in its cage. Didn't she realize we were on the verge of disaster? Mom would surely know what to do and could have shown us by example, but she was still upstairs with Bobbi Dwinnell, the daughter, collecting her dry cleaning.

"Now, dear," Mrs. Dwinnell, seated across from me, was holding aloft a dainty saucer of lemon wedges and a porcelain cream pitcher, "sugar, cream or lemon?" It had_all happened too fast. My thoughts were spinning. *Calm down. Collect yourself.*

"Oh, lemon and cream, please. Thank you," I smiled tightly at her.

"Are you sure, dear?" she responded, seemingly in concern.

*Well, for heaven's sake, what does it matter?* I thought grimly. *Why should you care <u>what</u> I put into my tea? I'm the one who is drinking it.*

"If that's what you want, then," and handed them across to me.

As soon as I poured in the cream and squeezed out the lemon juice, I realized my mistake. As if back in chemistry class, I watched the molecular transformation occurring before my eyes. To my horror, white chunks of curdled cream now dotted the surface of my tea like ice floes on a dark northern sea.

Tactfully turning to Gail, Mrs. Dwinnell inquired, "And you, dear?"

"Oh, I think I'll just have a glass of milk. Thank you."

*Coward!* I thought. Well, Gail could relax and enjoy her beverage, while I – what exactly was I to do with that cottage-cheesy looking brew before me? Lifting it to my lips, I sipped with a contrived expression of purest pleasure, swallowing a couple of the soft curdly lumps. "Just the way I like it," I lied.

My audacity amazed me. What Gail thought, I could not guess, because her eyes were still locked on the upside-down cockatoo. With no turning back now, I wondered whether I should ask for a refill.

Thank goodness, mom reappeared at that moment and said it was probably time for us to leave. We had not yet seen the crystal chandeliers, but Gail and I were more than happy to forgo the sight in order to escape the demands of high society. Mentally, we both vowed to be better prepared next time.

Gail

Sprague Avenue, the busy street in front of our house, proved to be a dangerous place for stray dogs and battered wives. One evening, deep in sleep, I was startled awake by police sirens and flashing lights. It wasn't until morning that I learned what had transpired. Apparently, an angry husband and his wife were driving down the street, and as their fight escalated, the man pushed his wife out of the speeding car. The unfortunate woman hit our driveway and rolled repeatedly over jagged rock and gravel before coming to a stop. Mom and daddy woke to her whimpering cries. She had been badly injured, lying unconscious on the grass. Daddy called the police, who arrived at the same time as the ambulance.

In the morning, neither parent said much, providing only minimal details to our queries. Fascinated by the strange event, I walked along the driveway; several rocks were stained with blood. Continuing my investigation, I was shocked to find a woman's eyeglasses and picked them up, turning them over in my hand. With this physical connection, I felt somehow bonded with her. Ironically, the design of her glasses was much like my own. In trying to re-create her identity, I speculated that she must be poor like me, with the same limited selection of glasses.

What, I wondered, could have happened to cause her husband to become so enraged that he would shove her out the door? Violence reared its ugly head in our household too, so I empathized with this poor woman's plight.

A chilling thought crossed my mind – maybe she wasn't pushed; maybe she had been trying to escape the violence, and in desperation had actually *jumped* from the car!

I remember mom once wanting to run away from daddy. She was holding baby Charles in her arms with Gwen and me at her side, the four of us walking aimlessly down Sprague Avenue. All we had were the clothes on our backs. After less than a mile, I remember mom saying to herself, "Who am I kidding? Where do I think I'm going?" With that, she turned us around, and we headed back home.

Did mom feel the same way as the poor woman in our driveway? That your life was so controlled by someone else that there were really only two choices – either you stayed and died slowly, or you grasped at your only other option and died quickly.

I believe this woman had made her choice.

Mom's life was a minefield of Sophie's Choices, a littered landscape of potential catastrophes for all of us were she to choose carelessly. And in that peculiar pathology of thought which determines choice, it seemed mom found herself more than a few times adrift in the nether realms of the subconscious. How else can we explain this remarkable event from her past?

In 1959, mom at 43 was in labor in a Spokane hospital in the process of giving birth to Del Curtis, her tenth child. Twelve years later in 1971 she was again at a local hospital for a long overdue gynecological exam.

"So, Rose," inquired the doctor, glancing up from his speculum, "When did you have your hysterectomy?"

Startled, mom replied, "Never! Why do you ask?"

"Because" – the doctor was now carefully choosing his words – "because you have no uterus; yet according to your chart you've given birth ten times!"

In astonishment, mom could only repeat she had never had a hysterectomy. And at appointment's end, clutching her prescription for massive doses of calcium to restore her depleted skeletal frame, she was utterly humiliated that such a thing could have happened without her knowledge or permission.

Not surprisingly then, in the years to follow, The Case of Mom's Missing Uterus generated a great deal of family discussion and conjecture. Since she had not been to *any* doctor in the 12 years subsequent to Curt's birth (and ruling out sorcery, witchcraft or divine intervention), it seemed obvious that her obstetrician had performed the surgery. But how could he have dared without her consent? Were not ethics still bound to the Hippocratic Oath? Or did the doctor think he was doing her a favor – this fertile yet malnourished welfare mother with a houseful of kids and possibly more to come?

A fine lesson in adult ways for us children. Was this how the world operated? With a different set of rules for the poor people? We could go to the hospital with pneumonia, TB, seizures – any perfectly respectable illness – and return home missing a vital organ or body part.

But then again, what if mom had agreed to the surgery, maybe while under anesthesia, and then had forgotten all about it?

Mom never did resolve the puzzle of her missing uterus, and would not consider a lawsuit against her obgyn when we suggested it – the (anticipated) millions of dollars in compensation dancing like sugarplums in our impoverished little heads.

Karen

There is no straight line to the past. Recovering personal memory is a thorny process, requiring a circuitous path, sometimes even the slow boat to China route and inevitably beset by emotional blockages and memory lapses.

I became a student of film and literature in part because both genres speak so powerfully to my subconscious, helping me come to terms with my childhood. Literary works can make order out of chaos, oftentimes in a symbolic manner, so that a frightening past becomes less intimidating, more approachable. Writers like Edgar Allen Poe, Sylvia Plath, Truman Capote, Edward Albee and the whole Theatre of the Absurd strongly appeal to my sensibilities. Like them, I seem predisposed to employ the bizarre, the Gothic, as a plausible if not accurate representation of reality. Dark humor, along with irony, especially when it bites, are effective ways of dealing with tragedy and troubled pasts.

So how do I come to terms with the woman I call mother – the passive, elusive figure she was reduced to through her marriage to my father?

I begin with family photos, looking up to a framed black and white snapshot on my mantel, an image of mom, me and my three sisters all standing together on my second birthday. Mom's blonde hair is shiny and styled; she is wearing a pretty dress and lipstick, so I know she is happy. We four little girls are well groomed, too, wearing smiles and short wool coats, like the Kennedy children, each holding a rag doll that mom made – the faces painted by dad.

Another photo of mom is especially becoming as she sits with the month-old twins on a slatted wood chair in the grassy meadow next to our house. The California sun shines through her loose, shoulder-length hair, giving it soft, golden highlights. She wears a patterned dress, holding Diane and Denae upright on her lap, the two of them in white cotton dresses. They are both screaming, mouths wide open, but mom has the most beatific smile. It is clear she is in love – with her new babies and with her husband – the unseen man taking the picture.

A photo from a few years later tells a different story; it is of mom, dad, Elaine, Denae, Diane and me. I'm holding a white chicken feather. Mom looks gaunt, frayed, her coat sleeves nearly covering her fingertips. Her hair is unkempt, her expression unreadable, as she leans slightly back from us, almost out of the camera's focus – as though she wishes to step away from the moment, away from her present reality. She once told me, "You can tell from the photographs when everything began to break down."

In the past it was always safer to remember only the comic, bizarre aspects of childhood. By reading the honest recollections of others, I was encouraged to put aside my rose-colored glasses, enabling me to use less painful memories as a jumping off point rather than a stopping place.

I am reminded of the first line in *Macbeth*: "So fair and foul a day I have not seen" –words intended to foreshadow the dual nature of its tragic hero. A fair summation of our own past, I think – the trick being to keep the fair and the foul in perspective, despite the daily contradiction of living with both.

In our family, the tragedies included, but are not limited to: five suicide attempts, (including my own); physical, sexual and psychological abuse; mental illness and alcoholism; torture, both physical and mental; crippling poverty; an abiding rootlessness that felt like quicksand; and the early deaths of our beloved youngest brothers.

What is it that can cause a man to put a loaded gun to his own wife's head? That can make a father so vicious that his children cower in voiceless terror, fearful for their lives? My worst memory is of the night when, in a fulsome rage, he ripped the skirt and blouse off my trembling body. I was only seven and stood there paralyzed. How does one think to do such a thing? Had it been done to him? What did he get out of it?

Daddy also smashed our dishware, broke windows and threw over the dinner table – not to mention pushing, slapping and punching our mother. He had no problem beating us kids with a strap, sometimes in the face.

Writer Sylvia Plath strikes a healthy balance between defiant anger and artistic control in her poems, "Lady Lazarus" and "Daddy." Without giving in to sentimentality or amnesia, she confronts and often exorcises some of the same demons we faced. So when she asserts, in her poem "Daddy:" "Brute heart of a brute…You do not do, you do not do," concluding with a wrathful, **"Daddy, daddy, you bastard, I'm through,"** it becomes for me a provocative meditation on patricide.

Dostoevsky dramatizes three sons' murderous feelings toward their father in *The Brothers Karamazov*, while Robert Graves goes even further in *I, Claudius* when he describes Caligula killing Germanicus, his despotic, depraved royal father.

Contemplated patricide. Actual patricide. These authors' bold strokes helped me to acknowledge, then discharge my own rage through vicariously experiencing the thoughts and actions of their damaged characters. I could carry my emotions to the very extreme of human behavior without fear of incarceration or institutionalization.

For me, Plath's poetry gave voice to interrelated demons of father, mother, loss and depression – a toxic combination, which can prove fatal. Thoughts of suicide and failed suicide attempts plagued the children in our family. Whether mom, too, considered it an option, I cannot say, but my own preoccupation was very much influenced by parental abuse and neglect.

I cannot forget a chillingly prophetic poem written by Diane in her early twenties, when we shared college classes at Quinnipiac University in Connecticut –a poem charged with latent elements of violence and doom:

*The jungle hides the lion*
*Growling around the thickest century*
*Us he devours*
*And struts among our suicides*
*Munching*
*And digesting*

"The first time it happened I was ten. It was an accident," writes Plath in "Lady Lazarus," her elegy on suicide. She continues, "The second time I meant… to not come back at all."

My own attempt came at 17, when I was a VISTA volunteer in Pittsburgh. After washing down a bottle of aspirins with MacNaughton's and diet coke, I called Denae in Spokane to say goodbye. Without telling me, she immediately called the police. Soon a fire truck was at my door. I came downstairs and convinced the emergency squad I was fine. They left, and I called Denae again to ask why she had interfered. Within minutes the paramedics were back at my door. Did I really want to die at that point in my life? I don't know. Mental health professionals say that every suicide attempt is serious, so I'll believe them.

I waited until my thirties to finally seek help, but not before finding one of my sisters who had also tried to kill herself. She was crumpled on the floor of her apartment, barely conscious. After being taken away by ambulance, she spent weeks in ICU at Yale/New Haven Hospital, with mom sitting by her side, tending to her through the long ordeal of recovery.

Denae

We would all agree, I think, that mom certainly tried to be a more present and nurturing person in her retirement by way of

270

countermanding the downtrodden, crazy-acting woman of our childhood. However, much as we all resolved to put the past behind us, its long sticky tentacles couldn't help but continue to mar our relations with mom and with each other. Doubts and questions were unavoidable; how much had she known of dad's sexual crimes against us? She wasn't blind, yet so often she did not see. But then again, had we been in her shoes could we have done any better?

Yes, we had all been damaged and knew from experience that our yearly get- togethers were *not* enjoyable occasions. The group dynamics, in spite of our valiant intentions, invariably collapsed into angry outbursts and misunderstandings. We were after all those same people from childhood... a crooked mother and nine crooked little kids who had been very much shaped by our father's perceptions of us: Mom was the "stupid Norwegian." Keith was Cabbage head; Diane, the Beauty. Elaine was the pariah and scapegoat; Denae, "the little mother." Gail was another substitute mother, while Curt was the Golden boy and Charles, the nobody – the invisible son. Karen was part family conscience, part loose cannon. Gwen was *Petsika* (the favored one).

And so it came to pass that just as dad perceived us, so also did we perceive each other and ourselves. For years we were trapped by these straitjacket personas. Sure, we got along most of the time, but the undercurrents were always there, undercurrents which caused fractious discords, seething resentments and sometimes even rivers... rivers boiling with unmitigated rage.

Competition for attention was fierce. Since individual excellence was a foregone expectation, one had to go into the realms of the extraordinary to be even casually noticed. One-upmanship became a means to survive. Resting on your laurels only guaranteed that you would fall behind in the unceasing quest for attention.

One does not easily discard what has taken years to accumulate. No indeed. So, wisely, we pared down the numbers in our family get-togethers, conceding that none of us were sufficiently healed to transcend the demons of the past.

The irony of this dilemma was well illustrated by the events of a friend's upcoming family reunion. She had requested me to act as photographer for the occasion. As we approached the designated park grounds, set up with picnic tables, balloons, blaring music and barbecuing meats, she confided that she had just taken two anti-anxiety pills, and was considering taking yet another. "But, why, Colleen?" I questioned, surprised because I knew how excited she was to visit with her siblings, in town for the gathering.

"It's the only way I can handle being with everyone, all at one time," she explained, her large brown eyes misting. "Most of us kids have to take *something* to calm ourselves down; there are so many unresolved issues that seem to erupt when we're all together."

Honestly, I wanted to laugh like a hyena after hearing this disclosure. My mind conjured up a fantastic image of this great big happy Irish family, assembling for their once a year reunion – all of them secretly gulping down, beforehand, great handfuls of downers, uppers, mood stabilizers or whatever it takes to "survive" the event. Who knew? So, our little clan was not the only maladjusted group having problems with family get-togethers. And it's such a normal thing to do, right?

Much later, I read in a self-help book that the worst possible thing dysfunctional families can do as adults is to participate in social functions, en famille. "It's a recipe for disaster," warns the author.

When mom retired in 1979 at age 62, she didn't exactly become Auntie Mame, but then again, she wasn't a frumpy, stay-at-home dowager, either. She fell somewhere in between as she traveled to New York City, Hawaii and the Fiji islands. In the interim, she often houseguested for weeks at a time with Karen in Maryland, or with Diane and John in Connecticut. She loved being inside "April Rose," Diane's bridal shop, chatting with the customers, all dressed up in the tea hats, lacy shawls and pearls that Diane laid aside for her. By modeling the boutique's inventory, mom felt she was doing her part to boost sales.

Denae, Mom, Diane

We were pleased with this new and different mother – more self-assured, enthusiastic – who was slowly rediscovering the woman she had left behind in her twenties. "Like a bird from these prison walls," she began to lift her wings and experience flight.

But the biggest change occurred with the births of Rachael Elizabeth and Heather Rose, her first grandchildren. Mom became Grandma Bubba, a very different sort of guardian than the one who had raised us.

Gwen

Mom was so anxious to be a grandmother. I always found that curious, since she never seemed to enjoy motherhood. She loved to hold, play with, laugh with – simply *enjoy* all her eight grandchildren. And when she finally moved out of the Greenacres house, she looked very specifically for a condo with a pool, since swimming was her grandchildren's favorite activity. She was so proud that they all learned to swim in her pool; it became the gathering place for most family events.

Mom's love for her grandkids bonded her to them, and consequently, me to her. When Heather Rose became pregnant at 15, mom was completely nonjudgmental, simply rejoicing in the upcoming arrival of her first *great*-grandchild. It seemed to have completed the circle of life for her. Jamison Curtis was born in July, and in December mom was able to "fly away to that home on God's celestial shore…to a land where joys will never end."

Heather Rose

When I was really little and stayed overnight at Grandma Bubba's, she always said the same thing to me after tucking me in and listening to my prayers. "Good night, good night," she would singsong, "sleep tight and don't let the bed bugs bite. If they do, I'll cut them in two and put them in your morning stew."

Thinking she was serious, I'd dread going to the table in the morning, afraid to look in my oatmeal for fear of finding the chopped up bedbugs.

Another time, we were all eating supper at grandma's condo – me, Justin and Ryan, the youngest at four. Grandma had the shakes really bad by then, so when she tried serving us from the bowl of peas, they spilled over the table. Thinking that was pretty funny, Ryan picked up the bowl, wildly shaking his hands up and down like grandma. "Would you like some peas, Heather?" he offered, as they splashed into our milk and down our shirts. Grandma Bubba just laughed with the rest of us. (Ryan later told me that he did this *not* to mock grandma, but to make her feel better by seeing that he had "the shakes," too).


Denae

And so it happened. We knew it would. But still we were unprepared. It came in on cat's feet, like the fog. Then it became bitterly cold, a winter frost that blackened the marigolds, chrysanthemums and geraniums which had been bright and alive with color the morning before.

Mom had tried to prepare us, like her mother had done years before, so it wouldn't be such a surprise. She had sat us down with her death and dying counselor, read her will, discussed her advanced directive wishes. But neither Gwen, Keith, nor I (those of us living in Spokane) believed her, not for a minute. She still looked healthy; her short hair was mostly brown, with barely a wrinkle on her face.

One question she put forth bothered us a lot: "Will you miss me when I'm gone?" We weren't really sure; we certainly hoped so. But this was no time for hesitation. When your 82-year-old mother puts such an important question before you, there's only one reasonable response. "Of *course*, we'll miss you. How can you ask such a thing?"

Several months later, she was in the hospital after a stroke – with her left side paralyzed. She was unable to speak and nearly blind. It was the day before Christmas, 1998. The weather was raw and freezing with drifting snow and high winds, the roads treacherous. In Connecticut, Kansas, New Jersey and Oregon, family members made hurried reservations to fly out Christmas Eve on the first available planes, hoping the unstable weather would not delay their flights. Travelers' warnings were broadcast hourly across the country.

"I had a premonition," Elaine remembers, "that I needed to be home for Christmas, that mom might not survive the year – she just wanted her life to be over. So I had already bought my ticket."

In Spokane, we prayed the airport would not be shut down. Still we whispered optimistically into mom's ear: "The family is coming; everyone will be home with you for Christmas."

Gail and Bud arrived first, from Portland. Their plane landed so hard they thought it was a crash landing. Once at the hospital, they leaned over mom to kiss her hello; Bud tucked his own father's rosary beads between her fingers, knowing how much they would mean to her.

Other family members followed – Elaine, Rick, Emily, Karen, Diane and John – brushing away the snow, the cold and their tears as they leaned over to greet mom.

A tableau of grace and sorrow in the semidarkness of her hospital room prevailed. The quiet and the dark suited the mood of mom's passing. We grouped about her, some sitting, some standing, others lying on the bed beside her as we massaged her feet, patted her face and stroked her hands. Her breathing had become labored, rattled, as her weakened lungs filled with fluid. We sang Christmas songs, "Silver Bells," "O Holy Night," to mask the horrible sound, so she wouldn't be frightened. Elaine, with her arm cushioning mom's head, pressed her face close and crooned such tender words to her. "My sweet little mommy, we release you into heaven. We forgive you, and hope you will forgive us." Then, from time to time, Elaine would look up searchingly into our faces, asking, "Do you hear the chimes? Such beautiful chimes playing 'Silent Night.' Where are they coming from? There's no church close to the hospital… but I hear chimes in the room."

Over and over we said, "We love you," hoping mom could still hear what we needed to tell her. Then in response, we heard her whisper indistinctly, but unmistakably, "I love you, too." *How could this be?* The doctors had told us her stroke had taken away her ability to speak! We gazed upon her face, into eyes that could no longer see –not anything of this world, anyway –and found them luminous, radiating love, pure sweet mother love to us all.

Christmas Day passed, and then the day after. Like folds of material, we were draped around mom and maintaining our vigil, continuing to sing her favorite songs: "I'm Dreaming of a White Christmas," "Brahm's Lullaby" – our voices taking on a timbre and beauty which we did not possess – a celestial choir sending ripples of music drifting into the still night air. "All is calm, all is bright…." It was so serene, so poignant, I almost felt like I was in a dream. "Sleep in heavenly peace…" The outpouring of love in the room seemed to push away the specter, the dreadful imminence of death. And when our tired voices got so raspy we could no longer sing, Gwen's husband, Kevin, serenaded mom in his beautiful Irish tenor with "My Wild Irish Rose" and "When Irish Eyes are Smiling."

Karen was with Gail at mom's feet. She said later, "It made me feel so humble, in awe to experience mom in such an exalted state of spirituality." Gail shared Karen's feelings, saying, "I was so overcome by what I was witnessing, so overwhelmed by mom's courage."

Truly, the significance of the occasion was so profound, it simply could not be registered on any conscious level. We all felt the blessings of heaven streaming down on us those many hours in mom's darkened room, knew the cleansing grace of forgiveness. The wounds of the past, wounds of both fact and perception, dissolved like chunks of ice beneath a summer sun. Mom was finally at peace, total peace.

Then, with us her family cradling her in the bosom of our love, she spoke out softly, hesitantly, those last words, "good mother…?" as a question to us all. I believe it was the first time in her life she had had the courage to utter aloud what must have been her greatest doubt, yet her dearest wish.

And it *had* become true, a statement finally of fact. "Yes," we responded heartily in unison, "You are a Good Mother." And we meant it sincerely.

Those two words, her final words to us, in that instant became both mom's epitaph and her wish fulfilled. A great burden had been lifted from us all. Mom had become and will remain, until the end of time, that which we had always wanted her to be – our Good Mother.

# ALL GROWN UP

Karen, Gwen, Denae, Gail, Diane, Elaine

*Toto, I don't believe we're in Kansas anymore*

*– The Wizard of Oz*

Childhood finally passed. Somehow, we remaining seven managed to survive the terrible darkness and unbearable lightness of that conflicted landscape. As adults, we began to pursue our own paths – each hoping to achieve a calm and potential that seemed nearly impossible in our youth. And we did so, most certainly, with the aid of a beneficent grace which watches over children everywhere.

Symbolic of that grace is a painting beloved by us all, Lindberg's famous lithograph "Guardian Angel," which hung in the various bedrooms of every house we ever occupied. How many evenings did we not say our prayers beneath its archetypal imagery? A towering, majestic, white-robed, angel with outstretched arms in a posture of beatitude smiles down on two frightened children attempting to cross a broken footbridge spanning a raging current, on a dark and lonely night. The sister tries to comfort her younger brother, but the scene makes clear that larger forces will keep the children from harm and return them safely home.

We all loved this picture because it spoke so clearly to our subconscious sense of danger and of love – the dangerous love we received from our parents. Its image could serve as a perfect hologram for our childhood, a mirroring of the forces of darkness and light that vied for supremacy in our young lives.

**ELAINE**

*Were I a bird, I could imagine myself as a yellow canary – once caged and mute – but now free to spread my wings and fly beneath the golden sunshine. I always wanted to sing, but it was not possible before. To have regained my voice and my freedom has made all the difference.*

*As an adult, one of my biggest challenges is to not always think of life in terms of work, always being busy. I have trouble saying no to people. We were so overworked as children, I still suffer from the resentment of those memories. I felt I belonged in public service, helping those in need, finding community resources for them, bringing joy into their holidays. I understand trauma, and that once a dike has been broken, it's harder to patch than if it had never been damaged.*

Elaine earned her master's degree in social work from the University of Oklahoma after first working in Vietnam for a year at the 24th Evacuation Hospital as a Red Cross social worker. Returning stateside, she earned an LPN license and spent several years in nursing at the Wesley Medical Center in Wichita, Kansas.

Denae

I recall Elaine's undergraduate days at the University of Hawaii, partly because she once shipped me two boxes of orchids, plumeria, ginger and hibiscus – fresh island flowers for a church luau I was helping out with. Each arriving guest was greeted with a fragrant lei, an unheard of party favor in the Greenacres of those days. Their expressions of delight provided me a deep sense of satisfaction, and the utmost gratitude to my Aloha sis.

Always generous, while stationed overseas with the Red Cross, Elaine visited a jewelry bazaar in Hong Kong and bought real gemstones for mom and all of us girls – garnets, pearls, rubies and aquamarines set in 18-karat gold. Says Gail, remembering that unforgettable moment when she opened her gift box, "I was only 15 years old, and it was my first real jewelry. I still have the beautiful alexandrite ring in a safety deposit box where I keep all my treasures."

Much of Elaine's professional career was with the Wichita school system. Always sympathetic to poor students, she often bought them winter coats, mittens and school supplies with her own money. She also worked in soup kitchens, served with a Mother-to-Mother ministry helping struggling single parents, and put in hundreds of hours at her church's clothing bank.

After falling in love with her soulmate in Kansas, Elaine and Rick honeymooned in Athens and Rome, then married in 1983, at a beautiful garden ceremony in Karen's backyard. They are especially proud of their daughter Emily, who earned her master's degree as a medical social worker, and now works in the Nashville school system.

## DIANE

*Peacocks and hummingbirds. I love the peacock for its exotic beauty, for the amazing color and design of its tail feathers. One feather by itself is so beautiful. But my heart belongs to the hummingbird.*

*The hummingbird darts; it is so quick, like a shooting star. You have to be very alert or you won't see them. It comes out of nowhere, hovers for a moment, and then is gone. Endlessly busy like myself, it tends to its nectar collecting while I tend to my brides' needs, jewelry designs, flowers and herb gardens.*

*The hummingbird is so fleeting, it almost seems invisible –just pulsating colors and a beak. This precious little being, a time traveler from the other side, reminds me of the visitations of angels, or of loved ones who have died. It is such a gift; each sighting always brings me a special message. I'm always, always waiting for the hummingbird.*

As children, we all thought Diane might become a famous ballerina, so highly regarded was she by her dance instructor. Somehow dad and mom came up with the money for one year of ballet classes, and our drab Greenacres living room became the Carnegie Hall stage on those afternoons when we watched her gracefully vaulting and pirouetting in her red velvet tutu and pink satin toe shoes.

A free-spirited hippie in her twenties, Diane was as inspired by the dancing of Isadora Duncan as she was by Janis Joplin's singing. After a summer spent hitchhiking with Karen through Europe and the Greek Islands (paid for by waitressing), Diane signed up as a VISTA volunteer and worked for a year in Georgia and Florida.

She attended classes at Quinnipiac University, finally earning her B.A. in English from Eastern Washington University. For a time she had her own silk screening business, designing shirts and headscarves, featuring butterflies and peacocks. Later, she studied jewelry design in New York City, and then opened April Rose, her bridal and jewelry boutique in Connecticut.

The outside of her shop is as gorgeous as the inside – a Mardi Gras landscape of trumpet lilies, geraniums, foxglove, begonias, verbena, camellias and ranunculus. Holidays like Christmas and Halloween find her home and property lavishly decorated, like Cecil B. DeMille stage sets. Bedazzled trick-or-treaters number in the hundreds each year, while the Christmas onlookers steep themselves in the fantasy, aurora borealis light show.

Sharing this slice of Eden is her scholarly soul-mate John, whom we affectionately call "Professor Cakes" – Professor Emeritus of Communications and English at Quinnipiac University.

Fashion has always been Diane's passion. As teenagers, we all loved studying the "before" and "after" sections of glamour magazines, to see the amazing transformations of wallflowers to goddesses. Diane, however, carried her interest far beyond ours, seeking out fashion-impaired classmates. She would completely restyle them, from eyebrows to hairdo to wardrobe – often redesigning their clothes on mom's old treadle sewing machine. Her most successful makeover was a plain-faced young nun who had left the convent. By the time Diane was finished, she was so gorgeous she could have been a runway model!

## DENAE

*I bonded long ago with the loon for its love of isolation and its attraction to remote, beautiful places. How can I resist its wilderness mystique, the amazing singular placement of its glittering ruby eye amid the complex black and white configurations of its lustrous dark plumage?*

*Loons are wary, reserved creatures; you can see them, but never know them, and certainly not ever pet them. They keep their distance.*

*I love their diverse sounds and rhythms –a rich repertoire of coos, wails, yodels and tremolos – enough to make the finest opera singer envious. Maniacal-sounding one moment, haunting and primitive-*

*voiced the next, their symphony of sounds shimmers like phantom skaters on the mist-shrouded surface of a woodland lake.*

*As an artist, I need quiet and isolation to do my best work. I also need to be versatile, painting landscapes, antique teapots, cave drawings, multi-flowered window boxes and jiving musicians.*

*My brother-in-law John says of me, "Denae is poor, but she leads a rich life." I wish the first part were not true, but nevertheless I appreciate his sentiment.*

Clearly, the vagabond gypsy life suited Denae, since she moved and changed jobs so often. Following her year as a VISTA worker in Danville, Illinois, she was employed as a youth counselor in California and Connecticut orphanages. While completing her B.A. in anthropology and women's studies at Eastern Washington University, she took extended leaves to work with Alzheimer's patients, recovering alcoholics and mentally disabled children and adults.

She created wearable art in the '70s, inspired by her twin's glamorous jewelry and feathered "tea-hat" creations. The Gallery of Wearable Art in New York City accepted her designs and showcased them on live models who exhibited them in display windows.

After earning her B.A., Denae returned to painting full time. Her artwork has been twice featured on the cover of *The Seattle Review,* the University of Washington's literary magazine. In fact, one of her favorite stories involves Dr. Charles Johnson, one of the university's best known faculty (now retired). In the early '90s, Denae had written seeking his opinion of a watercolor series she had just finished titled "Images of the Black Literary Tradition." At the time, Professor Johnson had earned the National Book Award for his novel *Middle Passage.* Not only did he love her art series, he encouraged her to submit the images for *The Seattle Review.*

As a result, her painting "The Cage of Obscene Birds," was selected to be the next issue's cover art. However, despite an exchange of correspondence and phone calls, Denae and the professor had not yet met – a fact that only increased her surprise over what happened next. Two weeks before the issue went to press, she received a call from the magazine's office manager describing an unexpected visit from Dr. Johnson.

"Denae," she began, out of breath with excitement, "you won't believe what has just happened! When Professor Johnson found out your cover painting was going to be printed in black and white because our budget couldn't afford color, he pulled out his checkbook and wrote a check for $1,200 dollars – printing costs for color – and handed it to me!"

You can imagine Denae's amazement. She could scarcely believe that a man she had never met had just shelled out a substantial sum so her artwork would be better represented. To this day she continues to sing his praises.

## KAREN

*I always have to resist my Don Quixote complex – that is, in plain language, Rescue 911. Having been successful in two lawsuits, one for sexual harassment, the other for unlawful termination of employment, I often think I missed my calling. Instead of teaching, perhaps I should have pursued advocacy law. But then my life would have been spent fighting windmills and I would have had no time for the stimulating world of art, literature and music.*

*Hummingbird is the bird I most identify with. My rooms are filled with images of this little fairy-winged spirit. Joyful, self-indulgent, it spends its time in the fragrant lush centers of flowers.*

*Native Americans consider it a symbol of love. Aware of this, two of my students once brought me two hummingbird feathers to tuck inside my necklace locket, hoping they would bring me success in finding my soulmate.*

Karen schooled at the University of Connecticut, University of California, Berkeley, and Quinnipiac University, where she earned her B.A. and master's degrees, and eventually received her Ph.D. in American studies from the College of William and Mary in Virginia.

As an undergraduate, she spent a year in Barcelona, Spain, teaching English as a second language, and traveling through Europe. Before that, she served as a VISTA volunteer in Pittsburgh, Pennsylvania.

Truly our family's political activist, while teaching at Spokane Falls Community College during the Persian Gulf War, she organized a schoolwide teach-in with a fellow colleague to better inform students and faculty about our Middle-East involvement. Later on, she organized a charity food drive to benefit displaced Kurdish refugees. At present she teaches composition at Quinnipiac University.

Denae

My favorite image of Karen is as a 17-year old at Chicago's O'Hare Airport on a layover en route to Pittsburgh to begin her VISTA year. Having prearranged to meet her, I drove up with my boyfriend, Chuck Hazelbaker, from Danville, where I was finishing my year in VISTA. This was 1967 – the decade of hippies, free love, civil rights, big hair and miniskirts.

Sitting with Chuck at the terminal, I watched as Karen approached. Three brunette hairpieces were piled high atop her head; her eyes were kohl-edged below stiffly mascared false eyelashes. She wore a French cut, gold minidress with matching coat, accessorized by a Jackie Kennedy-inspired black leather bag. In one hand she clutched a Louis Vuitton (look-alike) carry-on, gilded with travel stickers reading Venice, Copenhagen, Prague, Rome, Bahamas.

*"Enchante!* Such a pleasure to meet you," she smiled at Chuck, extending a perfectly manicured hand.

For a moment, I thought he was actually going to bow. In later conversation, he explained that her appearance so intimidated him, having never met anyone quite like her in the wind-swept plains of Illinois, that he could not decide whether she was a Hollywood star or European royalty.

That was Karen. Notwithstanding that she was on her way to serve as a $200-a-month worker in the war on poverty, her excitement at finally departing Greenacres to become a "citizen of the world" superseded her impaired vision of reality. With no formal mentoring outside of fashion magazines, television and the cinema, she had pieced together her own elaborate persona, containing elements of high society movie dialogues, Swiss boarding schools and political talk shows. To further ensure that *no one* would ever suspect the indigent nature of her background and cultural deficiencies, she concocted fanciful stories of our family's affluence.

Toward the end of her VISTA service, while visiting her one weekend, I was amazed to hear her roommate recount some of her tall tales: "Poor Karen, having to leave behind her red MG car and all her wealthy girlfriends. I understand a group of them have been in Corfu and Corsica for the summer, swimming and sunning along the Aegean coastline." *Hm-m-m-m-m-m.*

## KEITH

*A soaring eagle is the bird I most admire because of its strength, its power, its ability to build. Its nest is strong and secure, hanging from the tallest of trees. I admire its hunting and fishing skills, its ability to succeed from outside the flock. It is not the eagle's aloneness that appeals to me so much as its confidence.*

*Maybe it's presumptuous to aspire to being like the eagle. Anytime I have ever seen it in the wild, I have always been inspired. It represents leadership to me, the ability to stand alone and make sound decisions. Leadership is an important part of who I'm trying to be – something most guys get from their father. I didn't have that. How do you know how a man is supposed to act without that guidance?*

*The eagle doesn't have the flaws and problems of humans. It has no other choice but to be an eagle. Its traits are dependable, predictable – a safe, reliable role model.*

*As a parent, I aspire to the eagle's perfect timing in deciding when the young should leave the nest. After it has taught them everything it knows, it flings them out: "Okay, go fly! It's time to start your life!"*

A surf-and-turf kind of guy, Keith served his military duty as a Navy Seabee during the Vietnam War, traveling to Puerto Rico, Spain and California. While attending college at the University of Florida in Gainesville, he married his high school sweetheart, Judy, and they began their family of four children.

His inland roots were revealed one day at the Jacksonville Beach in the '70s. Bikini-clad coeds were limboing on the sand amid colorful beach umbrellas and hundreds of suntanned bathers. The water was congested with splashing swimmers. Idly scanning the waves as he dried off on his towel, Keith spotted an ominous, dark fin cruising quietly just beyond the line of swimmers. With bloody images from *Jaws* leaping to mind, and hoping to avoid a grisly repeat, Keith jumped up, pointing dramatically at the menacing fin. "SHARK! SHARK!!"

Several heads turned in that direction, then back to Keith in disgust. "Will you sit down – that's not a shark, that's a dolphin." Oops.

Once back in Spokane, Keith returned to the building trade, working his way up to supervisor, overseeing the construction of hospitals, schools and other large commercial projects. However, parenting has been his proudest achievement, raising his three sons and daughter.

A committed member of Alcoholics Anonymous, Keith is also a dedicated church leader and speaker at various men's groups. He actively serves the spiritual needs of his community.

Recreationally, he is a consummate boatman. Following the purchase of his first 17-footer, he's been in sailor's heaven ever since, spending as much time as possible at Priest Lake in Idaho, his family's favorite weekend hangout. He keeps a ship's log detailing all their sailing adventures and catastrophes.

## GAIL

*When I see the first robin, I know for sure that spring is here. Its arrival always inspires me to begin planting vegetable and flower starts in my greenhouse, cleaning up flower beds and distributing compost. As I work in the warm sunshine on my five acres of property, nestled in between the vineyards and nut orchards outside of Portland, I feel a camaraderie with this little bird.*

*He is such an industrious fellow with a keen sense of duty and commitment – foraging for worms to feed his growing family, re-structuring his nest, protecting his family– a true multi-tasker.*

*The robin is one of the first songbirds to sing at dawn and among the last to sing at dusk. I respect and identify with his work ethic and ponder how alike his days are to mine, as he above and I below tend to our busy schedules.*

Green Thumb might well be our gourmand, plant-loving sister's middle name. Much as she connected with mom during those long ago gardening days, she also bonded with the plant world.

She loved her classes at Western Washington University, but it was her Master Gardener's certification through Oregon State University's Extension Service that gave her the greatest satisfaction. Says her outdoorsy, sportsman husband Bud, "Gail gets more excited by a good pile of compost than by a handful of diamonds!"

For most of her professional career, she worked as a project administrator in the housing industry, combining both her administrative and design capabilities.

With all that chlorophyll running through her veins, Gail continues with her home business, Mountain Creek Gardens, and has supplied high-end food markets, restaurants and farmers markets with her organic salad greens, herbs and flowers. Surplus vegetables are donated to the Plant a Row for the Hungry program. She is ecstatic to be on the giving end of the food chain rather than the receiving end.

While cooking at our Greenacres house – struggling with the

lack of variety and shortage of ingredients – Gail dreamed of working within her own Provence-style kitchen, well stocked with the finest and freshest foods and state of the art cookware. She pored over food magazines and devoured cookbooks until the day, years later, when she could transcend from boiling pigs' feet for 5 to roasting Grande Marnier-glazed Cornish game hens for 25.

Her husband, Bud, gets the last word as we recall his oft-repeated expression acknowledging Gail's metamorphosis from the insecurity of poverty to becoming his self-confident and multi-talented wife: "That's my Gail – the Princess Queen of Everything!"

## GWEN

*Family is such a priority for me. What pleasure I have found in my back yard as I sat on the deck watching a quail family route its way, single file through my fence, looking for seeds and grass.*

*With their head plumes bobbing in unison, the mother and babies would emerge onto my lawn from the underbrush of an open field, as the father would fly to the top of the fence or roof. There he was quick to call out if he saw any sign of danger. Back and forth he would scan the neighborhood until the mother and chicks had eaten their fill. Only then would he fly to join them, and rustle for his own meal.*

*One day a baby quail flew down into a deep window well at our home, and did not have the strength to fly out. His concerned family stood in a semicircle on the metal rim above, peering down at its plight. By way of rescue, my former husband, Kevin, brought out a large serving spoon to scoop up the half-ounce bird. At his appearance, the father squawked in alarm, but neither he, the mother, nor any of the four chicks made a move to flee, despite their obvious terror. Only when the baby had been gently set down among them did they all lift their wings and fly away.*

Gwen received her B.A. in psychology from Eastern Washington University and her master's in education and guidance counseling from Whitworth College, after first raising two sons and a daughter. Her years as dedicated wife, mom and grandmom fulfilled her long ago desire to be a mother.

But it is to a solitary conversation in eighth-grade detention that she owes the substance and direction of her college choices and subsequent career. Flashback to Greenacres Junior High where blonde, brown-eyed Gwennie, cheerleader and femme fatale – also a rebellious adolescent – found herself sentenced to detention. Monitoring the roomful of teenage dissidents was Mr. McLeod, history and part-time special ed teacher, who intuited a depth and compassion to Gwen's character. "How would you like to be an aide in one of my special ed classes?" he had asked.

Amazed by his interest, Gwen accepted and became a responsible and perceptive classroom aide, continuing on in high school by working with special needs children. As a junior, she organized a group of students to help in re-patterning a severely brain-damaged teen. While majoring in special education in college, she also volunteered at the Spokane Guild School, a center for severely and profoundly impaired preschoolers, where brother Charles also worked.

Currently she is employed as a social worker with families in crisis. As counselor both to her own children and professionally to her clients, Gwen cannot forget how life changing a single conversation can be, when she reflects back to that hour in detention when an astute teacher took the time to mentor a defiant young eighth-grader looking for direction.

# PART THREE
# RE-CONNECTING

Dad with great-grandkids (Elijha, Isabelle) and Heather, their mom

*What is the price of Experience? do men buy it for a song?*
*Or wisdom for a dance in the street? No, it is bought with the price*
*Of all that a man hath, his house, his wife, his children.*
*Wisdom is sold in the desolate market where none come to buy,*
*And in the wither'd field where the farmer plows for bread in vain.*

–William Blake

Denae

I should have known something was wrong the moment I spotted the long, gleaming raven's feather. Instead, I stooped to pick it up as I approached my apartment building. Boldly accented against the powdery dusting of snow on the November ground, its stark blackness might have raised a note of alarm in some other's gaze, but not in mine. Loving ravens as I do, these Poe-inspired birds of magic and mystery, I felt lucky to have found such a fine specimen and was anxious to add it to my collection.

Moments later, inside my rooms, I noticed the red light on my phone blinking insistently, the caller ID reading – Valley General Hospital. Dismayed, I answered and was informed that my father had been admitted four days ago due to a serious fall injury. I hadn't seen him in twelve years. Why were they calling me? Who had given them my number?

The nurse's voice continued: "He's ready for discharge. Doctor wants to admit him to a short-term facility for convalescence and physical therapy, but your father is *refusing* to go. He insists that we send him home, instead."

In essence, dad had recovered sufficiently to no longer require hospitalization, but was still too disabled to be discharged to his own care, so they had given him an ultimatum. Either he go to a convalescent center, or he would be forcibly transported to Eastern State Mental Hospital.

*Had dad forgotten the months he had spent there some 50 years ago?* Red flags began flapping in my mind like the sails of ships caught in a hurricane. Always a major drama with him. Was this to be my reintroduction into his world of delusion and disorder?

Chilled by an ominous premonition, I flashed back to a bizarre hospital scenario I had shared with Gwen several years earlier in 1997 when we had attempted to visit dad after his quadruple bypass heart surgery. He never knew we were there.

A friend had called to notify us he was at Deaconess Hospital undergoing surgery. Since he was then in his late seventies, with many serious medical issues, his chances of survival were iffy. After alerting the out-of-towners, I collected some get well cards and a pink azalea, then rushed to the hospital with Gwen.

An orderly pointed us to Room 11, where through the half-opened door we could see an inert form beneath the disarranged bedsheets. What happened next defies description. Because it had been so many years since we had last seen dad, the suddenness of our visit gave us no time to prepare for a face-to-face. As we approached his room, no more than ten feet away, Gwen and I began to hyperventilate. Heartbeats racing, even our legs began to wobble and buckle. Gasping between breaths as though we were on Mount Everest, the closer we got to his door the worse our symptoms became.

In the intervening years since childhood, we had all been haunted by the specter of his abusive parenting and lived in fear of his death. Because with his death, any hopes for understanding or for reconciliation would vanish. So many questions would be unanswered: *Had he ever loved us? Was he sorry for all the pain and deprivation he had caused? Could he have controlled his actions, or was he simply a madman evolved from that unwanted, mother-orphaned child who had been passed around from relative to relative until he could finally fend for himself at age 16?* I recall Keith saying more than once through gritted teeth, "When dad dies, I'll go to his funeral for just two reasons: to be sure he's *really* dead, and to spit on his grave!"

*Did dad remember the events of our childhood? Or had the shock therapy at the mental hospital irreversibly damaged his memory? Obliterated his conscience, his ability to experience emotion?*

There was so much we did not know. When years later Keith read from his eulogy: "…Dad was a complicated man, and our relationships with him were very complicated," it was certainly true.


Gwen and I looked at each other in alarm; our eyes mirrored our thoughts. *What is happening to us? Is this delayed post traumatic stress disorder?* Somehow that brief glimpse of dad beneath his bed sheets had triggered the trauma of childhood all over again. Ten feet from his open door, we were stopped in our tracks, our hands palsied by tremors. We might just as well have been crossing into a war zone – Normandy, Guadalcanal, Da Nang – no weapons, no bulletproof vests as we stood there unprepared in our summer shorts and sleeveless blouses, gasping for air.

The battle would have to wait. Totally unnerved, we dropped onto a hall bench to regroup. Sitting there, silently contemplating dad's doorway, our sweaty hands soddened the cards and envelopes so thoroughly that the messages were unreadable. One thing was certain: we could not enter that room. Even my eyes resisted trespass to the top of his bed, so afraid was I of seeing his face and making eye contact. So we gazed instead at his bare feet. Not a speck of movement. He was, we reasoned, either asleep, unconscious or dead. But still we could not enter the room.

How had we gone so quickly from normal to almost catatonic? We had never behaved like this. Gwen's voice interrupted my thoughts, "We'll have to give . . . the cards and flowers . . . to a nurse to take in to him," stammering between gasps, "I can't go in there."

Standing up, swaying like drunkards, we lurched back to the nurse's station, afraid we'd pass out before handing off the azaleas. The charge nurse, looking like she was ready to call security, stared skeptically as we slumped against the granite counter for support. "Would you mind . . . putting these inside Room 11?" I squeaked out.

Her eyes scanned the 20 feet to dad's room. A stiff nod was her response as she accepted the wilting flowers.

"Two wheelchairs" would have been our next request, so we could get to the downstairs lobby. But we decided against it, fearing her patience was exhausted, and the security guard still loomed as an option. Somehow we made it unassisted down the eight floors to the parking lot.

That was six years ago, and now Valley General Hospital was awaiting my arrival so I could persuade my obstinate father to enter a nursing home – the very place we had sworn on the Bible to keep him from half a lifetime ago. Good grief. The ghosts and fears of the past were colliding big time with the present.

Convalescent center, short-term care, extended care – pure semantics. For dad, they were all one and the same – the dreaded "nursing home." Junkyard, graveyard, he believed it was a killing factory for the displaced, sick old folks that no one wanted. And seemingly, fate had designated me to open the door for him.

Years ago I had declared him dead, dismissing him as *Francois*, a Frank Veselits look-alike, who coincidentally inhabited my father's address. Now, apparently, he was to be exhumed. I thought of the Haitian zombies who were buried alive, then later dug up, expected to resume their previous lives as best they could – notwithstanding that the experience of premature burial had rendered them so psychically deformed that they were shunned by the entire community. Was this to be my father's fate as he returned to life, very much alive and kicking at Valley General and on the verge of being readmitted to Medical Lake?

How was I to greet him after so many years of no communication? What would he look like? He was now 85 years old. Was he still dyeing his hair? Those odd shades of red and orangish brown that I had glimpsed in random passings, unnatural colors that had not fulfilled the rich browns or blacks promised by the bottle's label.

He had never apologized for any of the terrible abuses. None of it had ever been discussed. Did he know that some of his children had been diagnosed with post traumatic stress disorder? Did he have any idea how much damage had been done? Elaine, Karen and Gwen with decades of therapy, along with Diane, Keith, Gail, Charles and myself in intermittent therapy, AA groups, Al-Anon, ACOA and other self-help programs. Would he feel bad to know of the thousands of dollars we had spent on Valium, Lorazepam, Prozac, Paxil, Lithium, Trazadone, Wellbutrin – the psychotropic drugs which ease our depression and help us sleep?

How much did he recall? Was his mind an untroubled tabula rasa while ours were littered with hieroglyphic horrors? Did he realize the extent to which we had suppressed or forgotten entire sections of our lives? Buried them so deeply that for some all that remained was a handful of hazy, disconnected images.

Only Elaine and Karen had confronted dad about the past. Two decades earlier, under the guidance of her therapist, Elaine had written dad a long letter listing his criminal abuses and their crippling impact. With two suicide attempts behind her and years of therapy ahead, she hoped this appeal might elicit from him an admission of guilt, or, at the very least, an expression of regret – some sign of concern for her well-being. Elaine also mailed each sibling a copy of the letter, excluding Curt, because he knew nothing of dad's crimes. Since he was only six when dad left home, we never told him about the past.

"How *could* she write me such a letter?" was dad's response, calling upon family members for sympathy and redress. He was terribly upset that such long "forgotten" misdeeds could be dredged up so callously. "The past should remain the past. Digging it up doesn't solve anything. It's all over and done with," was his final statement. End of discussion.

Karen, too, had attempted to address the past with the help of a therapist. At age 37 while suffering a nervous breakdown, she was encouraged to "gently" confront dad with her recollections to help her heal. Not surprisingly, as the day approached, she was quaking with nerves. Hoping to forestall her panic, she recruited mom as a supportive observer, while Gwen, overhearing, asked if she too could come along to vent her own issues.

Purple foxglove and scarlet geraniums bordered dad's shady front yard as they pulled into his driveway. "I can't do it! I'm too scared to talk to him," croaked Gwen from the back seat, diving to the floor for refuge. "I'll stay down here where he can't see me. Maybe I'll hear some of your conversation with the window rolled down."

Mom sat on the front porch steps alongside dad as Karen, with pounding heart, recounted her grievances, seeking answers. "But that all happened *years* ago! I thought it was all over and done with," choked dad, tears spilling down his cheeks. "Why in god's green acres do you want to bring up the past?"

The therapist had only rehearsed Karen in disclosing her feelings, the intent being to find *her* voice, not to assuage dad's conscience. "After you have said what you want, then leave," had been his advice. So Karen did, taking mom and Gwen with her. Nothing had been explained by dad, but at least Karen had the satisfaction of speaking her mind.

The hospital staff at Valley General was still waiting. As I drove the eight miles, I carefully observed the speed limit, being in no great hurry. Mentally, I tried to prepare myself for this strange, unexpected reunion with dad. So many years of estrangement – even though I knew, of late, both Karen and Diane had been sending him letters and photos. Safely residing on the east coast, 3,000 miles away, for them it was a non-threatening correspondence.

My thoughts were scrambled by anxiety. Would I hyperventilate again, like the time with Gwen? Would I stutter, lose my voice completely – faint dead away? This was no Sunday afternoon in the park I was walking into. I didn't need to consult the Oracle at Delphi to tell me that. Even with such misgivings, little did I guess this was only the beginning of a two and a half year journey with dad. A journey requiring our passage on the night train into No Man's Land, where we would be subjected to a series of crashes and derailments, careening on and off course until we finally reached the Valley of the Shadow of Death.

Indeed, metaphors aside, this was to be a real journey with real souls – souls that were imperiled, teetering on the brink of calamity, while at the same time desperately seeking reconciliation, forgiveness and redemption.

How could I have known that dad's obsessive fear of nursing homes, which now so squarely confronted him, was inconsequential compared to the gravity of the jail which really imprisoned him – a steel barred cell of his own making. Alcatraz . . . San Quentin . . . Sing Sing . . . Hell? Its name was not nearly so important as the face of its jailor – a fearsome face marked by disease, old age and a battered, uneasy conscience. He was locked up good and tight, all right.

This was not a journey for the faint of heart. I knew it the moment I walked up to him sitting on his bed. His gown was stained with orange juice, and dark flecks of chewing tobacco stuck to his stubbly chin, dotting his white sheets. His hair was gray and matted, his eyes cloudy and dull.

"Hi, dad. Well, you've got yourself in a real pickle this time," were my uninspired words of greeting after twelve years. Then, before we could launch into "father-daughter catch-up," a middle-aged woman wearing glasses interrupted us with, "I'm sorry, Mr. Veselits, but I'm here to do a mental assessment before your discharge. It'll take about an hour." Glancing over at me, she added, "You can stay if he has no objections." Good, I thought, this will give me a chance to observe him and his mental state.

It wasn't long before his evaluator, with laptop and a notebook of questions, asked, "How many children do you have, Frank? Can you tell me their names?"

The five-dollar questions, I mused. Let's move on to the *fifty* dollar ones.

A few minutes elapsed and dad had only pulled up two names. I stared at him hard, a sickening feeling rolling into my gut. "Diane . . . Karen . . ." still echoed in the air while creases of effort wrinkled his brow. Apparently, he was too stumped to continue.

Curt and Dad

Come on, dad, I'm thinking, This is an easy one, a no-brainer.

"Let's see. Was one of them called Bert? Or no, maybe it was Curt?"

My stomach was a thick burl of undigested road kill. A tsunami of tears welled up behind my eyelids. *Unbelievable*! Dad had actually forgotten our names! He didn't remember his own children. You want to know what hell feels like? Forget the flames. That's nothing compared to sitting next to your father, and he doesn't remember you.

In an instant, the incredible pain I felt over dad's forgetfulness turned into acute sympathy. What in the world had happened to him to place him at such a desolate crossroads that he had forgotten his own kids? Especially little Curt, the apple of his eye.

Had dad been over-medicated with drugs? Had the years of drinking finally pickled his brain? I was moved to help him with a little prompting. "Hey, dad," I teased halfheartedly, "There were nine of us. Come on, you're pulling her leg, admit it. You've got Diane, Karen and Curt. Didn't Diane have a twin?"

"Oh yeah," a glimmer of a smile crossed his face. "Denae. ... Oh, that's you! Of course, how could I forget?" he responded, smacking his palm against his forehead. Fifteen minutes later, with dozens of giveaway clues, he could only recall three more names. Not wishing to humiliate or distress him further, mercifully his evaluator moved on to his employment record – all of which he had forgotten, except for the year he had worked as a bridge inspector.

Finally, her evaluation was complete. Even though I would have liked to have curled up on a hospital bed myself (with a cup of morphine), so upset was I by dad's lack of memory, still, I needed to return to my original mission. "Okay," I said, plumping up his pillow, "rest your brains while we sort out this discharge business."

Dramatically, I overstated what he could expect at the mental hospital as opposed to a couple weeks in a short-term care facility.

He finally agreed, thank goodness. Apparently, his fears of going back to the "looney bin" overshadowed his paranoia of nursing homes. I was hugely relieved because I was pretty sure if they took dad to the psych ward he'd probably die there. Somehow I couldn't bear the idea of my father dying in the nut house – too much of an affirmation of what we had all tried so hard to escape from. Surely that was not the fate that destiny intended. However, in terms of our journey together, I would have been very surprised had I known then that we hadn't even left the train station yet!

So began my new life in 2003, as advocate, nurse and caregiver for dad. Much as I did not want to be so deeply involved in his life, I had no choice. His medical profile was both dismal and astonishing; dismal because he had so many illnesses, astonishing because he had been so healthy and active his entire life. As a child, I don't recall him ever being sick. When had he become a walking *Merck's Manual* of diseases? More to the point, how could he still be *alive* with his long list of maladies? He was being treated by 13 doctors. Thirteen! Since I kept their phone numbers posted on his refrigerator, I counted them one day, amazed at the total.

Because dad had rejected dialysis, his low-functioning kidneys were in chronic renal failure. He had a leaking heart valve, high blood pressure, diabetes, severe gout inflammation and deformation in both hands and feet, and compromised liver function due to his years of alcoholism. He was blind in one eye and nearly blind in the other, along with glaucoma complications.

Nearly every month he had to be hospitalized with severe urinary tract infections, which caused his whole system to go septic and his temperature to spiral up to 105 and 106 degrees. His cumadin levels required constant monitoring, as did the pressure sores on his feet. In the midst of this medical melee, his kidney specialist warned that the excess toxins in dad's poor-functioning, filtering system could travel to his brain, resulting in sudden-onset psychotic behavior – for which we were to immediately call the paramedics. Never a dull moment with dad. Ever.

There were times, I must confess, that were not only *not* dull, but in fact were surreal, utterly out of context with my present reality. For example, I refer to a sublime October afternoon when the lengthening purple shadows beneath the vividly colored canopies of elms, hemlocks and maples made me long for my tubes of paint and brushes. Gwen and I were assisting dad up the sidewalk to his room at Maplewood Gardens, a short-term convalescent center, on a return trip from his doctor – our inaugural experience as his medical team. We were filled with misgivings as to the manner and extent to which we would be participating in his care.

Gwen, pretty in pink and looking like a Dutch school girl even though she was in her forties, walked a few steps behind, carrying his catheter bag (discreetly wrapped in brown plastic), which was attached to dad by an umbilical, tail-like tubing. Coursing through that narrow chute was a not-so-invisible yellow stream originating in the headwaters of his compromised bladder.

I, in turn, walked alongside dad, supporting his faltering steps with my shoulder while my left hand clasped his gout-crippled, purplish, swollen fingers. In my other hand I carried his spare cane and exam results. To think, a short two weeks ago we had been blissfully unaware of any detail of his existence. And now the three of us were an intimate mini-parade advancing in dirge-time up the sidewalk to his room.

Turning slightly, I caught Gwen's eye and whispered, "Aren't we the spectacle? Who would have guessed a month ago that we would become dad's valets?" We were hit with a massive attack of the giggles and had to concentrate on restraining ourselves. Dad may have been hard of hearing, but he could still see – and we certainly didn't want to hurt his feelings by laughing at him.

After reconnecting, my greatest fear was that I would be the lone sibling attending to dad's crisis calls and medical needs. To be perfectly honest, I did feel like a traitor who was consorting with the enemy. After all, most of us had been deliberately out of contact with him for years and had every intention of continuing to do so.

Nevertheless, I was desperate for allies. But all five potential recruits expressed their regrets similarly, saying they were "not interested." At all. Period. And don't call back. End of story. Goodbye. Good luck. Only Diane, 3,000 miles away in Connecticut, had immediately conveyed her concern and committed herself to helping out.

What could I say? I knew exactly why everyone was estranged from him. As a matter of fact, I agreed with them, wanted to still count myself as *one of them*. This was a crossroads of sorts, I realized, and I needed to make a decision about my siblings' unwillingness to help. Being mad at them would just alienate me, jeopardizing our good relationships. Since they had sound reasons for their distancing, it was not my business to judge them. I would just have to respect their convictions – no matter how many bullets I had to bite to staunch my disappointment.

But I will tell you in advance, every single member of the family eventually rallied, coming to dad's and my assistance. It didn't happen overnight, but it didn't take months either. Within weeks, each person had transcended his or her bitterness, rage, or pain to show dad love and support through those final difficult two years. Diane, from Connecticut, pledged to call dad every night after his dinner – which she did, faithfully and with good humor for the duration. She and her husband John also sent me monthly checks to subsidize my living expenses.

Elaine, from Kansas, wrote sweet cards and letters, spilling over with colorful photos of the mountains, forests, and fishing streams which dad so loved, but could no longer experience.

Karen, from New Jersey, drove home for the summer with her dog Valentine –to keep him company, tend his flowers, and assist in his care.

Gail, from Portland, penned dad a long and thoughtful letter before resuming any interactions. On reading our copies, we felt her sentiments very much reflected our own.


March 8, 2004

Dear Dad: I'm not going to go into minute detail regarding our relationship as it is not my intention to make you feel bad or to punish you.

For my well being, I need to have relationships with people that I feel are solid, healthy and reliable. I also need to feel that I get something back from the other person. Unfortunately, none of these traits are your strong points. I've spent a good part of my adult life trying to understand and heal from our difficult childhood. I believe that part of that healing was moving away from you physically and emotionally. That was not easy, and I have never felt totally certain that it was the right thing to do. It's not that I didn't want to have a relationship with you, it's just that I don't know how to have one without getting hurt. I never felt you cared very much about me or you certainly would have tried to communicate with me. I felt it was your place to make amends and make the first move toward some reconciliation. Well, you never did that. You always seemed so preoccupied with your own life.

Ten years ago, I did try to open the lines of communication. Shortly after I moved into my current home, I invited you to visit with Denae. I had great plans for my property, thinking you could share by becoming involved in some of my projects. You said you would help me by doing some drawings of different gardens and landscape plans. Well, that was 10 years ago, and I never heard from you again. The message I received was that you didn't wish to share any part of my life, hopes or dreams. That was a painful and major disappointment, so I closed my heart to you.

I tried to reconnect with you many times by sending you birthday and get well cards, but I never received any reply. I heard that you had responded to other family members' cards, but not to mine, so I stopped writing you.

Although there has been a lot of pain, loss, and sorrow, I do hold some good memories of you. I remember you working hard putting a bike together for me one year for Christmas. You didn't know I was watching as you worked on it in the garage, and couldn't believe you were doing this for me. I always wanted you to take care of me when I was sick because there was a certain gentleness about you at those times. You also took us on some wild adventures that I doubt most kids ever would get to experience.

You gave us strong bodies and healthy minds. You always taught us to reach high and dream big and that being ordinary was never good enough. I learned to have a strong work ethic and be self-reliant, which has served me well all my life. You instilled an appreciation for art, music and books. You nurtured in us our love for the natural. The greatest joy I feel is when I'm tending one of my gardens. I don't know if you know but I became a Master Gardener a few years back and had a business growing organic salad greens, herbs, and flowers. It was one of the happiest times of my life, and I hope to continue with it when I retire from the business world.

I always admired your artistic abilities, intelligence, strength and perseverance. You are a maverick, and one of a kind.

I thank you for these gifts and feel they partly make up who I am today. I think you would be proud of me and what I have become and accomplished in my life. I only wish you could have known me better.

As you face the next passage in your life, I want you to know I hold no malice toward you – it is not for me to judge. Your life has not been an easy one, and my prayer for you is that when your time comes, I hope you go in peace to a happier place.   Your Daughter, Gail


Over time, a father we never knew existed revealed himself to us. Still eccentric, still the "compleat" individual, he surprised us with an outrageously funny wit and a heroic stoicism in accepting his chronic pain and infirmities. The doctors, nurses and other hospital personnel *loved* him, often bringing in other consultants or interns to duel wits with him.

The other reason for their unannounced visits was to view and examine his amazing gout-deformed hands. In explanation for this extraordinary interest, one elderly physician clarified for me: "Most medical practitioners will never see such an advanced state of gout – the patient usually dies before it can be this deforming."

Almost like elephantitis of the hands, dad's knuckles were obesely swollen, red and misshapen; his lumpy fingers –curled under like claws –were riddled with subdural crystallization. An especially distressing condition for an artist, I might add.

"Say, Frank, do you mind, could we look at your hands one more time?" A group of doctors would appear at the door, and dad would grin in response, blue eyes twinkling. Drawing out his "paws" from beneath the white sheets, he would hoist them dramatically into view, as though objects of incomparable worth. Along with the gratified expressions of awe and disbelief would come the inevitable request to view his lower extremities, as well.

Yes, I mused wryly, spectator to their amazement, "the Eighth Wonder of the World" – my father's club hands and club feet.

# ROOM WITHOUT a VIEW

Great Expectorations
Denae

For as long as I can remember dad had no faith in banks, hiding his money instead under mattresses, beneath chair cushions, or wadding it into empty soup cans to be stashed in the attic crawlspace.

On one hospital visit, Gwen and I were gloved and gowned up preparing to visit dad in his quarantined, orange-flagged room. Surprisingly, he was sitting up in bed and marginally coherent, despite having been shot full of high-powered antibiotics for a urinary tract infection, now in his bloodstream, which had upped his temperature to 104 degrees.

"Boy, am I glad to see you guys," he greeted us. "Did you remember to bring that cotton pickin' wallet of mine? It's got all my money. Someone could break into the trailer. I've *got* to have it."

Then pausing for a moment in his distress, a sudden beatific smile crossed his flushed features. "Say, and while you're at it, could you pick me up a couple cans of 'Cope' – I'm almost out." Wink, wink.

Our *least* favorite errand. And he knew it. Dad loved his Copenhagen like a bear loves honey. So Gwen and I were facing the dreaded "Copenhagen run" or "C-run," as we often abbreviated it. We loathed the habit, loathed even saying the word and used every euphemism or abbreviation possible to circumvent mouthing the repulsive syllables. Our childhood was marked as much by trials involving dad's tobacco addiction as it was by trials with his violent, erratic behaviors.

*Grizzly, Chew, Snoose, Skoal, Kodiak, Cougar, Snuff, Red Seal, Timberwolf* . . . . Plenty of names to describe the dreadful stuff. But it all boiled down to one thing – to avoid it, at all costs.

Not an easy feat. Because at our house, it had been everywhere. Under his bed, under *our* beds, under the table, beneath the sofa, under armchairs, under car seats. Rule number one when cleaning the house or dusting: *Never* reach into a dark empty space without first shining a flashlight into it. Such an oversight would surely bring you into a close encounter with that deceptively small tuna can *filled* with the odious black spittle. One bump and your lily fair hands would be flooded with mouth excrement. No amount of turpentine, bleach (forget the soap), or even DDT could entirely cleanse your skin or memory from the experience.

As we followed behind dad from room to room to car to camping tent in our daily routines and assorted misadventures – no matter how diverting the activity – *never* did we lose sight of the necessity for caution. It was a yellow, black-edged road sign in our minds: *BEWARE the COPENHAGEN*. Especially hazardous was sitting behind dad in the car on road trips. Rolling down your window was unthinkable, no matter how stifling the air – an action certain to expose you to flying spittle and slimy, dark plugs of tobacco.

Buying it for dad was in the same category as a mother asking her teenage son to buy Tampax for her. So when faced with this request, we sought small, isolated gas stations or Qwik-Stops where the clerks were strangers and where there would be little chance of running into friends.

Once at the checkout stand, there was a script of sorts which we followed in making our purchase. We usually suffered through a couple false starts before finally choking out, "Two cans of Copenhagen, please," *immediately* followed by, "It's not for me, it's for my father."

As if that were not sufficient, we would launch into lengthy accountings of his failing health (Why else would he not be buying it himself?), nationality, blood type, identifying birth marks – to further convince the by now completely annoyed clerk that it really was for dad, and not a habit which *we* had acquired.

By this time, rather than having established our disdain for chewing tobacco, we had instead raised suspicions as to our mental stability, or that our presence might be motivated by a darker agenda than simply purchasing dear old dad's Copenhagen. In short, we usually left these outpost stations in haste, as though we had indeed committed a crime.

Meanwhile, back at the hospital room, a glassy-eyed dad was completing his instructions to us. "I'll wait right here until you get back... Remember, the wallet and the Cope. Try to hurry."

Within an hour we had his wallet – past searches had familiarized us with his hidey-holes. This one was inside the metal-toed front of an old hiking boot, which also contained a discolored set of lower dentures. Back in his room, as we counted out the twelve-$100 bills, we persuaded dad to let us deposit his wallet and money inside the hospital safe.

Later that evening at home, I received an urgent call from the charge nurse reporting that all dad's vital signs had gone up alarmingly. "Perhaps you should consider returning to the hospital. Things are looking pretty bad for him."

I could have guessed. There he lay, knotted in his bed sheets, handfuls of Copenhagen sprinkled like peppercorns through the layers while his blue eyes were bulged out in panic. "Some son of a bitch stole my wallet! Every goddamn dollar I have is in it. You've got to find it! I'll tear this room apart with my bare hands if I have to. It's *got* to be somewhere!"

Back to the downstairs vault to retrieve dad's fortune. Within minutes all his vital signs had returned to normal.

"Sacre bleu! It's safe!" he rejoiced. "I'm going to hide it under my pillow. They'll never think to look for it there."

I waved goodbye to his bowed head, where he was laboriously counting each hundred-dollar bill with his club hands. A happy ending, I thought. So I wasn't prepared the following morning when Gwen and I stepped up to the nurse's station. A wild-eyed nurse waylaid us before we could even pick up the pen.

"What a night I've had! At 2 a.m. when I went to check on your father, I found hundred dollar bills all over his bed and floor – like someone had just robbed a bank! What on earth would possess you to leave so much money with a sick old man??!!"

# OF HUMAN BONDAGE

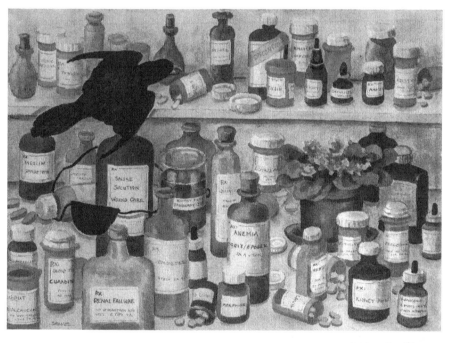

painting by Denae

*Deep into that darkness peering, long I stood there wondering, fearing...*

–Edgar Allan Poe

The Greeks were a smart bunch. They had a pretty good idea what life was all about, creating the two-sided face mask to express the dichotomy – tragic on one side, comic on the other. Like yin and yang, to be complete the two must be in partnership, creating a whole and perfect balance.

Denae

Somehow the sublime truth of this concept would be magnified to a blinding glare when interacting with my father. As artists, we both realized that to a certain extent our hands were our fortunes, our tools for creating art and beauty. I remember reading with horror of Pierre-Auguste Renoir in old age, valiantly struggling to paint with brushes strapped to his fingers – his arthritic grasp too weak to hold them. How much more aggrieved was I to see my own parent's hands, blackened and crippled by years of gout, resembling the ruined remains of a Chinese woman's feet, bound by centuries of tradition. Surely this was the unkindest cut for an artist to lose the use of his hands.

For months his painting room door had remained closed with orders that no one was to enter. Desperately missing his means of creativity, dad asked me to set up his easel near the couch where he lay, directing me in assembling canvasses, drawing papers and brushes. I also laid out his pastel chalks, pencils, charcoal sticks and tubes of oil along the easel's shelf, in readiness for the master.

Each morning with the sun, dad would sit up in anticipation, amidst his rumpled pillows and quilts, readjusting the black patch over his dead eye –a pirate among the ruins –then would study the waiting easel and chair. Clumsily, he'd rearrange the chalks and brushes, prelude to painting. Leaning back for a moment, he would consider aloud possible subjects: an eagle in flight, a mountain waterfall, a mother bear playing with her cubs. Around him, hanging on the walls like old friends, were portraits he had done of great American Indian chiefs: Sitting Bull, Red Cloud, Crazy Horse, Chief Joseph and Black Elk.

"Montage of a Dream Deferred" – he couldn't even hold a coffee cup, yet he hoped to produce one last magnum opus. Some days I could hardly bear to look at him sitting on the couch next to his easel, Still-Life with Artist, as he gazed longingly at the brushes and paints, hoping for a miracle to uncurl his stiff swollen fingers.

Buddy, his yellow-crested cockatoo, would perch without song on the tilted drawing board, like Poe's raven on the bust of Pallas, staring motionless at dad, while he, equally motionless, stared at his empty canvas… "What immortal hand or eye dare frame thy fearful symmetry?"

As long as his "studio" remained there next to his couch, he could still believe he was an artist, capable of creating beauty. "Tomorrow," he'd say, "tomorrow I'm going to sit in that damn chair and start drawing. I've got it all worked out in my head." But tomorrow faded into yesterday, and finally we put his studio back in the painting room. Neither he nor we ever mentioned it again.

Over a two-year period – with dad entangled by a dizzying routine of emergency room visits, short-term-care stays, then back to home – it became impossible to keep up my own painting and gallery shows. Even with his 9-to-5 schedule of caregivers, there were still evenings, doctor's appointments and emergency room visits to cover. Gwen had a family of her own, as well as three grandchildren, while Keith had his family responsibilities and a full-time job as a construction supervisor. For him, the old angsts and resentments simmered uneasily just beneath the surface. So my calls to him were infrequent and usually of a desperate nature: "Dad's in ICU again, Keith. I'm *sure* he's going to die this time. Could you please come and sit with him? I've got to go home and get some rest. He's running a 105-degree temp and is unconscious. It'll probably be your last chance to see him alive."

"Okay, sis. But only because *you* are asking. I'm only doing this to help *you* out."

On those teeth-baring, horn-locking occasions when dad, at home in his trailer, refused emergency medical intervention or ambulance transport, Keith would be summoned as the final voice of reason. Usually he was able to override dad's resistance. But one wintry December night dad's refusal was so absolute that Keith saw no recourse except to spend the evening as nurse and guardian – a sacrifice of the highest magnitude, since in the decades since childhood he had never spent more than an hour or two alone with him.

With medical crises occurring like clockwork, dad was at death's door about once a month. Gwen and I would stand toe-to-toe with the grim reaper behind the hospital ICU windows, staring in at his feverish form while spinning fans whipped the 30-degree frosty air against his bedsheets, causing them to rise up at right angles, like boat sails, in an effort to lower his temperature.

"Should we alert the out-of-towners? Call the relatives in Canada so they can come and pay their last respects?" This same scene of imminent death played itself out over and over in his hospital room like some demented dress rehearsal for disaster. "Enough already," we felt like screaming. "We know our lines!"

Family members dutifully, concernedly, would fly in – Diane and John from Connecticut, Elaine and Rick from Kansas, Karen from New Jersey. With them they would bring flowers and tears, along with new ideas for dad's eulogy, or a different photo for his obituary.

Then he would rally. Once again, return flights would be booked, goodbyes exchanged – and a few months later the tableau would begin all over again. Final scene. Take 22. Action! Twice, we called the parish priest to administer last rites. The holy oils would be applied to his forehead, along with the sign of the cross in preparation for Eternity. Both times, like Lazarus, he revived –happily returning home to tend his geranium-filled window boxes and patio pots of red carnations.

Meanwhile, Waiting for Godot, Gwen and I felt trapped between alternating states of dad's near death and then resuscitation. We seesawed precipitously through anticipated loss and then recovery as dad succumbed to more illnesses, and then improved. Not normally given over to dark humor, we found ourselves in semi-hysteria, referring to him as The Man Who Would Not Die. We were imprisoned, the three of us, in some macabre, absurdist science fiction movie where the intended victim is drowned, shot, buried alive, burnt at the stake, fed to the wolves . . . but he does not die; he *refuses* to die. Poisoned, a stake driven through his heart, bound to a cliff for vultures to devour – still the victim eludes death. Some final, crucial detail of his execution seemed always to be overlooked, left undone, so that in each instance, with death certain – once again the grim reaper would depart the scene unaccompanied. Simply put, dad either would not or could not die.

Don't get me wrong. I'm not saying we wished for his demise. Quite the contrary. Mirabile dictu. By now we had actually begun to *enjoy* his company; were in admiration of his indomitable spirit; entertained by his irrepressible, earthy wit; and, quite frankly amazed by his heroic disdain for his chronic pain and multiple afflictions. His right foot, now black with gangrene, was slowly rotting away from uncontrollable infection. Doctors could not amputate because he was too old, his immune system too fragile. To forestall the inevitable, with the assistance of my friends Bridget and Elizabeth O'Reilly (sisters and nurses), we took turns changing dad's dressings and bandages, while he crooned to Buddy and admired the orange hibiscus sitting next to its bird cage.

Dad, Bridget,
Elizabeth

Several months earlier we had signed up dad with hospice, after he was discharged from the hospital with a 7 percent kidney function. Nothing more could be done. The paramedics returned him home as flat and lifeless as the gurney board he lay upon. But, guess what? He improved. Within weeks, his kidney function had rallied to 25 percent, so hospice gave him his walking papers. They mailed him a document headlined with "I'm off Death Row!!" dad's jubilant response to the director's phone call, days earlier, congratulating him on his "pardon." The paper, signed by every person on staff, became a permanent fixture on the wall above dad's couch, testament to his gritty determination to survive. Each of us was mailed a copy; dad was so proud to be one of the few people ever discharged from hospice.

So, no, we did not wish him dead, not at all. We just wished he would make up his mind. What really bothered us, was beginning to obsess us, was this unnatural state of events. How could such a gravely ill man of 88 be pronounced near death so often by his doctors, and then not succumb? In utter defeat, I submitted to Gwen a final resolve, to end once and for all any future debates on "Should we call the-out-of-towners to come (again) and say their last goodbyes?"

"Never again, Gwen. Clearly, dad is *not* going to die. Let's pack up our wills, advanced directives, do-not-resuscitate orders and leave them in his desk drawer so he can pass on our wishes. Forget the obituary. Forget the eulogy. Dad is immortal – his symptoms are an illusion, a hallucination."

I continued, speaking faster, recklessly, "We've been tricked, bamboozled, hoodwinked. It's all a hoax – his Great Big Fat Czechoslovakian Joke! He played us like a violin, and we played our parts to perfection. But now we're leaving the stage. Forget the bows. No encores, thank you. Let's just get back to normal life. As for dad, we'll continue to visit him, but without all the anxiety, since we no longer have to worry about him dying."

# AN INTERLUDE

painting by Denae

"Sometimes a great notion ..." Well, I had one, notwithstanding, it came at a terribly inconvenient time, smack dab in the middle of all the exhausting madness related to dad's care. In retrospect, I do think I was crazy to have begun the project in the first place. However, as an artist, I have learned that when inspiration or opportunity come knocking, I'd better open the door.

My idea was to create a Van Gogh tribute painting, something I had long thought about. When complete, if it adequately fulfilled my vision, I intended to send photo copies of it to Mssr. Dominique Janssens, president of the Institut Van Gogh in Paris, and then await his response.

For years I had been in love with Vincent – in love with his radiant expressive art, in love with his earthy inspirational spirit. Zealously, I had studied his life, family, friends, and his published correspondences to absorb as much as I could of what was most dear to him.

By way of making our admittedly abstract relationship more real, I superimposed a photo of myself onto a copy of one of his self-portraits –the end result being a side-by-side image –both of us wearing matching blue green shirts and straw summer hats. Diane, my twin, calls it our engagement photo. I do not disagree.

A year earlier, a poet friend, observing my passion for all things Van Gogh, penned this verse in tribute:

> *You should have been the lover*
> *of Van Gogh, or Gauguin's mistress,*
> *passionate lover; the colors*
> *you might have taught them to use*
>
> *you might have been the one*
> *they fought for the night Van Gogh*
> *lost his ear, your carmine red*
> *is what made him bleed.*

*And when Gauguin fled to Tahiti
it was for you he left his wife and children,
all so he could taste your tropical blue,
find the dark chocolate of your skin.*

Michael Magee

I did not disagree.

After two and a half months of wrestling with an extremely difficult composition and equally difficult color choices, I finally completed the 36-by-48-inch oil titled "The Artists' Room, Entrance to Heaven." In essence, it was a tableau of Vincent's funeral. How ironic, I thought as I applied pigment to the canvas, that I should be painting this beloved artist's death at the same time that I am preparing for my own father's death.

Despite the somber subject matter, my idea had been to make it vivid – celebratory! – a tribute to the triumph of art and life, Van Gogh's legacy to us all. Within its composition I replicated 24 of his masterworks. Some were arranged on the walls around his sunflower-draped casket; others were embodied in the figures of the mourners, as well as in the bouquets of sunflowers decorating the room.

"The artists' room" (used for painting or displaying artwork) was a small room at the back of the *Auberge Ravoux* in Auvers, France, where Van Gogh had boarded and painted the last two months of his life. Because he committed suicide, the Church at Auvers wanted nothing to do with his funeral service. So, while poor Vincent was slowly decomposing in the intense summer heat, his brother Theo was making hasty arrangements with Mssr. Ravoux, the innkeeper, to use the artists' room as a replacement.

Deliberately, I had left out the ceiling, exposing the small chamber with its mourners to a serene blue sky and orange yellow sun/moon. And why not? Vincent was never bound by conventions; he reveled in his luminous starry, starry nights. My painting's intent was to depict his soaring spirit in an affirmation of that poignant line written to

Theo: "Just as you take a train to reach Rouen or Tarascon, you must take death to reach a star."

With the artwork completed, I mailed a letter with photos to Mssr. Janssens in Paris, signing off with the universally hopeful, "Looking forward to your response."

Well, what are the chances that a struggling artist living in Spokane, Washington, on the basis of a letter and three photographs is going to hear from a wealthy, international businessman who just happens to own and manage the Auberge Ravoux, now a celebrated museum and restaurant (renamed the *Maison de Van Gogh*), as well as being director of the prestigious Institut Van Gogh?

The odds were not in my favor. But still I kept my fingers crossed and continued to hope for the impossible. Two years earlier, I had sold an entire 18-painting oil collection to the Rosalie Whyel Museum near Seattle – an almost unheard of accomplishment for *any* artist. If one miracle could happen, why not two?

In the meantime waiting for a response, I returned to recording dad's urine output, taking his blood sugar readings, and ferrying him to and from doctors' appointments. Trying not to think about an important letter from France which might never find its way into my mailbox.

Three weeks later, the phone rang: "Paris calling." Two months and several transatlantic conversations later, Mssr. Janssens had invited me to Paris and generously offered to guide me through Auvers-sur-Oise, adding, *"S'il vous plait, Mam'selle*, I would be delighted to have you dine with me at the Auberge Ravoux."

I accepted. Everyone in the family donated money, allowing me to make the trip. I flew to Paris in April 2005, and had the time of my life –walking in Van Gogh's footsteps through the pastoral village of Auvers where "Wheatfield with Crows," "Portrait of Doctor Gachet," the "Church at Auvers" and so many other famous works had been created. If ever there was a princess in fairyland, surely it was me. How, I marveled, had I been transported so effortlessly from Spokane, taking care of my ailing father, to being squired about Paris and Auvers by a handsome, urbane host, who months earlier had been a total stranger?

It all seems like a dream now, a Cinderella story that I must have imagined. But it really did happen; I have the photographs to prove it.

"What do you want me to bring you from Paris?" I had asked dad the day before I left.

"All I want is a picture of you standing next to the Eiffel Tower," was his response (He was not entirely convinced of my trip –the photo would have been proof).

So that's what I gave him. It's my favorite image from the entire trip.

Mssr. Janssens continues to e-mail me now and then – the last time, from Shanghai. And "The Artists' Room, Entrance to Heaven" still hangs on the wall in my painting room –waiting like me, for the day it will become part of the permanent collection of some art museum.

In the meantime, we regard each other with an unspoken bonhomie, reminiscing about my incredible Paris adventure – the trip of a lifetime.

The Artist's Room, Entrance to Heaven

# AMAZING GRACE

painting by Denae

<u>Denae</u>

If dad was The Man Who Would Not Die, one auspicious Wednesday in October became The Day That Would Not End. Since dad was again convalescing at Maplewood Gardens, a two-member evaluation team from Social Services had notified him they would be reassessing him for discharge, hoping to determine whether or not he could care for himself at home.

A big day for dad, who was chomping at the bit to be out of this facility, irrespective of the fact that he was utterly incapable of cooking and cleaning for himself, much less maintaining his personal hygiene. In sympathy, I had signed on as co-conspirator in a willful plan to deceive his evaluators. How could I not? "Misery, thy name is Frank" could have been posted above his doorway, so depressed had he been during his two months back in Assisted Living.

Not once had he gone downstairs to dine with the other residents. In fact, he had not left his room in weeks, except for the few times I pushed him in his wheelchair along the corridors in an attempt to get him to mingle. Stubbornly, he refused even to make eye contact with the passing denizens, instead muttering loudly in their wake, "Why in hell did they put me here with these decrepit old geezers? They've all got one foot in their coffin, the other in the grave. I'm not one of them. By God, I can still climb a mountain or two before they start shoveling the dirt over *me!*"

The one time he did speak to a little white-haired granny cruising along in her four-wheeled walker, I was too embarrassed to even look up at her. "Say, you're looking pretty good today," dad purred. "Who's your undertaker!?"

All week dad had been running 101-degree and 102-degree fevers, but he made me promise I wouldn't tell his medical team for fear they would postpone his evaluation. So I was pressed into service as maid-for-a-day: washing his clothes, doing dishes and preparing his meals in our gambit to portray him as dischargeable.

Seven a.m. the next morning found me unlocking his door, a full six hours before his appointment, hoping to troubleshoot any minor emergencies that might thwart his homecoming. I stepped into chaos. How in 24 hours one sick old man could so destroy one tiny space is beyond me.

From across the room the first thing I noticed was a huge brown puddle on the beige carpet encroaching into the shadows beneath his bed – a stagnating pool of …. what else? Copenhagen juice. Somehow, he had overturned all his spittoons, the dark liquid studded with dropped green, pink and blue pills, looking like M&Ms floating on the surface.

"Out, out damned spot" assumed new meaning as I stood there contemplating the scene with detergent and water bucket. Three hours of scrubbing, rinsing and rescrubbing. Next, dishes in the kitchen sink, diarrhea in the bathtub and vacuuming up tobacco bits on the carpet.

Meanwhile, dad, in the deepest of slumbers, had not moved, his face ominously flushed. The underarm thermometer registered 103 degrees. Great. Diarrhea in both his bedsheets *and* in his pajamas. Spray the room with Febreze, Lysol, then a piney air freshener. One hour to go. "Dad, can you get into the wheelchair? This is D-Day. We need to get you changed into some clean clothes. Your assessment team will be here within the hour."

"Sure, sure," he grinned, prominently displaying his gums. Where were his teeth? They were in his mouth when I left last night.

"Dad, where are your teeth?"

"Hell, I don't know – maybe under my pillow. Check under the bed, too, while you're at it."

Frantic, I lifted his mattress, emptied drawers, unrolled mismatched socks before I found both uppers and lowers submerged in the murky waters of a coffee cup. "Okay, you're nearly ready!" (which included three layers of pull-up adult diapers to slow down the unstoppable diarrhea). Even though I had dressed him in a warm navy blue sweater and gray sweatpants, I could see he was beginning to chill, so I wrapped an Indian-patterned wool blanket around his shoulders and then spritzed him with Old Spice. The thermometer reading was now 103.8 degrees and rising.

Great. "Now, dad, are you sure you can pull this off? You're running a pretty high temp."

"Hell, that ain't nothin'. I've been in blizzards up in Alaska worse than this. Don't worry about me. I can fool them, easy."

Several seconds before the doorbell rang, I finished dusting his flaming cheeks with baby powder to bring them down to a more acceptable pink – then greeted the two smiling women standing officiously before me. "Hey, dad, look who's here!" While he babbled out a gravelly, "How're you gals doing? I'm doing *great*! Come on in."

Both women had laptops and pages of questions. They sat on either side of dad, intent on their screens as they entered his responses. One hour passed and then another; dad's eyelids sagged, drooping lower and lower against his moist flushed cheeks, the dampness making a paste of the baby powder. His answers had slowed down to a whisper.

"You know," I said, addressing the ladies, so busy with their data entries that they had not noticed dad slumping into unconsciousness, "this is the time of day when dad usually naps; I can see he's getting tired. How about if I answer for him so he can get a little sleep?" – the unmistakable smell of diarrhea wafting up from his sweatpants, only inches from their nostrils.

*Please God*, I implored mentally, checking his pantlegs and ankles for the tell-tale brown streaks. *Don't let his chances for discharge be ruined when he is so close.* At the same time thinking, *How in the world can they not notice how sick he is?*

"Sure, we're almost done anyway. He's probably just worn out with all the questions."

Twenty more minutes passed. Dad was now clearly unconscious, out like a light. And still the two women, oblivious, were chatting pleasantly as they closed their laptops and pulled on their coats. "Tell Frank goodbye for us. . . He looks so peaceful . . . like he's really in a deep sleep. (*Coma*, I thought.) He passed the evaluation. We'll put our signatures on his discharge papers and turn in the paperwork."

*Good grief. Goodbye!* Within seconds of their leaving, I had dialed the facility's nursing staff and requested two nurse's aides, STAT. As soon as they had bathed and changed him into clean clothes, I called an ambulance. We were at the hospital within minutes, where he was admitted for treatment, beginning with an IV for severe dehydration. Five days later, when he was discharged, I drove him to his trailer – his assessment team none the wiser for all the considerable drama they had missed. Dad and I both felt we deserved Oscars for our amazing performances.

Despite my recent resolve to accept dad's immortality, I still could not help pondering the unnatural resiliency of his health. Most of his illnesses made no sense at all – the diabetes, kidney failure, near blindness, leaky heart valve, crippling gout, severe urinary tract infections. He had no prior symptoms or genetic disposition for any of these conditions.

Even his brain was an anomaly. After the last MRI, his doctor had handed him a black and white photo of its interior. Over one-quarter of his brain mass had decomposed into a network of waterways, looking more like a map of the Mississippi River and its tributaries than any flesh-and-blood cerebrum and cerebellum. Shaking his head, the doctor had commented: "Even in hundred-year-old men, you don't normally see this much water sloshing through the brain cavity."

And what about his ferocious stoicism? His superhuman disdain for the 104 degree and 105 degree temps; the pain levels of "9" and "10" from his urinary tract infections and other maladies? Nothing, it seemed, could provoke a complaint from him. Unbelievably, he appeared to *embrace* his diseases – the more, the better. "Pile it on" seemed to be his response. "There ain't nothing you can hand me that I won't accept."

How about those dreadful skin rashes that itched worse than a dozen cases of measles and chicken pox? To keep him from scratching deep wounds into his flesh, I would cut old sheets into long strips. After creaming him with a thick topical antibiotic, I would wrap his back, shoulders, neck, arms and legs with the white cotton swathes, effecting the appearance of an Egyptian mummy – which he found hugely amusing. Joking to his morning caregiver, he would quip, "So what are you going to feed the mummy for breakfast today?"

Ever the conundrum, dad and his condition occupied my thoughts obsessively, until one day an epiphany of sorts came to me. Only one explanation made sense. Somehow dad must be trying to atone for all his sins. If he could suffer long enough, with the worst possible afflictions, especially without complaining, then maybe, MAYBE the Almighty would forgive him and spare him from an eternity in hell. For once in his life, I realized appreciatively, he had not turned to his children, *expecting* us to help him out. To his credit, he was enduring the trauma of his maladies, silently and alone.

Honest to god, no other explanation made sense. I thought back to my college literature and mythology classes – back to the stories of Orestes, Agamemnon, Clytemnestra and Electra, those infamous characters from the ill-fated House of Atreus. Were we the 21st-century reincarnation of this lineage? An ancestry seeking blood revenge, demanding retribution for the decades of atrocities? The Furies, those black-winged vixens, had already quarried their victim, their long talons buried deep into dad's flesh, right down to his beating heart. Clotho, Lachesis and Atropos, the three Fates, stood grimly over him – like the witches of Macbeth – scissors in hand, waiting for the signal to sever the life cord. Was this the destiny that awaited him?

My answer came not many days later when one of his caregivers, Teresa Terry, a kindly, reserved young woman, walked in at 8 a.m. to begin her shift – she and dad alone in his cramped trailer. Hurrying to the kitchen to begin his breakfast of oatmeal and bacon, she heard a deep, unearthly moan, as of a soul uttering his last words before falling off the cliff into hell. There could be only one source for this disturbing sound: "Frank, is that you? What's wrong? Are you all right?" she asked the crumpled form on the couch in the next room.

"The wind tapped like a tired man at the window…" as dad's voice, ponderous and low, rumbled up from his blankets. "It's all over for me; I don't know what to do. I'm going to hell, I know it. I've done such terrible things."

A deeply religious woman, Teresa carried her Bible to work to read in her spare time. Rushing over to dad, she pulled up a chair. "Frank, what do you mean? There is *no* sin so great that God will not forgive it."

"Well, He's not going to forgive me. I've done so many terrible things; I can't even forgive myself. I'm headed for hell. I don't deserve forgiveness."

Reaching for her Bible, Teresa opened it to a specific page, then gently laid it on his chest. "Frank, have you heard of the Sinner's Prayer? It's like knocking on Jesus' door and asking if you can come in. Do you want to say it with me? That's all you have to do to be forgiven."

So dad repeated the words after Teresa, with absolute sincerity. And that was it. He must have believed her because he died a week later, with his cockatoo Buddy on the couch beside him.

There is a postscript to this story. It happened three days before dad's death. I had been staying overnight because of his extremely fragile state. In the morning, awakened by woodpeckers drumming on the roof, I walked into the living room and found dad in a heap on the floor; apparently, he had fallen from the couch during the night. I winced to see his 85-pound skeletal frame, bare except for his white pull-up briefs. Try as I might, I could not get him back on the sofa. So I called Keith, who was already at work, to ask for help.

Within 20 minutes, he was at the door, all 6 feet, 190 pounds of him. As he approached dad, uneasy thoughts crabbed through my mind. *Be gentle*, I thought, *he's so vulnerable. Try to forget the past.* I needn't have worried. Bending over dad, Keith lifted him as carefully as though he were a wounded butterfly. Standing still for a moment, he looked down at our father, draped in his arms. A vision came to me then, of the Pieta – that transfiguring moment at the end of the Via Dolorosa, when Mary supports her fallen son with such ineffable sorrow and love. That image manifested itself into the present as I gazed at my brother cradling our gravely ill father.

A holy light seemed to wash over them, as together they faced the gates of Eternity. *What was happening?* With tears in my eyes, I thought I knew – but asked Keith afterward, just to be sure.

"It was all gone in a moment," Keith said quietly. "All the anger, the resentment, the bitterness. Such a lightness I've never felt before. I knew all the old terrible feelings would never return. When I looked down at dad, all I felt was love … nothing else."

# GOING UPSTREAM

Denae, Diane, Gail, Gwen, Keith

*...I shall never do what I might have done and ought to have wished and pursued.*

–Vincent Van Gogh

<u>Keith</u>

Some people you experience in life seem to always be headed in a direction that does not fit the norm – a direction that makes no sense and has no logic connected to it. They make decisions and choose paths that defy understanding. My father was one of them. No amount of conjecture or analysis can adequately explain his behaviors or mental processes. I have tried, but every time I seemed to be on the verge of understanding, I would be confounded again by his next action.

Much of my life was spent trying to make sense of my relationship with dad, usually ending with frustration and heartache. After his passing, I came to realize that not only did it not make sense to me, it didn't have to. Some things in life just are, with no other good reason. With that thought in mind, I find comfort in *not* understanding.

In the events leading up to his passing, one huge problem loomed. Since it was a never-discussed subject, none of us kids really knew how to deal with the eventual reality of dad's funeral. Most of us had spent a good part of our lives trying not to hate him for the awful things he did while alive. "Staging" a funeral, with all the glowing testimonials about the person's life and what he meant to those left behind seemed extremely hypocritical, since most of what we felt to be true about him was unflattering, to say the least.

So what do you do? If you don't have a funeral, then you take away people's opportunity to say good bye – people who may not necessarily share the same opinion as you. Such was the case with dad's close friend Eva. For reasons, again completely unclear, she loved him unconditionally. So in consideration to her, we decided some kind of service would be necessary whether we wanted it or not. We had no idea what was in store for us.

Our arrangements began with Gwen asking her pastor to preside. Dad had never been a regular churchgoer; in fact, his primary involvement was in making sure that we kids went regularly. Maybe he thought he could be saved vicariously through us, or possibly he thought it made him appear a good parent. In any case, Gwen's pastor requested some personal information about dad so he could speak knowledgably. We all supplied what we could drum up, hoping that there would be enough to make a go of it. Somewhere in the process a miracle began to take place, which, as was true for everything else in dad's life, was hard to explain.

Two words come to mind as a result of the planning and completion of the funeral: "redeeming value" and "love." I thought I understood these words, but both took on new meaning by their relevance to dad's death.

One misgiving we had about his funeral was that no one would show, but many people did come and were moved by the service. One biker type guy, whose name I will not mention, was found at a tender moment with tears in his eyes. To my amazement, I heard testimonies about good things in dad's life from people he had touched in a positive way.

We children were able to come up with some affirming stories of our own, as reflected in the eulogy:

> *"... Ours was a father who was not sensible, not cautious and not conventional. For dad, there was no word for 'impossible' – He thought his children capable of doing anything. He dared us to be more than we ever thought we could be. His expectations of us even bordered on the dangerous: when he had us swimming rivers that were too swift; climbing mountains that were too high; playing in places as children where truly 'the angels feared to tread.'*
>
> *Yet we survived, and we know we are stronger for it... The last thing he said to me in a moment of clarity was: 'Don't get lost, Keith,' followed by a playful smile.*

*It could have been the rambling of a delirious, ill man,
or maybe it was God speaking through him, advising
me not to get lost in hate and bitterness and regret, but
rather to be found in His love."*

I felt the pastor really put dad's life in perspective when he talked about his abundant potential and how little he had done with it. He advised us all to avoid finding ourselves some day in that position. "Redeeming value" was to be found in a life not squandered – an opportunity for others to learn from his failures. But for me, learning to love through the process of dad's dying was probably the more remarkable of the two.

Each family member took a slightly different approach in coping with this long ordeal. Some stayed by his bedside giving help from a place in the heart that many of us could not access, while others kept their distance. One sister called all the time, while others visited some of the time, and still others, for a while, could do neither. None of us were wrong; I think we were all learning something about love which came to fruition not only during the service, but also in the days that followed. We each learned to love dad through the avenue we found most acceptable. And we were reminded, as we shared childhood stories, of our love for each other and the power of that love to not only help us survive, but also to redeem our lives for good purposes in the years to come.

All of this from dad's funeral – go figure.

For most of his life, dad wrestled with guilt and shame from the atrocities he had committed. He carried this baggage with him always, and one can only guess at the extent to which it affected his life. He probably could not find a way to forgive himself because he had never known or acknowledged God's forgiveness. I believe because of his act of repentance in saying the Sinner's Prayer, he was finally able to let go of this life and no longer fear the next.

After the cremation, we were faced with another dilemma – what to do with dad's ashes? The ashes of our mother and two brothers rest side by side in the same mausoleum, but it did not seem the appropriate place for dad. Since he was a self-proclaimed "free spirit," Gail suggested we sprinkle his ashes in the Spokane River, where he had found so much enjoyment. I was not confident that it was legal to do this, so choosing the spot to carry out the private ceremony my sisters had planned was important to me on more than one level. I wanted it to be meaningful, but also somewhat remote so we would not be arrested.

A sheltered area downstream from Plantes Ferry Park was selected – albeit a little too close to the public walk bridge to suit my taste. As we climbed down the embankment, I could see the current was pretty strong, an important consideration guaranteeing the ashes would travel downstream quickly.

Standing there together at the river's edge, Diane, Denae, Gail, Gwen, my wife Judy and I solemnly recited the Lord's Prayer and the 23rd Psalm, then everyone turned to me to complete our ceremony. Carefully opening the bag of ashes, I proceeded to empty them into the water, while my sisters tossed long-stemmed red and pink carnations alongside. To my utter amazement, the ashes started flowing *upstream*! How could this be happening? The river was flowing in the *opposite* direction! Even in death, dad seemed to have the ability to go against the grain. We all watched in disbelief –until eventually the eddying current joined the main stream, carrying with it dad's ashes, our flowers and the prayers of his family.

Saying good-bye

# END THOUGHTS

*Star light, star bright, first star I see tonight*
*I wish I may, I wish I might, have the wish I wish tonight.*

Gwen

I remember Gail at nine teaching me that verse as we lay on our backs in the yard behind our house watching the stars. I am sorry now that I cannot remember what our childhood wishes were, because those wishes were our best efforts at guiding our course. But I do know we kept wishing upon stars, year after year, hoping to visit that place "where troubles melt like lemon drops" – even when our wishes went unanswered, or continued to collide with a darker reality. Hoping that someday we could "wish upon a star and wake up where the clouds are far behind us."

We never did learn how to fly over the rainbow, no matter how hard we tried or how many times we wished. I guess broken wings take a long time to mend, if at all. But no matter, we still gaze at the stars, a continuing source of mystery and fascination –God's way, perhaps, to keep us looking up.

Denae

I cannot forget one long ago special night, when as a family we came pretty close, I thought, to soaring above the rainbow – or at the very least, in Wordsworthian terms, "trailing clouds of glory." It was the year dad had decided on a more novel approach to the Christmas season.

"Why not try something different this year?" he had remarked, studying the tree's tinsel garlands as we were washing up the supper dishes. "There's a lotta poor buggers living in the derelict joints and flophouses along skid row, downtown. I've been thinking about them; what kind of holiday are they going to have?"

Pulling out some loose change from his pocket, he continued: "How about I give you each a couple of dollar bills, some dimes and quarters – the money Rose and I would have spent on your presents – and we'll drive around Christmas Eve handing out money to them bums? Well, whaddya say?"

*Hmmm-m.* Reluctance hung thick in the air. Little as we usually got at Christmas, our collective assent would mean this year we would get *nothing.* Slowly, stiffly, one by one we nodded our heads in agreement –like prisoners of war reconciling to torture.

Flushed with enthusiasm for his still hatching plan, dad went on: "Instead of caroling the neighbors, you kids can pick out a couple of the seediest dives and go inside to sing your Christmas carols to them. Hell, Rose could even bake a big batch of cookies – we'll bag them up and hang them outside those poor cotton pickers' doors. How about it? Are you with me?"

Only two days to prepare. Our old upright piano was fairly jumping with "Sleigh Bells Ring" and "Holly Jolly Christmas" as mom pounded the pedals and keys for an all-day practice, like Jelly Roll Morton thumping out ragtime. From the kitchen, we older girls sang along as we baked ginger snaps and sugar cookies, which were stuffed into sandwich baggies and tied with neat little red bows by the younger kids, Keith, Gail and Gwen.

No midnight mass at St. Mary's church that night. Dad distributed the dollar bills and change, and then we all piled into the car, zipping up our jackets and clutching nearly fifty bags of cookies. The sky was black as Hades, with fat, wet snowflakes drifting down to melt against the windshield.

By the time we reached skid row, the only signs of festivity along the dim streets were colored neon tavern lights spelling out "Budweiser," "Coca-Cola" and "Hot Sandwiches" in reds, blues and yellows. A few transients were crouched together in alleyways for warmth; a lonesome-looking three or four more were passing lopsidedly through bar doorways, while others were shuffling in the direction of the Union Gospel Mission for a free blanket and cup of hot cider.

Carefully, we selected our favorites, pointing them out to daddy so he could pull the car alongside. Then, leaning from the window, we'd hand them quarters and half-dollars still warm from our curled fists – the braver among us occasionally squeezing out a "Merry Christmas!"

On to the flophouses, as daddy called them. Never having been in one before, we were quaking, nervous as cats before a bath, all the more so because daddy and mom had decided to wait in the car. We were now in the worst section of town –Murderers' Row, from our perspective. Newspaper reports of muggings, transient knifings and drunken back alley brawls were most often cited from this area.

"I was petrified!" recalls Diane, "expecting to be shot or kidnapped at any moment."

Images of yellow crime tape and flashing scenes from Hitchcock's *Psycho* occupied the rest of our thoughts. No one wanted to be in front as we stopped at a metal-barred wooden door standing ajar, and peered up into the darkness of its narrow stairwell, leading to the second floor.

"You go first; you're the oldest," Karen whispered to Elaine, pushing against her shoulder.

Thinking "Bates Motel" as we climbed the steps, fearfully we clung to our bags of cookies with one hand, while with the other we pinched our noses against the suffocating, sour stench of dog urine, boiled cabbage and stale cigarette smoke.

The upper-level corridor was even spookier than the climb up. But we were at the point of no return. It was 9 p.m. and graveyard quiet, just like in the poem "…and all through the house not a creature was stirring, not even a mouse." The only lights to be seen were pencil thin streaks beneath the doors of the 20 or so rooms stretching down either side of the long passageway.

Our fingernails bit ridges into our palms. We were intruders, after all. What if the tenants demanded we leave when we started singing? We weren't exactly the Vienna Boys Choir – not a nightingale in the bunch. Diane couldn't even carry a tune. Her husband John once likened her voice (after sitting through two verses of "Happy birthday to you..") to that of an Indian elder with adenoids chanting beside a campfire.

Carefully, quietly, we attached the cookie bags to the doorknobs with rubber bands, then boldly, Elaine punched PLAY on the portable tape deck she had brought for background music. Ready or not, we launched into "I'm Dreaming of a White Christmas." No applause when we finished, but no yells for our departure, either.

Song after song, we plodded on, our volume increasing with our confidence. For percussion, Keith occasionally shook the string of tiny silver bells we had tied to his wrist. In the middle of "Chestnuts roasting …" I noticed a shaft of light slitting the darkness as one door, ever so slowly, creaked open. We kept singing. Another three or four doors opened an inch or two, and we could identify here and there a thatch of hair, a rheumy eye, part of a whiskery cheek pressed against a door frame.

We waited for the words "Get the hell out of here!"

It didn't happen. Something else did.

That stinky, dank passageway which before had seemed so frightening was now faintly illuminated with rays of light from the partially opened doors – like a church at midnight with moonbeams slanting in through stained-glass windows. We were singing "Joy to the World," our closing song, and we felt the joy – all around us, inside of us. What a strange and grand moment, such a dizzying grand feeling. For once in our lives, the poor Veselits – the hard up, put down, hand-me-down, charity case Veselits – were the bearers of Christmas instead of the recipients. Joy to the world, indeed. Were we not soaring this night – blazing across the inky vastness of the wet December sky, a veritable comet? And trailing clouds of glory, every single one of us.

# Acknowledgments

We owe much gratitude to the caring community of generous adults who aided in our survival for so many years – relatives, teachers, clergy, food-banks, neighbors and community services. A heartfelt thank you to David Meil for his unshakeable faith in our memoir; for introducing us to Zeno's Paradox and other esoteric dogma; as well as for the invaluable, detailed and witty manuscript review, which we affectionately call, "the Condensed Version." We are indebted to William Claflin for rescuing this project in its time of need, and for his unfailing and gracious hospitality.

Many thanks to our brilliant nephew and niece, Kris and Alicia Veselits, for their computer wizardry and for their abilities to act as "sounding boards" in the reworking of difficult passages. Special thanks to Naomi Judd and Christina Crawford for their kind words and encouragement early on in the process. We so appreciate Bob Banger and Marsha for their unwavering support and insightful comments. Much gratitude to Carol Santos for the many years of zealous support, and also to Jim Kjeldsen, Father Tom Colgan SJ, Don and Connie LaPoint, Suzanne and Karl Fleming, Mary Jo Rudolf and Marilyn Mc-Conaghy for their commitment throughout this book's evolution. We could not have completed this memoir without the expert advice and kindly guidance of Kimberly Hitchens (Hitch) of Booknook. You're the best!

Finally, there is no thank you large enough to convey our gratitude to my boyfriend, Neil Claflin – editor, reader, project developer and videographer extraordinaire. He saw a dream deferred and interceded to make it happen.

Made in the USA
Lexington, KY
10 July 2017